Black Magic &
Purple Passion

This book is dedicated to all those who love
black plants and to my mother for creating an individual

Aeonium 'Zwartkop'

Black Magic &
Purple Passion

A complete guide
to dark plants

Karen Platt

First published in 2003 by
Karen Platt.

British Library Cataloguing in
Publication Data

Platt, Karen
ISBN: 09528810 98

35 Longfield Rd
Crookes
Sheffield
S10 1QW
England

Cover Design by Alan Coventry
AC Design
www.acdesign1.co.uk
alan@acdesign1.co.uk

Printed and bound in Singapore.

Title Page : Fittonia albivenis
Argyroneura Group
page 2: Aeonium 'Zwartkop'
page 3: Solenostemon 'Merlot'
page 4: Colocasia 'Black Magic'

Front Cover: top, left to right:
Begonia 'Helen Teupel',
Viola 'Blackjack', Helleborus
'Harvington Shades of Night'.
bottom left to right:
Aeonium 'Zwartkop',
Zantedeschia 'Schwarzwalder',
Catalpa erubescens 'Purpurea',
Back Cover: top left to right:
Solenostemon (Coleus) 'Merlot',
Tulipa 'Queen of Night', Ajuga
reptans 'Braunherz' (Mahogany).
bottom left to right:
Trifolium 'Dark Dancer',
Colocasia 'Black Magic', Ipomoea
'Black Heart'

Also by Karen Platt:

THE SEED SEARCH

PLANT NAMES A-Z

GROWING FROM SEED

GARDEN SURF

FOUNDER OF THE
INTERNATIONAL BLACK
PLANT SOCIETY
To join visit the website or send a
stamped addressed envelope to the
address on this page.

www.seedsearch.demon.co.uk
k@seedsearch.demon.co.uk

CONTENTS

INTRODUCTION

Why a second edition? After the success of the original book, black plants have caught the imagination of many and the enormous interest and demand for black plants has prompted this expanded version with more than 1,000 additional plants. This second edition is completely rewritten and fully expanded with over 300 new photographs.

There are so many wonderful plants in the plant world. So, why black plants?

Of all colours in horticulture, it is black that is mysterious, captivating and alluring. Black plants are complex, with secretive qualities, a colour that can portray the opposite of what it appears to be. It can stand alone or work in harmony with other colours.

The fascination for dark plants in the garden is all to do with the striking depth of colour, its ability to mingle, its power which focuses the eye, the allure, the chic. Dark plants make a statement; they have that little bit extra to offer. Black is the most unusual, astonishing colour in the garden and I aim to show that it is the easiest colour to incorporate in the garden in any quantity.

Black plants first caught my eye ten years ago, and they enchant me still. I have been growing and promoting them ever since, not just as a highlight, but for black borders too, not just as a contrast but as the main colour in the garden.

Whether you are starting a garden from scratch, or looking for something to uplift an old border, black is the colour. There are black plants for every garden situation. Enjoy them wherever you garden.

Gardeners who find the colour black difficult to place in the garden, will find a solution in the completely new section embracing the use of black plants in the garden. Share my growing experience regarding dark plants in more depth with personal accounts of plants, their habits and qualities.

The plant market on both sides of the Atlantic has been taken into consideration owing to colleagues in the U.S. and to my increasing knowledge of the U.S. market and USDA zones are now given. I have had the opportunity to travel more, to meet breeders, to see in situ, to photograph and to portray many dark plants in watercolour.

You will find here all dark plants currently known from the myriad of classifications in horticulture, including those in regular cultivation and rarities which increase the pulse rate and excite the compulsive collector.

This is the book for you, if you adore black plants and want to make your garden a little bit different to stand out from the crowd. Something a little sexy and indulgent perhaps, or something ultra modern, or even elegant and nostalgic, black plants have it all.

Not just the colour of the moment, it has the right qualities to maintain its place in the garden, just like that fashion classic, the chic little black dress. I do not follow gardening trends, but I appear to have created one. However, black gardening is not merely a fashion. Black is here to stay.

To dismiss black plants as a fad or craze, does them a great disservice. Black is the buzz word with garden designers, breeders and retailers alike who recognise black as the quickest selling plants. Black plants are increasingly available to the discerning gardener.

I recently launched The International Black Plant Society to further the knowledge of these wonderfully dark plants. My range of 'Black Magic and Purple Passion' plants has been launched in the U.S. with Proven Winners. So, it is natural that I should rewrite my book and incorporate the latest developments from the U.K. and the rest of the world.

Karen Platt
January 2003

BLACK PLANTS
AND HOW TO
USE THEM

Athyrium nipponicum

BLACK IN PUBLIC PLACES

*Black is increasingly used as an
anchor colour to attract the eye.*

Colocasia 'Black Magic' and Victoria amazonica

In the UK, a number of gardens open to the public are incorporating black plants into their planting schemes. However, black is still mainly seen and used in the private garden. It has yet to reach its potential in the public garden.

HRH Prince Charles in his garden at Highgrove has a black and white planting, a design of perfect harmony in the sundial garden. Some of the plants you will find growing at Highgrove are *Tulipa* 'Queen of Night', *Aquilegia vulgaris* 'William Guiness' and *Dahlia* 'Bishop of Llandaff' with its red blooms disbudded for the desired black magic foliage effect. Dark plants were also used in the tapestry garden created for HRH Prince Charles at Chelsea in 2001.

Christopher Lloyd at Dixter was the first to widely use *Dahlia* 'Bishop of LLandaff' and like me he does not disbud them as they are grown at Highgrove, and where they would naturally be entirely out of place in a black and white garden, but enjoys those fabulous scarlet blooms which are so excellent and so very welcome in a hot border. Christopher is also partial to dark-leaved *Canna, Aeonium* 'Zwartkop', the elegant dark *Arisaema ciliatum, Euphorbia cotinifolia* and *Colocasia* 'Black Magic' amongst others. He is also the plantsman who discovered one of the finest dark spring plants, *Ranunculus ficaria* 'Brazen Hussy'.

The Tapestry Garden at Chelsea

10

Japanese Garden at Kew

Black plants are intermingled in borders at Great Dixter to great effect. A visit to the garden leaves one marvelling at the skill with which Christopher Lloyd uses black plants as part of the whole, mingling so well with an array of colourful plants. Evidence that black plants reign supreme in combination with other plants of any hue or colour.

Christopher Lloyd says *"In flowers and plants, black as a living colour is comparatively rare, but is glamorous and sophisticated and therefore greatly to be desired"* (with kind permission of the great man).

At Sissinghurst where the white garden still reigns as queen, we find black plants are being used in other parts of this garden too. Fabulous specimens of *Aeonium* 'Zwartkop' in the border, *Clematis recta* 'Purpurea', the purple leaves are green by the time it flowers, dark *Helianthus annuus* (sunflowers) and *Salpiglossis* as well as dark-leaved *Eucomis* are spread throughout different borders. Will the future see a black and white garden at Sissinghurst?

Black is always a favourite at Chelsea, champion of all that is new and trendy in horticulture and purple foliage plants became tops with the garden designers but we still sadly see the same half a dozen plants used over and over again. Dark *Canna, Oxalis triangularis, Ophiopogon planiscapus* 'Nigrescens', *Geranium phaeum* as well as dark *Berberis* and *Phormium*. Good use of certain black plants can be seen at Wisley, the RHS garden where there is a wonderful bed of *Ophiopogon planiscapus* 'Nigrescens' combined with a golden foliage *Acer*, specimens of *Fagus, Cotinus* and dark *Acer*, but black is not much in evidence here. Likewise at Kew, where there is a superb planting of black *Colocasia* with the giant waterlily, *Victoria amazonica*, and wonderful dark species Begonia, in addition to the many dark plants in the hothouse.

Graham Fraser has created a dark border at the National Trust property, Stoneacre in Kent.

In the U.S., Disneyland at Los Angeles used black plants to create a garden outside the haunted house. At the Chanticleer garden in Pennsylvania, there is a superb courtyard planting of *Alocasia* 'Frydek', *Ipomoea* 'Black Heart' and a variegated *Schefflera*.

Many private gardens on both sides of the Atlantic feature black strongly in the overall garden design and I welcome the day when public gardens are unashamedly black. Black fever is catching.

A trio of darks at Chelsea. Phormium, Canna and Oxalis triangularis ssp papilionacea.

11

THE COLOUR BLACK

Colour is used to evoke a mood. The use of black is exciting, by no means morbid, dismal or ghastly.

A black garden designed by Proven Winners at the San Diego Fair.

Colour is important in the garden, it reflects a mood. It is a powerful communicator. Black used correctly is dynamic. The most evocative and provocative colour in the garden. No other colour has at one and the same time such a subdued tone with such a sensual aura. No wonder it is a firm favourite for gardeners to incorporate in the garden. Never dull, always exciting. Not menacing, but magical. Hardly funereal even in its darkest representations in flower form, but often mysterious. Many dark flowers have the luxurious quality of black silk or velvet. Sumptuous flowers associated with an opulent touch of luxury. Equivalent to the finest deep red wines, the velvet Syrah or an excellent burgundy, as sensuous, full and fruity as the Australian reds and just as heady. Like opening a box of your favourite dark chocolates and letting loose your sensual side. In essence, they are plants about which to become passionate. They speak of indulgence, having a sensuous, sexual quality which no other colour possesses. Dream plants with that extra quality of which plant lovers never tire. Imagine the joy when the dream becomes a reality and the plants are incorporated into your garden. A touch of black, a hint of the splendour of the Arabian nights. A dramatic bed of black flowers and foliage with the sunlight shining through petals and leaves. The garden is your stage, plants are the protagonists, have courage and faith to create the garden you most desire.

Black is the most misunderstood colour in the garden since it represents different things to different people. The words of Coco Chanel when she described the little black dress, can be applied to the best of black plants. "I have said that the little black dress is everything. It is sheer beauty. It is perfect harmony." Sometimes more is said by less, when wearing all-black, it makes a statement all on its own, but the elegant string of pearls adds just the right touch. Apply this to the garden, all-black looks good with some dark plant combinations, but the addition of the equivalent of the string of pearls is strikingly simple and elegant. Black is the colour of the sophisticatd garden. It is truly elegant.

Black is also seen as sexy, seductive and mysterious. Black plants have an immediate attraction, an irresistibility, like a magnet. They are alluring and enticing, glamorous too. The sexual attraction cannot be denied. This is not just an association with the flower colour, but the undeniably phallic spathes of aroids. We are seduced by not only the depth of colour, svelte and suave, but by the shape and suggestiveness of such plants. Black plants are dressed to thrill.

Intriguing and curious too, the shading on many black plants requires a closer look. These are not plants you walk past and forget easily. The mystery is revealed on closer inspection of these oh so noticeable plants which demand our attention.

Desirable. Black is the single most sought after colour in the plant world. These are plants which one wants to possess. Understandably so, they are quite elusive and always have been, but fortunately for black plant lovers they are becoming increasingly available. Testifying to their popularity is their place in the top ten of polls run by many societies such as the American Iris Society.

On the other hand, black can be perceived to represent evil, rebellion and death. The latter are things we need not fear, we are talking plants, there is no evil, no face of death in a black plant. Black is not necessarily gloom and doom. White plants are more commonly used as funereal plants.

Gothic, maybe, but this is not my perception of them at all. Dark, towering with a hint of menace that I would not associate with black plants. Witches and spells are not the magic connections I make, rather that old black magic called love. Menace and fear are torments of the unknown and I cannot apply these irrationalities to plants.

Black is often associated with midnight, however black plants disappear into the night, being consumed by the dark and reflecting no light themselves, these are definitely plants to see in the full light of day.

Black is a colour of contradiction, representing two opposite forces of evil and beauty, horticulturally the beauty comes out on top.

An unusual colour for the garden and some of the most unusual plants of the plant kingdom are dark. The black or purple aroids, the curious purple pitcher plants, *Amorphophallus*, whose name says it all. A monster of a plant with a very dark spathe, one reason to stay out of the rain forests of Borneo where it is found, but what a sight this must be. *Stapelia* and *Huernia* also come in dark shades. But if the colour has its fair share of the more unusual plants, it also has more than its fair share of real beauties. Testament to this are dark orchids such as *Paphiopedilum* with near black petals or pouches, the superb black *Zantedeschia*, the beautiful forms of dark *Arisaema* and *Helleborus orientalis* as well as dark roses to name but a few.

Just as popular and desirable as the dark flowers are the darker foliage tones usually designated as bronze or purple. Purple represents wealth, royalty, sophistication, intelligence, spirituality and dignity. However, in Brazil and many European Catholic countries, it is the colour used to represent death.

Whatever your perception, black is certainly the trendiest colour in the garden. The discerning gardener appreciates black as the colour of the modern garden. It is seen as fashionable. Fashions come and go. However, black plants are not just a passing fancy, there are so many good dark plants capable of making a real contribution to the garden. It is a plant colour of the past as well as the present and the future. Black is the ultimate classic surpassing all fads and fashion and so versatile that it can be used anytime, anywhere, anyplace.

Sombre, spooky, macabre, menacing or funereal are all words misused to describe black plants. To me, they are sexy, fantastic, desirable, glamorous, mysterious, sophisticated and utterly stunning with a velvet quality found in few other flowers. At once, so nostalgic and yet so modern; funereal to some and yet so chic and sexy; dark and mysterious and yet not sombre.

*Black and purple are magical,
passionate plant colours.*

Paphiopedilum 'Black Monarch' x callosum

A dark Helleborus from Heronswood Nursery

IS IT BLACK?

*Black in horticulture is not solid and devoid of hue,
but a mysterious intermingling of rich, velvety tones
which look black in certain light.*

Viola x wittrochiana 'Blackjack'

It is frustrating that black plants are dismissed as not being truly black. There are shades of all colours, and a range of hues to consider. Are all red flowers truly red? What about those true blues? All colours are perceived in a subjective way, and colour within the plantworld is used loosely. Very few black plants are jet black. Jet, incidentally, the incredibly black precious gem, the real thing found in the north Yorkshire seaside town of Whitby, in England, comes from the fossilisation of *Araucaria araucana*, the monkey puzzle tree.

The colouring of most black plants is not actually black for this would mean a total abscence of any other hue or overtone. One can argue the point, but black is in the eye of the beholder. In certain garden settings, with the correct light and backdrop, plants can appear black. To be near black is not a disadvantage; use the wonderful tones which enhance not distract in harmony, as part of a whole.Just as not all reds are the same hue, and not all blues are the same tone, blacks differ too. Black flowers have a dark intensity which is deep without being dull, intense without being sombre. It is the blackness we ultimately seek, made apparent by the tones and shades of velvet reds, intense blues and purples. The variations will work to your advantage.

Black is the most argued over colour in the garden

Black flowers fall into categories usually with a bias of black-blue which appear cooler; black-purple which are warmer, glowing and black-maroon so wonderful with a dusky, rich, glowing intensity in their depth of colour. These are the ones I often feel evoke the mystery of 'black plants'. All three often possess a luxurious velvet quality. Just as popular and desirable are the darker foliage tones which verge on purple, purple-brown, purple-black and bronze-brown.

See plants in flower and leaf if at all possible before you buy, bearing in mind that the colour of the latter may be stronger in one particular season as in good dark spring growth or autumn colouring. These dark plants, flowers or foliage, are treasures. Some are very rare, others disappear fast, but it is always worth the wait to obtain a good black plant.

WHY ARE PLANTS DARK?

Colour is perceived by the eye which absorbs some colours and reflects others. When you mix green, red, yellow and blue, each one absorbs more light so there is less light to reflect and you end up with black. The argument that plants are not black, perhaps should be that black is not a colour at all. What is actually black? Take a felt tip pen and draw a dot on filter paper, add drops of water and be amazed. Yes, there are colours in there that together make black.

The overall effect of dark plants is to perceive them as black, and for ease of reference, this is the way I prefer to think of them.

Most of us know about chlorophyll and its role, but there are other pigments which are important. These are mainly seen in autumn when chlorophyll breaks down and carotenes and xanthophylls predominate leading to glorious autumn (fall) colour. Anthocyanins are responsible for purple colours in plants, the pigment usually being triggered by cool temperatures. Purple plants usually have sunlight independent pigment, which is why new growth is often not dark. Wheat can exhibit purple colouring when phosphorous is in limited supply and when soil level pH falls below 5.5. In addition B genes are dominant in dark plants. These are some of the factors contributing to dark plants.

Horticulturally, black is represented by the darkest near-black flowers with rich overtones of blue, magenta or purple. Deep aubergine (eggplant purple) and plum purples and the richness of imperial robes together with inky velvet purples, deepest indigo blues and sumptuous deepest magenta.

In foliage we find a range of brown to bronze through purple to black. True blacks are hard to find. What we have within this colour, horticulturally designated as black plants, is the darkest range of plants known in horticulture.

IS NIGER BLACK?

It is worth noting that the latin specific epithets (the second word in a given botanical name) such as *niger, nigra, nigricans, nigrescens* are not always an indication that a plant possesses dark flowers or foliage. In *Betula nigra,* the specific epithet refers to the dark bark, for *Helleborus niger* it refers to the root, and with regard to *Hydrangea* 'Nigra' it is the black stems that are black.

The same is true with common names, where there is little indication of the colour of the plant even when it is named black. So too with the use of the word black in cultivar names, which again does not necessarily signify that a plant has black flowers or foliage. Often it is the cultivar names which are odd, bizarre or strange, not the plants themselves. One must always remember that black is a selling point. So a darkish plant will often be given the name 'black'.

THE DARKEST OF THE DARK

The black enthusiast searches for the blackest of all. The darkest plant is thought to be *Eustoma nigrescens (Lisianthus)* from Mexico, sadly very difficult to bring into cultivation.

Most 'black' plants do not exist in the wild, they have been hybridized. In cultivation, with current breeding work, we can expect yet more dark plants to appear on the market.

Iris chrysographes black forms are probably the darkest plants you will find readily available. Many bearded *Iris* are extremely dark. The darkest regal *Pelargonium* is 'Springfield Black'. Aroids such as *Arisaema speciosum* and *Arum palaestinum* also provide us with near black spathes. *Viola*s and pansies offer good midnight black flowers.

One of the finest black-maroon plants I ever saw, was named *Scabiosa* 'Satchmo', and how I wish I still had this, incredibly dark, a big flower, very beautiful, much finer than any of the other dark *Scabiosa*. I grew it in 1995 and I recently spoke with the importer of

The black foliage of Ophiopogon planiscapus 'Nigrescens'

this and he is trying to obtain it again. The best black-blues are without doubt found amongst the bearded *Iris*. The finest black-purples also amongst bearded *Iris* and in *Streptocarpus* 'Black Panther'.

The most incredibly black foliage plant is without a rival, *Ophiopogon planiscapus* 'Nigrescens'. *Solenostemon (Coleus)* are becoming darker and darker with the near black foliage of *S.* 'Dark Star' and *S.* 'Black Prince'. With good heat and light *Ipomoea batatas* 'Black Heart' and *I. batatas* 'Blackie' are hard to beat for the depth of colour in their leaves. Foliage of *Dahlia* from the latest breeding programmes in New Zealand have produced some good, very dark blackish foliage with little or no green showing, such as *D.* 'Midnight Sun' and *D.* 'Fire Mountain' superior to the colour previously available.

Positioning of black plants is more important than that of any other hue

Tones change in relation to sunlight. It is not improbable for different tones to appear dominant at different times of the day or when viewed from different angles and positions.

17

Photographing plants at different times of day is an eye-opener. Looking at a plant from different angles reveals the plant as a whole. Even with modern colour reproduction and printing, one still has to bear in mind the limitations of the photographer, the scanner and the printer in capturing the true colour of a given plant. Dark plants are notoriously difficult to photograph well, usually involving under exposure, a practice I have not employed. Dark plants photographed in late afternoon light give good dark tones, quite a different tone to that of harsh midday light. Colour of dark flowers and foliage alike is affected by the amount of light falling upon it, rendering positioning of dark plants in the garden of chief importance. Dark plants usually colour best in full sun, but bear in mind that some of the darkest *Hemerocallis (day lilies)* will fade in strong, direct sun. The glaucous purple foliage of *Rosa glauca* is attractive in full sun and much planted, yet in shade it presents an altogether different aspect, a sad greyish-green with a mauve tinge. This apparent change in colour is applicable to many dark foliaged plants whose green tones will come through stronger in shade.

The soil in which a dark plant is grown and the amount of water and feed, light and temperature, even the root run are all factors which can contribute to the depth of colour. Some plants such as *Strobilanthes anisophyllus* and *Ipomoea batatas 'Blackie'* are greatly affected by light and heat. Generally speaking, for best colour, place with the sun behind, and watch the fabulous effect when the sun shines through the leaves of dark foliage such as *Fagus sylvatica* 'Purpurea'. Many dark flowers look darker when the sun is low and coming from the side. The play of light in the garden is one of the biggest joys I encounter, being able to use light to its full advantage is one of the secrets of good planting. The fall of light onto the leaves of Heuchera and other purple-leaved plants is fantastic, transforming them into sparkling jewels.

Juxtaposition of plants can also play an important part in how dark plants appear. *Tulipa* 'Queen of Night' is a good strong dark tulip. Planted with white, the depth of colour is enhanced greatly. Good contrasts make the colour appear darker than it is in reality. White is the obvious contrast for its luminosity but pale pink and pastels work equally well.

From flower to flower, the colour can change, understandably so where foliage or flowers are at different stages of growth. Some black plants have a tendency to fade, offering yet another variety of hues. If growing from seed, you will often find many variations in colour from one seed packet and it is advisable and necessary to rigorously rogue out and select the darkest plants, this is best not done at seedling stage as colour in leaf and in flower often only comes with maturity, as with *Antirrhinum majus* 'Black Prince'.

Buds can be enticingly dark, offering an irresistible promise, sometimes they do not disappoint, but they are not always an indication of the darkness that lies within. On the other hand, some *Pelargonium* are quite pale in bud to begin with until they open into those lavishly dark, velvety petals.

Curiously, dark foliage and flowers rarely come together, two exceptions being the sweet william, *Dianthus barbatus* 'Sooty' and the snapdragon, *Antirrhinum nanum* 'Black Prince'. Both are grown from seed and in both cases the darkest foliage and flowers is only found in rigorously selected plants.

The enticingly dark Iris 'Black Knight' in bud.

18

BLACK IN THE GARDEN

Black is a powerful colour which can be used with subtlety or the full force of its dynamism.

A black garden designed by Proven Winners

DESIGNING WITH BLACK

Whether you want to use black as accents and highlights or as the main colour of your garden is a matter of choice. Either way black is a dramatic colour. It is so versatile, harmonising with other colours or taking pride of place on its own.

Blended into existing borders to uplift tired plantings or as the main colour for a newly created garden, black easily fits into many garden themes. Use it to its full potential in any garden situation.

Powerful focal points are easily created. Let the drama of black plants work their magic in the garden. The exquisite and unusual beauty of black flowers cannot go unnoticed, their arresting quality demands attention. Love them or hate them, they cause much comment and attract attention.

All plant designs and planting suggestions, are given here as an introduction, adapt, change or use them as a starting point. Be bold and brave. Employ highlights and contrasts as you perceive them to fit into the overall scheme, without being bound too much, if at all, by rules and regulations of garden design or colour restrictions. Experiment and be flexible. Use your own eye to judge if you have it right.

Black breaks the mould, it is the most powerful colour in the gardener's palette. Be prepared to break all the rules.

BLACK ON BLACK

Black plants are no longer fashionable for the few, black has become the must-have colour. Above any other, I would always plant a black plant, for the intensity of colour in foliage or flowers; I believe nothing can compete as long as it is a garden worthy plant. Does the plant look good, is it well-behaved, does it retain its colour for a sufficient length of time are all questions the gardener needs to ask.

Limitations in gardening to one colour are often discouraged in many ways, and I am not proposing that we all suddenly dig up our gardens and plant black alone. I believe it can be achieved in a limited space, but it is not an easy task to do well. I frequently put black plants together on their own and favourite combinations are demonstrated throughout the book. The selection of plants is of utmost importance. When placing darks together plants must be in varying degrees of 'blackness'; choose the varying hues to complement one another. *Ophiopogon* works better with the purplish-black *Viola* 'Barnsdale Gem' than it does with the silky black, nearer tone of *V.* 'Molly Sanderson'. The black mondo grass also looks like a dream with the brownish foliage of *Ranunculus*. The tones of dark plants are wide and varied and can be used effectively as excellent companions. Aim to create a pleasing tonal scheme, to attempt the creation of a one-toned black garden would fail miserably, just the same as any other one-toned, one colour garden. If it needs contrasting or complementary colour, add it. I do believe most firmly and emphatically that there are instances where black can work alone.

The dark garden is not dull, but dusky in a sensual way. Full of mystery, of a new adventure. Black is the colour for the most adventurous gardener. Used imaginatively, you can create an aesthetically pleasing dark garden.

Two darks working togeher Ophiopogon planiscapus 'Nigrescens' and Ranunculus ficaria 'Brazen Hussy'

THE PERFECT PARTNER

However good black is on its own, one of the best reasons for using black in your garden is the fact that it goes with almost any colour. Used as a contrast, black is not over-dominant, rendering it so very easy to accommodate in the garden. Not only is black a good complementary colour, but the plants themselves are easy to adapt to any planting scheme, be it formal or informal, the creation of a cottage garden or the latest, most bizarre aspect of modern designer gardening which seems to include more hardware in the way of furniture, decking and lighting than plants. Black is an excellent companion to sparse modern planting. Concrete and black go hand in hand. A gravel garden with nothing but a large container filled with a black specimen plant such as *Colocasia* is perfect. Furthermore, it is just as adaptable as green for foliage effect, in fact it can be used effectively as if it were dark green and makes a good foil for lighter shades. Black has so much to offer and is deserving of a place in the garden.

Cotinus coggygria 'Royal Purple' and Berberis thunbergii 'Aurea'

Black goes with anything. I enjoy it on its own or with the whole spectrum of colours. In my garden I have a black border in its own right where I have planted several shrubs and perennials interspersed with bulbs and annuals. I also have created a black and red border with white and pastel highlights, a black and blue border and a black and green border. The possibilities are endless.

Exploit the perfectly contrasting flowers of dark-leaved plants to their best advantage. Dark foliage plants come in all shapes, sizes and textures and if variety is the spice of life, black plants have it all as they are found across numerous genera and are therefore ideal in many situations in the garden. This is the great appeal of black plants. There is a dark plant to suit any garden situation, any type of soil, any container or border. Dark plantings are easily extended with the use of stem, bark or berry.

Think black, think again, think endless possibilities for using the tones and hues together or as contrasts.

Lysimachia ciliata 'Firecracker' offers a perfect foil for Astrantaia major

21

BLACK AND WHITE

White gardens are undeniably beautiful, Vita Sackville-West knew what she was doing when she created the white garden at Sissinghurst, the most imitated garden in the world. Fairy-like, a harking back to childhood, the longing for an elusive quality of something once possessed. It is one of my favourite gardens, there are so many white flowers I enjoy. Black is undeniably beautiful too. Imagine using the two together to form a symphony of contrasting colour. The qualities of each colour, the one luminous, the other tenebrous, light and dark become one whole. White flowers serve their purpose to make the darks appear even darker, whilst blacks enhance the luminosity of the whites. If we find blacks are not truly black, many whites are not all radiantly white. Yet, it is the cream or green-white tones which are so welcome and not so radiantly stark as 'pure' whites. A secondary contrast completes the planting admirably, the addition of silver plants or ornamental grasses are the most effective combinations.

Black and white is sophisticated and smart like formal dress.

The black and white theme is a popular one; a formal, ordered representation of tone. Style and elegance should be in every garden. Achieve it by using this union of two opposing colours.

In a predominantly white garden, black is used as a focal point. When making a black garden with white highlights, select and position plants carefully. Balance is the essence of all contrast. Classic black and white plantings are easy to create. Foliage and texture come into their own in a garden of stark contrast.

Use bulbs, in pots or borders to extend the season. Spring would not be spring without the most classic black and white combination for its simple elegance, *Tulipa* 'Queen of Night' and *T.* 'Purissima', is truly breathtaking. It may seem odd to talk of a black plant which personifies purity, but *T.* 'Queen of Night' is purity itself for me. Plant with *Salvia officinalis Purpurea* Group, the silvery *Cynara cardunuculus* and clouds of *Myosotis sylvestris,* forget-me-nots.

In the border black and white sweet peas, intermingled with *Clematis* form an excellent backdrop for *Allium, Penstemon, Centaurea, Scabiosa, Dianthus, Papaver* and *Pelargonium*, all abundant in black and white. Admirable in this setting is *Geranium phaeum* 'Album' and *G. phaeum* itself, or *G. phaeum* 'Samobor' which has the added attraction of good black leaf markings. Allow *Ophiopogon planiscapus* 'Nigrescens' to creep through the near white succulent rosettes of *Sedum spathulifolium* 'Cape Blanco'.

A cherished planting of mine is the simple juxtaposition of black and white *Lathyrus odoratus (sweet peas)* which is very easy to accomplish and always remarked upon. I have also grown *L. odoratus* 'Midnight' climbing amongst *Dahlia* 'Chat Noir' which was awesome, two darks, working very well together. This combination gave me great pleasure.

Picture a pond of black and white *Nymphaea (water lilies).* Majestic plants, but never more so than in the intensely deep red, overlaid with black *N.* 'Black Opal' in conjunction with the purity of *Zantedeschia aethiopica* 'Crowborough' and dark *Colocasia* 'Black Magic'.

Create a dramatic frame for the main entance to your home with *Wisteria x formosa* 'Kokuryu' and a good white flowered *Wisteria* such as *W. sinensis* 'Alba'. Another exciting way to use these fabulous climbers with amazing pendulent flowers is an arbour where the whole structure is covered with the plant and it becomes almost den-like. Be adventurous with your choice of plants and even more so with how you use them. Great gardens are made by gardeners who are willing to try anything.

Black and white schemes can also make use of flowers which nature has already endowed with a combination of these two sought after colours.

The most used example of this is the excellent border plant *Aquilegia vulgaris* 'William Guiness' ('Magpie'). This mixes handsomely with *Dianthus* 'Black and White Minstrels'. A fabulous looking plant, deep maroon and white petals, but one I find in my

A pond is a good dominant feature of a black and white garden. Employ the moisture lovers Colocasia and Zantedeschia, teamed with Nymphaea. Raised beds are easily maintained filled with black and white foliage and flowers. Pots placed around the central pond overflow with Ipomoea, Colocasia, Heuchera and white Hosta. Walls are clothed with climbers.

experience to be a weak grower. Dark-leaved, white-flowered plants are few, Dahlia 'Fusion' is one of the best, its flowers having a pinkish tinge.

Enhance black and white schemes by using the blackest foliage, *Ophiopogon planiscapus* 'Nigrescens' is deservedly the chief protagonist. *Aeonium* 'Zwartkop' will appreciate increased light levels and reward you with almost true black shining petals. Employ my cheat's guide to using black plants and include a little purple foliage too. None better than *Ajuga* for ground cover, use *A.* 'Valfredda' ('Chocolate Chip') and *A.* 'Mahogany', snip off the blue flowers if you want to keep it pure black, purple leaves and white flowers. Talking about snipping off flowers, use plenty of *Solenostemon* such as *S.* 'Merlot' in frost free areas. *Trifolium* 'Quadrifolium Purpurascens' ('Dark Dancer') is good in containers, divided frequently, it grows at an astonishing rate and looks good in spring.

Another latest trend is in white foliage, I saw the release at Chelsea of the first white-leaved *Hosta* in the U.K., but there are others already out and about in the U.S. such as *H.* 'Mostly Ghostly' and *H.* 'White Wall Tyres'. A must-have all white *Ophiopogon* 'Snow Dragon' sounds far too good to be true. A white leaved *Trifolium* with dark markings is quite astonishing. *Colocasia* 'Nancy's Revenge' is a show-stopper. Whitish leaved *Caladiums* and *Hypoestes* 'White Splash' would be interesting to use in warmer areas or as summer fillers.

A favourite combination of white and black is a mixed planting of *Aruncus dioicus, Astrantia major* 'Hadspen Blood', *Stipa barbata* 'Silver Feather', *Heuchera* 'Velvet Night'. Near the poolside, or in retentive soil try *Astilbe* 'Snowdrift', *Actaea (Cimicifuga) simplex* 'Hillside Black Beauty', *Rheum palmatum, Ligularia* 'Desdemona' and a white leaved *Hosta*. I also have a penchant for *Sanguinaria canadensis*. Any of the white daisies such as *Argyranthemum* look good with dark *Heuchera*.

In a large pot, try black and white flowered Viola around the base of the darkest *Cordyline* or *Phormium* you can find, my preference would be *Cordyline* 'Black Tower' and *Phormium* 'Platt's Black',

with the darkest *Pelargonium* possible, choose *P.* 'Springfield Black' or *P.* 'Black Butterfly' or the trailing *P.* 'Tomcat' and I would not object to the redder tones of any of the dark *Pelargonium, P.* 'Lord Bute' is a good performer and therefore always one for which I can make a space, although this is no longer the darkest by far. A mixture of *Pelargonium* can be quite effective. *P.* 'Vancouver Centennial' with its dark bronze leaves and vivid flowers also combines well with *Phormium*. A cloud of *Gypsophila paniculata* is welcome to break the solidity of plantings with its airy quality. *Crambe cordifolia* is also a plant which blends well in most plantings.

White shines in the dark, choose a shady spot for white flowers and they will literally glow in the dark. Another airy plant, and one I love very much is *Gaura lindheimeri* 'The Bride'. *Corylus maxima* 'Purpurea', *Anemone hupehensis* and *Digitalis purpurea* 'Alba' look superb in a shady setting; not too much shade for the *Corylus* or the colour will be lost.

The deep, shiny purple foliage of *Berberis thunbergii* 'Bagatelle' looks good with *Clematis* 'Early Sensation'. Enjoy the combination of *Heuchera* 'Chocolate Veil', *Anthemis cupiana* and *Gypsophila cerastoides* in a sunnier spot. The tubular white flowers of *Nicotiana sylvestris* 'Only The Lonely' are a joy. Annuals such as *Nicotiana* 'Domino White' and *Nigella damascena* 'Alba', with that most wonderful of common names love-in-a-mist, are always welcome, lifting a planting if it has become too dark and filling unwanted bare ground. Allow *Nigella* to seed itself where it wants to be. Valuable for its lovely feathery foliage and the addition of superb seedheads. There is now a seed strain called 'Albion' with black and green seedheads.

BLACK AND SILVER

Silver foliage plants are often used in white gardens. Softening a scheme dramatically, the contrast is not as harsh as a clear cut black and startling white. Silver-grey associates well with the darkest foliage in black or purple. Incorporate these plants in schemes to achieve a subtle effect, softening the stronger tones of black plants. The best silver plants are feathery *Artemisia*, my favourites are *A. stelleriana* 'Mori's' form and *A. ludoviciana v albula*. Silky *Celmisia semicordata* is a superb plant with sword-like, hairy leaves. Tender silver-grey *Convolvulus cneorum* makes a useful mound. *Cynara cardunculus* is used for its immense stature and dramatic effect of its large sculptured leaves, valued for leading the eye upwards. Its purple flower heads are not too out of place in the black garden, especially where purple foliage has been used. *Pulmonaria saccharata Argentea Group* is a plant for which I can always find a space. Furry *Salvia argentea* with its superb rosettes of densely hairy leaves; smooth or intricately lacy. *Senecio cineraria* in either lacy or smooth leaves. The soft, woolly, felted leaves of *Stachys byzantina* which are so wonderful to touch. The dead nettles *Lamium maculatum* 'White Nancy' or *Lamiastrum* 'Herman's Pride' for underplanting, their silvery leaves are most useful in shedding light in shade. Tender *Lavandula lanata* is a wonderful contrast with its densely woolly leaves and dark purple spikes of flowers, deserving to be more widely used. A substantial silvery shrub is found in *Salix lanata* making a good mound against which to plant darker foliage and flowers. The beautiful tree, *Pyrus salicifolia* is hard to beat as a specimen of shimmering, shining silver foliage. The white stems of some *Rubus ssp* would not be out of place in such a scheme.

All these examples offer valuable different shapes and textures capable of producing stunning planting associations. Felted or woolly leaves appear silver. Use them amongst dark grasses, including *Ophiopogon* which is not truly a grass, and the darkest foliage of *Heuchera, Dahlia, Solenostemon (Coleus)*, hardy *Geranium and Canna*. Black and silver on the same plant is not a common occurence, *Heuchera* 'Green Spice' is therefore favoured for its combinations of silvery-green foliage with superb black-purple veining, a capital plant amongst new *Heuchera* which are so useful both in the garden and in containers. Combine with the dark mini foliage of *Ajuga* 'Valfredda' (Chocolate Chip) for a stunning combination. *Heuchera* 'Velvet Night' just glistens in the border and is superb underplanted with silver or golden foliage. You can almost feel the sap pounding through those black veins. *Heuchera* with large, metallic scalloped leaves are superb dramatic backdrops for many other colour contrasts. The undersides of these plants are often just as fascinating as the leaves above.

A window box of *Solenostemon (Coleus)* of varying darks such as *S.* 'Dark Star', *S.* 'Black Prince' and *S.* 'Merlot', the blistered and puckered *S.* 'Molten Lava' an easy seed strain, the dark dusky *Antirrhinum nanum* 'Black Prince', *Begonia semperflorens* bronze foliage and silvery *Senecio cineraria* works well.

Deep red magenta foliage such as *Beta* Bull's Blood or *B.* 'Macgregor's Favourite' or *Plantago major* 'Rubrifolia' are an excellent foil for silver plants.

An interesting combination is found in *Papaver orientale* 'Black and White', a dark *Heuchera* such as 'Ebony and Ivory' or *H.* 'Plum Pudding' and the silver foliage of *Convolvulus cneorum*.

Dark foliaged *Sedum* such as *S.* 'Lynda and Rodney' or *S.* 'Purple Emperor' associate well with the shimmering foliage of *Artemisia absinthium* 'Lambrook Silver', superb with a dark rose behind, *Rosa* 'Ruby Celebration' fits the bill admirably. The grace of the wands of the angel's fishing rod, *Dierama pulchellum*, whose flowers can be suitably dark in a true form of *D.* 'Blackbird' look even better with their bare stems hidden by *Stachys byzantina* without detracting from their delicate beauty.

Try concentric circles of black and silver around a dark central specimen plant.

Silver softens schemes

THE BLACK AND GOLD PLOT

When creating a black, purple and golden scheme there is tremendous scope for eye-catching, dramatic colour combination. Scintillating combinations are easy with these colours and it is simplicity itself to make a garden that glows golden and glamorous.

Gold foliage provides the perfect accompaniment to dark foliage from black to purple. Just as there are few true blacks, gold is a nicer way of saying yellow. The problem with golden foliage is that it often suffers badly in sun and can look sickly. Not so with the new breed of golden foliage plants beginning to emerge. Excellent grasses to use are *Carex hachijoensis* 'Evergold' for its broad yellow central stripes on the green leaves, or the fabuously gold *Carex elata* 'Aurea', *Milium effusum* 'Aureum' the deservedly well-loved Bowles' Golden Grass or *Hakonechloa macra* 'Aureola', the wonderful grass that always appears as if its cup is over-flowing. Grasses blend well with dark foliage and solid leaved plants such as *Bergenia, Solenostemon (Coleus), Heuchera* and *Geranium* and are a perfect compliment to so many plants found in the dark garden.

Dan Heims introducd *Heuchera* 'Amber Waves' which retains its golden tones throughout the season, making a perfect foil for dark foliage.

In addition, there are also numerous shrubs and perennials from which to choose to add a golden glow to your dark schemes. Ensure a balance when combining these strong contrasting colours. Deep, dark foliage often has yellow or orange flowers, offering natural ready-made contrast for a real sunshine garden. Succulents are a good choice. Allow *Sedum* 'Angelina' to interweave into your dark plantings, it is a truly golden addition to the garden, looking superb with *Ipomoea, Ophiopogon, Ajuga* or *Solenostemon (Coleus)*. Many *Berberis* have yellow flowers such as *B. x ottawensis* 'Superba' to combine with the purple foliage. This is a taller and more vigorous plant than *B. thunbergii f atropurpurea.* The

light purple foliage of *B. thunbergii* 'Golden Ring' is narrowly margined in golden yellow. *Dahlia* are like the sun coming through the clouds when you choose dark-leaved varieties with yellow flowers. Planted en masse these are very uplifting to the spirits. *D.* 'Midnight Sun', one of the newly bred *Dahlia* to come out of New Zealand, has deep yellow flowers over almost black foliage on tall plants. The soft yellow and vermilion flowers of *D.* 'Moonfire' are quite distinctive combined with the dark purple foliage. *D.* 'Yellow Hammer' has perfectly contrasting almost black foliage. I am very partial to garden worthy *Euphorbia*, and they fit suitably into the black, purple and golden scheme, at their best in spring, offering maroon to purple colouring. *E. dulcis* 'Chameleon' and *E. cotinifolia* are the darkest. In damp ground, employ *Ligularia dentata* 'Dark Beauty' with its smallish, star-shaped yellow flowers and dark leaves as a striking contrast to yellow flowered plants enjoying such conditions.

Ranunculus performs a spring spectacular, with many dark-foliaged forms having yellow flowers. *R.* 'Brazen Hussy', discoverd by Christopher Lloyd, is still probably the best of an ever-increasing number of dark forms.

For a truly striking display, try a round bed of *Hakonechloa macra* 'Aureola' with a dark *Acer* or surrounding *Berberis* 'Helmond Pillar'.

Good yellow plants with green foliage which can play a part on this stage include Inula helenium or I. magnifica, yellow bearded Iris as well as the fabulous Lysichiton americanus which has startlingly brilliant yellow spathes.

Just as there are white plants with black centres, we encounter a range of creamy yellow plants with dark centres which are sumptuous. Chief amongst these is *Hibiscus trionum*, a superb annual and truly beautiful flower. *Helianthus debilis* 'Italian White' is pale yellow with dark centres which will stand well beside dark flowered sunflowers. Another possibility is x *Halimocistus wintonensis* 'Merrist Wood Cream'.

Gold glows and uplifts, whilst darks focus the eye in a drift.

> Gold is sunlight,
> Black is midnight

This black and gold design was created for
The San Fransisco Flower Show. Pots on
the patio teem with Colocasia, Ipomoea,
Heuchera and Solenostemon.
The colour scheme is reflected by four
dominant succulent towers created by
LivingWreath.com and echoed by
the backdrop of shrubs.
An archway gives a view of the
garden to the reflective area
at the far end.

© KAREN PLATT 2002

27

THE COTTAGE GARDEN

The cottage garden style still retains its popularity though other trends come and go. I love the idea of clothing walls around the doorway with scented roses or wisteria, rather vigorous for this purpose, both of which are available in dark forms. Employ dark *Clematis* on walls, obelisks or growing through shrubs, I believe *C.* 'Romantika' to be the darkest, its flowers are almost black on opening, deepest purple when open. Beware the sun which can fade dark clematis. *C. x jackmannii* is still one of the best purples. The free flowering, almost untidy look of a cottage garden in charge of its own destiny, not clipped and over-trained and tied up by the master's hand, has great appeal. No lawns, no bare soil, just plants in abundance, even overflowing onto paths and tumbling down walls. What joy!

Superb flowers evocative of the cottage garden include *Alcea rosea* 'Nigra', beautifully dark and combining well with *Crambe maritima* which makes a fabulous white haze in front of those rather large, but not too handsome hollyhock leaves along with *Malva moschata f alba*. Dark, mysterious *Dianthus* 'Sooty' and *Antirrhinum nanum* 'Black Prince' which should reward you with dark maroon-black foliage, purplish red on the underside, and dark dusky red flowers with that magical velvet touch. Both look good with *Nicotiana* 'Only The Lonely', *N.* 'Domino White', or choose *N. alata* if you wish to be a night flower-sniffer. *Rosa glauca* enhances the effect whilst *Stachys byzantina* adds a shimmering silver touch to dark combinations. The stately spires of *Delphinium* in ever deeper shades, some with an attractive black bee work well with *Veratrum nigrum* and its white counterpart in front of the deep dark foliage of *Cotinus* 'Royal Purple'. *Digitalis purpurea* 'Alba' would mingle nicely.

Dark sweet peas add interest climbing on willow supports. Enjoy their flowers indoors too, picking regularly to maintain flowering. Gallica roses are favourites of cottage gardeners, partnered with *Sedum* 'Purple Emperor' associating perfectly with *Artemisia* 'Lambrook Silver' to add a sparkle to the whole. Choose the darkest *Potentilla* 'Etna' to add a neat dark accent to the border along with easy to please *Hebe*. *Euphorbia amygdaloides* 'Purpurea' is a charming addition along with *Geranium phaeum* and *Aquilegia vulgaris* 'William Guiness'. Choose *Dianthus* (pinks), *D. barbatus* (sweet william), *Centaurea cyanus* (cornflowers), *Helianthus annuus* (sunflowers) and *Erysimum* (wallflowers) as all these firm cottage garden favourites are now available in the darkest shades. *Papaver somniferum flore pleno* black (listed in seed catalogues as *P. paeoniflorum*) is a must for this setting; seeding itself effortlessly, thereby enhancing the planting with its silky dark petals. *Lavendula* too is an essential cottage plant, emitting a welcome fragrance, dark purple appearing black in tone. *Scabiosa atropurpurea* and *Knautia macedonica* add button flowers; *Knautia* is usually the paler of the two and is smaller and more compact. *Allium* are valued for their large globe heads, still earning their part in the garden as they go to seed. Dark leaved or dark flowered *Dahlia* and *Salvia* make a valuable late summer contribution.

Use *Astrantia major* 'Hadspen Blood' coupled with *Aruncus dioicus*. A dark climbing rose adds height, interplanted with a white *Clematis*, dark and white *Paeonia* in the foreground, stately dark bearded *Iris*, with mysterious, dark *Dianthus* in the foreground intermingled with the purity of white *Iberis*. Dark *Penstemon* can be used to advantage in this setting. *Viola riviniana* 'Purpurea' makes groundcover, perhaps a little too easily, so keep your eye on it, and do intervene with this one's progress. *Primula* 'Garnet' will greet the spring with its velvet red blossoms, looking good with *Pulmonaria* 'Sissinghurst White'. Dark *Tulipa* will happily follow. Allow the darkest *Aubretia* to tumble over walls, combined with *Sedum spathulifolium* 'Purpureum' or 'Cape Blanco' to provide contrast where needed.

Plant up window boxes with dark *Pelargonium*, *Impatiens tinctoria*, dark leaved *Tropaeolum majus* (nasturtiums) 'Red Wonder', and black *Viola x wittrochiana* (pansies).

The essential English cottage style garden is effective when planted dark. Wisteria, Clematis and Lonicera clothe the walls hand in hand with dark shrubs , Berberis 'Helmond Pillar' and Ilex meservae lead the eye upwards. Dark Ajuga, Heuchera, Lavandula and Salvia tumble onto paths, with Hebe, Dianthus, Dahlia, Pelargonium, Sedum and tall Alcea completing the picture.

A cottage garden

A ROMANTIC ROSE GARDEN

Roses growing alone is something I am not in favour of, but roses I must grow. There is nothing like a rose. There is nothing so romantic as a dark rose. Romance is still alive, it has just turned a shade darker. Romance enters the twentieth century with near black roses instead of the usual red. The rose to me is the ultimate symbol of love. Dark roses are a foretaste of heaven. Forget the English front garden with a dozen ill-pruned roses struggling with black spot and other infamous rose diseases. Know how to use them, cultivate them and you will love them. Use them in a mixed border, but never plant directly underneath as roses have shallow roots. Be aware that soil can become rose sick and you will not be able to replant in the same soil for some years. Buy a good plant to start with and you have almost won the battle.

Roses look wonderful over pergolas or arches of any kind. I like to see roses growing on great swags across the garden, this adds height and gives wonderful summer colour, choose scented varieties that waft on the breeze and you will forever want to be in the garden. I look at my roses almost every day. From the moment they are in bud, they hold a fascination for me. The rose is one of the plants I associate with my childhood. An old family friend grew R. 'Josephine Bruce'. The perfume, the deep red velvet flowers are forever associated in my mind with his garden. It is still a favourite rose of mine. Shapely, fully double flowers, available as a modern hybrid tea and even better as a climber, strong and vigorous. Sometimes plants obtained under this name have little scent and a weak neck, but it is one of its parents you have bought if you find it to perform in such a way . Not the darkest, but lovely nonetheless, it is not sentiment alone which makes me love this deep velvet rose.

I grow R. 'Ruby Celebration' , R. 'Deep Secret' for its fabulous scent, black buds and new foliage appearing reddish. R. 'Black Beauty' an excellent cutting rose is to be recommended. R. 'Louis X1V' is admirable for its almost black flowers and fragrance, R. 'Nuits de Young' which is one of the darkest of the old roses and R. 'Tuscany Superb', a large gallica bearing semi-double blooms of the deepest, darkest crimson. Alongside roses, grow bearded *Iris, Paeonia, Camilla, Geranium phaeum* 'Samobor', a dark *Heuchera*, the darkest but slightly tender *Lavandula* I have seen and grown to date, *L. stoechas* 'Regal Splendour', there appears to be some black in here, and the little bunny ears have veining verging on black. In my rose border I have two dark-leaved Hebe, one pink, the other deeper flowered, a white rose, *R.* 'Iceberg' (which was already in the garden), and a dark *Fuchsia. Geranium* 'Ann Folkard' with its deep magenta flowers centred black, sprawls over the whole all summer long. To the back are *Lonicera* 'Dropmore Scarlet' and *Jasminum officinale* with its heady scent, so reminiscent of the East, close my eyes and I am in Tunisia once more with a thousand stars in the sky above me. It's a wonderful effect of dark red roses and a pinkish mist. At ground level to the fore are *Viola* in black and white, a pink *Sedum* 'Herbstfreude' (Autumn Joy) and purple *Sedum* 'Purple Emperor'. *Scopolia carniolica* 'Zwanenberg' gives a terrific spring show along with *Dicentra spectabilis* 'Alba'. *Scopolia* are interesting plants, allied to *Atropa belladonna* (deadly nightshade), but not nearly so poisonous, its sumptuous deep purple bells are accompanied by much green foliage. I inherited a pink *Rhododendron* here, which I have kept. When I am favoured the white *Agapanthus* makes a show in late summer in between the dark roses. It does not always favour me, the fault is mine alone, the plant is rather overcrowded and it likes elbow room to perform well. Any gaps I fill with different annuals, usually of dark red, pink or white. *Cosmos* 'Sonata' worked well one year. *Scabiosa atropurpurea* is good too. The idea is to have very little soil on view. It is a border which is almost maintenance free, a little autumn pruning if necessary; my style of gardening.

The darkest of roses are the most romantic

30

ORNAMENTAL GRASSES

Drifts of herbaceous perennials and grasses are an easy theme in black and purple. Colour is in general on the paler side and the effect is wispy, giving a desirable, airy contrast to more solid plants. Ornamental grasses are such fabulous plants, they deserve to be in every garden. The wispy, airy, soft appearance of many grasses adds another dimension in planting. Plumes, often arched are truly graceful and enchanting. Their use in structure and movement are invaluable.

No grass guru would want to be without *Carex*, offering as it does lovely, bronze foliage, like butterscotch and toffee, these warm tones are welcome in the garden. *C.* 'Toffee Twist' is an excellent container plant with delightfully wispy foliage with wonderfully warm bronze tones. Usually grown for their foliage, some *Carex* species such as *C.* atrata and *C.* dipsacea have black flowers.

Uncinia, the hook sedge, is also useful, darker than *Carex* and with much stiffer foliage, these sedges enjoy damp or moist soil. *U. egmontiana* I find to be the best of these. All bear dark plumes and seed now and then. Clumps need to be replaced fairly regularly.

Tall *Miscanthus* make a statement and are superb specimen plants but also mix well in the border. *M. sinensis v purpurascens* has foliage which turns purple-green with pink midribs and spikelets of purplish flowers in autumn. Leave these in place for the seedheads which look so wonderful in autumn. The dark crimson plumes of *M. sinensis* 'Morning Light' are another possibility. *Panicum miliaceum* 'Violaceum' is an erect annual with purple-violet leaves and graceful, deep purple spikelets in nodding heads borne in late summer. *P. virgatum* 'Shenandoah' makes a small and neat clump of purple foliage topped by airy plumes to 90cm (3ft).

Pennisetum are wonderful grasses with good purplish foliage. Very touchable, very soft, resist stroking if you can. *P. alopecuroides* 'Moudry' is quite a rare black-seeded fountain grass, so too *P.* 'National Arboretum' which has black-blue fruits. The leaves of *P. setaceum* 'Rubrum' are dark purple, a favourite with me for its wonderful soft, deep crimson plumes from midsummer to autumn. *P.* 'Red Riding Hood' is a dwarfer version of the above and a superb choice for front of the border or containers. Leaves, stems and flowers are a rich burgundy. *P. setaceum* 'Burgundy Giant', on a larger scale is deepest burgundy throughout. Sadly, British summers are often too cool and far too short for *Pennisetum* to flower well here, if at all, they need a good long, hot summer such as in the Midwest of the U.S. where they flower happily until first frosts.

If you have never grown *Melica altissima* 'Atropurpurea' now is the time to do so. An immensely attractive grass bearing erect spikelets with densely flowered tips of a lustrous deep purple from May onwards, paler as they age throughout summer. This graceful addition to any garden increases slowly. It stands well as a specimen or in the border, best in woodland soil, in sun or shade.

Uncinia rubra tries to cheer this doleful container

31

Pennisetum setaceum 'Rubrum'

Large grasses are an excellent companion for big, bold perennials such as *Eupatorium rugosum* 'Chocolate', dark-leaved *Actaea (Cimicifuga)* with white bottlebrush flowers and *Macleaya cordata* (Plume Poppy), the botanical name is a mix-up and the plant is very much on the vigorous side. They work equally well with dark-leaved *Canna*, the big dark leaves of *Colocasia* 'Black Magic' and *Ensete ventricosum* 'Maurelii'. Grasses look good together whether large or small, there are some excellent grass island beds to be seen at gardens open to the public. Grass-like plants such as *Ophiopogon and Uncinia* blend well with most grasses, and look good as 'hair' for containers. The majority of grasses complement other plants perfectly and are equally superb on the patio in pots.

The dark purple spikelets of *Molinia caerulea ssp arundinacea* 'Moorhexe' on erect stems will also prove very useful as would *M. caerulea* 'Edith Dudszus'. *Schoenus nigricans* is a black sedge with clumps of wiry stems with blackish long-tipped clusters of spikelets with a long, stiff pointed bract at stem tips. This 75cm (30") tall aquatic is invasive. *Saccharum* 'Pele's Smoke' (*S. officinarum* 'Violaceum') is an ornamental sugar cane with dark purple stems from Polynesia. A very different and dramatic container plant with its elegant leaves on woody segmented canes. Ornamental oats, *Avena sativa* 'French Black' make a certain dark exclamation mark and the wheat *Triticum* 'Black' or 'Black Tip' are possibilities to explore along with dark varieties of the ornamental broom corn, *Sorghum*.

Phyllostachys nigra has stems which take up to four years to colour well, but it is well worth the wait. Its slow growth is suitable to containers. It makes a decorous, see-through screen. *P. violascens* is a clump-forming then spreading bamboo with swollen green canes at first striped purple, becoming violet. The narrowly, lance-shaped glossy green foliage is glaucous on the underside. *Fargesia nitida* has purplish young stems, often requiring lots to drink in summer as leaves curl when dry.

Ophiopogon planiscapus 'Nigrescens'

32

THE HOT BORDER

The hot border is a theme which lends itself particularly well to the dark garden and one of the first ideas I adapted for the use of black plants. As with all the schemes, the idea is to juxtapose the colours, in this case, black, red, orange and yellow, with the black, green and purple of the foliage.

Grown with the sun behind, purple leaves become translucent, a very magical effect which will be much appreciated. Cotinus provides a superb dark backdrop for other plants. The insignificant flowers rise like plumes of smoke from the bush and hence it is commonly called the smoke bush tree. It associates well with silver, gold and red. *Physocarpus opulifolius* 'Diablo' is a relative newcomer and the colour of its foliage has been criticised, but I find it attractive. *Lysimachia*, although attractive, is not quite as good a colour as the other two. Its variability is perhaps owing to seed-raised plants. It looks best in a clump on moist soil and is very hardy. *Prunus cerasifera* 'Nigra' could also be used as a backdrop, to keep it as a hedge, trim after flowering. Excellent colouring can also be had with *P.* 'Royal Burgundy' or *P.* 'Thundercloud'. *Berberis thunbergii* 'Atropurpurea' lends a dark mound of foliage with yellow flowers. Additional dark foliage is found in the large, palmate, exotic leaves of Ricinus communis 'Carmencita' or *R. communis* 'Impala', the former having the added extra of red flowers. An unusual source of dark foliage is found in Kale 'Toscana di Negro' a superb plant for use in the border with foliage so dark that it appears black from a distance. *Heuchera* adds a dark accent too in the form of *H.* 'Velvet Night'. *Ophiopogon planiscapus* 'Nigrescens' and *Ajuga* 'Valfredda' (Chocolate Chip) complete the dark planting admirably. In contrast bright flowers are provided by *Dahlia* 'Bishop of Llandaff', *Fuchsia* 'Thalia', *Lobelia* 'Queen Victoria' and *Lychnis x arkwrightii* 'Vesuvius', all four have the added bonus of dark foliage. *Dianthus barbatus* 'Sooty' for its dark flowers and foliage, the annual *Nicotiana* 'Domino Red' and an excellent contrast of foliage from the red blood grass, *Imperata cylindrica* 'Rubra', which shines like rubies with the sun behind. The whole scheme benefits greatly from backlighting.

Hot reds to use vary in shade from the darkest *Dianthus barbatus* 'Sooty' to the bright scarlet red blooms of *Dahlia* 'Bishop of Llandaff'. The emphasis is on bright, shocking reds or the hotness is lost. *D.* 'Fire Mountain' with its fire red blooms against almost black foliage will not disappoint. On standby would be the superb old variety *D.* 'Grenadier' with double scarlet flowers and dark blackish foliage or the single scarlet flowers of *D.* 'Preston Park' with almost black foliage. Adapt the planting, substituting one plant for another, always keeping the ratio of dark to red to maintain the effect. If you prefer a yellow to orange bias use *Lychnis x arkwrightii* 'Vesuvius' with its brilliant orange flowers. The standby is again *Dahlia*, such as *D.* 'David Howard' with its superb dark foliage and double light orange flowers taking centre stage, admirably accompanied by a supporting cast of *D.* 'Ellen Huston', a superb double-flowered orange-scarlet with contrasting dark purple foliage. Bringing yellow blooms into play would be the deep yellow *D.* 'Midnight Sun' which has an attractive vermilion ring and distinctive dark purple foliage. The yellow flowers of *D.* 'Yellow Hammer' will play a part too against almost black foliage. *Dahlia* are superbly easy plants. I like to bring them into growth as early as possible. Given my limited space, I still think this is worthwhile as it is so easy to get many plants from one tuber which has been stored frost free over winter. Lay the tubers on top of fresh peat and watch them shoot. It is not unheard of for 100 cuttings to be taken from a tuber. Grow on and these can go outside in the garden when danger of frost has passed. Staggered cuttings result in a succession of flowers in the garden. The yellow to orange theme can be continued in autumn for a blaze of colour with *Helianthus, Helenium* and *Rudbeckia*.

The hot border remains hot when summer temperatures are cooling down.

> Hot colours look at their best with a dark backdrop

The hot border is a wonderful scheme to use in the garden and an easy one to adapt. Easy too to extend the season. Add *Helenium* and *Helianthus* in burnt reds for more autumn colour.

The preference could be for yellows and oranges instead of scarlet reds. In spring use *Ranunculus ficaria* 'Brazen Hussy' for a bright display, teamed with *Anthriscus sylvestris* 'Ravenswing'. Add *Inula*, *Ligularia* in a damp spot, *Helenium* and *Helianthus* in shades of sunlight yellow. *Dahlia* 'Moonfire' and *D.* 'Yellow Hammer' will bring another ray of sunshine to this scheme.

For the Hot Border illustrated below
Choose *Physocarpus opulifolius* 'Diablo', *Cotinus coggygria* 'Royal Purple' and *Lysimachia ciliata* 'Firecracker' for the backdrop to this hot scheme. The fabulous leaves of *Ricinus communis* 'Sanguineus' add interest. This is a dramatic plant capable of reaching large dimensions if fed the diet of a giant. On the boundaries towering mounds of Kale 'Negro di Toscana' will wow all who see it, marvelling at the blistered leaves which definitely look black from a distance.

In the foreground plant *Ophiopogon planiscapus* 'Nigrescens', *Ajuga reptans* 'Braunherz' (Mahogany) and *Heuchera* 'Obsidion' and *Beta* 'Bull's Blood'.

Two small shrubby *Berberis* such as *B. thunbergii* 'Atropurpurea Nana' complete the dark colours.

Hot colours shout out against the deep colours of the contrasting foliage. Darkest red *Lupinus* hybrids, *Lobelia* 'Queen Victoria' which will appreciate being kept moist, the shrubby *Fuchsia* 'Thalia' with its bronzed leaves and interesting dark flowers, deep red *Nicotiana* 'Domino Red', *Dahlia* 'Bishop of Llandaff' not only for its scarlet flowers but also for its deep dark foliage and *Dianthus barbatus* 'Sooty' set the planting afire. *Imperata cylindrica* 'Rubra' adds a glow of its own, superb with the sun coming through its leaves, complementing the darker colours as they are transformed by the sun. This is a striking grass but I have never been able to please it.

This scheme looks good from late spring to the first frosts giving excellent long season colour.

A hot border

TROPICAL TOUCH

This is a scheme I adore, even though I live in the north of England, or perhaps for this reason. Tropical plants are so lush and so full of life. The feeling of being surrounded by plant life, so dense, so abundant is one that has immense plant appeal to me. Some tropical looking plants are hardy but most are tender and if you cannot wrap and keep plants hugged through winter, you will either need to lift and store or over winter indoors, often an impossibility with large plants. The only alternative is to discard plants and start again the following spring. However, it is not all green. Exotic tropicals come in dark foliage forms too.

The hard core background planting comes in the form of *Phyllostachys nigra*, the loveliest of bamboos, with its attractive, lance-shaped foliage and dark black canes. Use *P. violascens* here too for its violet canes and narrowly, lance-shaped, glossy green foliage. It is hard to imagine a tropical garden without a palm, but if you do not want to include too much green, you might have to sacrifice them altogether. An interesting addition is the tender *Cyrtostachys renda* with its red stems which will contrast well with exotic red flowers of *Canna* and *Lobelia*, but this will not tolerate cold temperatures. If willing, include the hardiest palm, *Trachycarpus fortunei*, hardly a compromise as this kind of scheme benefits greatly from a contrast and the form and colour of this marvellous palm will fit well into any tropical scheme. *Phormium* are very useful in this kind of setting. *P. tenax* and its cultivars are the hardiest, offering a good choice of dark-leaved forms from brownish-bronze to purple-brown. One *Phormium* stands out as darker than the others, a near black of compact, slow growth, *P.* 'Platt's Black' and I am jolly pleased that the darkest flax is known by this name. *Phormium* provide a good silhouette, large varieties making a good evergreen background and smaller varieties useful towards the front of a border. Their silhouette is matched by that of *Cordyline*. Similar plants when young, but forming a trunk as they mature, when they resemble a palm. *C.* 'Purple Tower' and the slightly darker *C.* 'Black Tower' are the two to choose. Others border on bronze-purple tones such as *C. australis* 'Atropurpurea'. The colour range of both *Phormium* and *Cordyline* extends into some useful reddish foliage and copper shades too.

Although not true exotics, plants which have the appearance of exotic foliage can be used. That excellent performer and standby *Cotinus coggygria* 'Royal Purple' could also find a place in this type of planting scheme. Its purple foliage will add another splash of colour of a different hue. It combines wonderfully with hot orange and red. Include *Sambucus* 'Black Beauty' for its superb dark foliage. Cut back every year, this remains on the small side. Combine with tropical looking grasses such as *Arundo* or golden foliage plants.

Tender components can be mixed and matched to achieve a different effect every year. *Canna* will need to get as early a start as possible to produce their fabulous flowers. But the foliage alone, wow! Given the right conditions, you will be rewarded with exotic flowers which come in many striking shades. Statuesque plants, *Canna* look like lonely sentinels on guard duty sticking out high above smaller plants. They deserve to be mingled. Either keep them under glass in winter, or lift and store, but never allow the somewhat large rhizomes to dry out completely. *C.* 'Black Knight', *C.* 'Australia' and *C.* 'General Eisenhower' are favourites for their big, bold, dark foliage and exotic flowers.

Canna are good with *Ricinus* which I start early from seed. Both plants are gross feeders, requiring a rich diet and ample water. Given this diet, they reach excellent proportions and have real impact. The bigger they are the better the overall effect. The paddle shaped leaves of the *Canna* complement the deeply palmate, wonderful *Ricinus* leaves. For a permanent, palmate partner, choose the hardy *Rodgersia podophylla*. Its fabulous foliage is a good underplanting to larger plants, but it does prefer moist, boggy areas where it colours much better in this

Create a dark tropical paradise with dense, lush foliage and exotic flowers

type of situation, especially in cooler areas. Best autumn colour is produced in full sun with damp feet. *Rheum atrosanguineum* is another choice for moist ground. A third companion is another big plant, and quite a fast-growing one too, *Ensete ventricosum* 'Maurelii' a dark-leaved banana relative. What could be more exotic? Keep out of windy areas where the leaves will be torn in unattractive shreds. This is not hardy outside in Great Britain, but is nevertheless an excellent plant to use in summer months. Excitement mounts as I just think of it. None more exciting than a new black-leaved ginger, *Zingiber* 'Midnight'. This has to be seen to be believed, fabulous shiny dark leaves rivalling those exotic dark-leaved *Philodendron*. Tree ferns can also play a part in the exotic garden, *Dicksonia antartica* is about the hardiest and gives a primeval feel to the garden. Wrap well in winter. If you can plant *Xanthorrhea australis*, the black boy, do so. This is so wonderful, the kind of plant I would move to warmer climes just to grow. A black plant collector's must have. The grassy, green top overflows from the black trunk, like a wild hairdo.

Large leaves reign supreme in the dark tropical garden. Supreme amongst black plants has to be *Colocasia* 'Black Magic'. We are talking dramatic foliage here, a plant no-one can ignore. Its dark, near black leaves are large, arrow-shaped, handsome, on the dullish side, no shine or gleam, but what a plant. For depth of colour this is truly magnificent and quite adaptable, it has been over-wintered at 0°C and is more or less evergreen. *Colocasia* 'Illustris' makes an equally dramatic statement. Other large-leaved plants with something to say include *Alocasia* and *Anthurium*. There are some superbly dark bromeliads which fit in well here with almost black, or black-striped foliage, most with a superb sheen. The choice widens with purple types too. *Orthophytum gurkenii* has purple-brown leaves barred with silvery lines. *Pitcairnia sanguinea* bears low, flat dusky rosettes with a violet blush to the underside of leaves. The lovely *Aechmea* with black and almost white stripes and the dark striped *Vriesea* (recently re-classified) are all favourites of mine, but these require humidity to grow

well. *Cryptanthus* are available with near black leaves. *Neoregelias* are usually purple at the base of green leaves. *N.* 'Pepper' is a magenta hybrid, liberally peppered in purple-brown. The open vases of *N. schultsiana* are a brilliant red-purple. *N.* 'Vulcan' x 'Black Night' produces leathery rosettes with rose tinted leaves splattered maroon. Grow plenty of *Solenostemon* (Coleus) for this kind of scheme, keep them as standby fillers in pots. Easy to grow, there is a seed strain *S.* 'Palisandra' but I do not find it to be stable, I would therefore recommend you buy plants of the darkest, such as *S.* 'Dark Star', *S.* 'Merlot' and others, to provide the right complementary tones. *S.* 'Life Lime' is an excellent addition with its chartreuse foliage and the odd speck of maroon. The variegated leaves of *Codiaeum* (Croton) make a valuable addition too with their fascinating leaf shape, often with wavy margins, some thin like extended fingers, some rounded, with spots or splotches of vibrant colour. They look like they have been splattered with paint.

Episcia, the flame violets are tender, evergreen perennials from the forest floor of tropical areas. Leaves are puckered and bronze-black. *A. cupreata* 'Mosaica' has the darkest, near black leaves with a sheen. These are suitable in hanging baskets as well as for summer bedding, where their creeping habit will fill gaps. *Eucomis* 'Sparkling Burgundy' is splendid in this scheme. Its fetching, strap-like purple foliage forms dark burgundy rosettes which is best in full sun.

The garden can almost stand with foliage alone, but the addition of flowers, some with dark foliage, raises the whole temperature and brings the scheme to life. Indulge yourself by using really hot colours. I like to use the reds, oranges and yellows we find with dark foliage and hot colours. Choose vibrantly coloured flowers and dark foliage offered by *Anthurium, Canna, Colocasia, Dahlia, Ricinus*, purple-leaved *Eucomis, Ipomoea, Lobelia, Phormium, Codiaeum, Cordyline, Solenostemon, Hibiscus* and black-stemmed tree ferns for a riot of colour. For orange flowers add *Kniphofia* and *Crocosmia* which raise the heat, in inferno colours, *C.* 'Lucifer' is just one which will set the planting ablaze. *Amaranthus* would not be out of place, with regard to foliage or flowers. The deep red tassel like flowers of *A. caudatus* are exotic. Leaves of many *Amaranthus* cultivars are suffused red-purple. If red hot and tropical is to your taste, dark foliage and flashing, fiery flowers will be your joy.

A smaller planting is easily achieved by choosing favourites which work well together. *Hibiscus acctosella* 'Coppertone' (Red Shield) with leaves of brilliant maroon-purple, *Ricinus* 'Carmencita', *Canna* 'Wyoming' and a good dark *Solenostemon* works wonderfully. The lusher the better. The foliage in a planting such as this will offer every shade of purple to almost black, flowers will be blazing and hot in shades of red, orange and yellow.

The Vulcanicity Garden at Hampton Court Flower Show

POOLSIDE PLEASURE

There are immense possibilities for creating a dark area around a pool, by the side of a stream or in a pond. Water gardening has become more popular which will present no problem for lovers of dark plants. There are many dark plants which enjoy constantly damp, but not water-logged soil in full sun. Some *Astilbe* bear dark bronze leaves in spring and enjoy such conditions whilst associating well with other moisture lovers. *A x arendsii* 'Obergartner Jurgens' is one of the darkest and the foliage contrasts well with the red flowers. *Darmera peltata* is only on the reddish side in autumn, but has superb large leaves. A member of the saxifrage family, it revels in moisture at its feet. *Eupatorium rugosum* 'Chocolate' bears dark bronze foliage and perfectly contrasting white plates of blooms late in the year. It colours best in sun, although it is capable of tolerating some shade. *Rheum* and *Rodgersia* are two good companions for this situation. Both are superb foliage plants, both with hints of bronze.

Damp soil is not a problem for dark plants which revel in it

Other damp lovers include *Actaea (Cimicifuga)*, *Colocasia, Helianthus, Hemerocallis, Lysimachia, Persicaria* and *Ajuga* which will give good ground cover in damp soil. The sultry *Cosmos atrosanguineus* prefers damp soil as do bronze-leaved *Crocosmia, Euphorbia dulcis* 'Chameleon', the foliage plant *Haloragis erecta, Iris chrysographes* black which must never be allowed to dry out, some *Fritillaria, Ligularia, Lobelia* such as the dark, desirable *L.* 'Queen Victoria', much easier to overwinter if its feet are actually wet in the shallow part of a pond. *Ophiopogon planiscapus* 'Nigrescens' prefers moist but not wet soil. *Osmunda regalis* 'Purpurascens', *Plantago major* 'Rosularis', and *Ranunculus* do not appreciate dry soil at all. *Sambucus, Trifolium and Zantedeschia* are not opposed to wet feet either. *Scrophularia auricula* 'Variegata' is a little bit loud in its variegated foliage of green and cream, but can be admittted for its very dark brownish-red flowers and it does appreciate a position in damp shade.

In a pond, try the combination of *Zantedeschia black, Nymphaea* 'Black Opal' and *Trapa nutans,* the water chestnut with its red stalks and hard black fruits, with *Lobelia* 'Queen Victoria' adding dramatic red flowers as well as good dark purple foliage, and the incredible *Colocasia* 'Black Magic' contributes the right touch. This planting could be further enhanced with the use of moisture loving grasses and rushes such as *Typha*, the bullrush, one of the first plants I loved as a child, I still like those dark brown seedheads on this interesting plant, even though on the invasive side. *T. minima* is the only species suitable for a small pond, however narrow spikes do not have quite the same impact as the larger *T. latifolia. Schoenoplectus lacustris* bears brown spikelets of flowers and adds contrast with green foliage. *Acorus gramineus* 'Ogon' fits in well here with its golden and green variegated foliage. Add more flowers with moisture loving *Iris* in shades of contrasting yellow.

A streamside planting is superb with bronzed *Astilbe*, the magnificent fern *Osmunda regalis* 'Purpurea', *Plantago major* 'Rosularis', *Eupatorium, Actaea (Cimicifuga), Angelica sylvestris* 'Purpurea' which is an impressive plant with leaves, stems and flowers suffused deep purple. *Angelica* have excellent ornamental value in the garden especially by a stream or in damp woodland. Damp-loving *Hosta* make the ideal contrast to these dark plants.

A more informal poolside planting would include many of the plants mentioned above, especially those big leaves which add such an impact. Soil that retains moisture in the border is often a problem with some plants rotting off, discard them and plant up with *Ranunculus, Ophiopogon* and *Ajuga*. The latter has some superb foliage offerings in metallic shades and good deep purple-blacks. I have a very good form of *A. reptans* 'Atropurpurea', retaining wonderful colour year round. Most *Ajuga* are accompanied by brightish blue flowers, but there are now some with pink flowers, too, equally useful in shade, where they increase happily.

By a pond or stream plant moisture lovers such as bold Eupatorium and Actaea (Cimicifuga) with Ligularia, Rheum, Rodgersia and Darmera palmata which turns reddish-purple in autumn. Colocasia, Zantedeschia and Lobelia 'Queen Victoria' will enjoy dipping their toes in water.

WOODLAND EDGE

Some of my favourite flowers and black plants are woodland plants. Impossible to choose a favourite, this is one area where I have no objection to being spoiled and possessive, I want them all. How does one find words to describe these plants? Fabulous *Fritillaria*, hedonistic black *Helleborus*, terrific *Trillium*, seductive *Scopolia* and my treasured aroids, including amazing *Arum*, attractive *Arisaema*, aberrant *Arisarum*. Last of all, alluring *Aristolochia* and *Asarum*. There are some breathtaking plants here. Add to these all the shade lovers such as *Anemone*, *Bergenia*, *Actaea (Cimicifuga)*, *Corydalis flexuosa*, *Dracunculus vulgaris* will grow in partial shade, *Epimedium*, *Euphorbia*, *Geranium* and *Heuchera* tolerate shade on moist sites. *Liriope*, tender *Maranta* appreciate shade, *Podophyllum*, *Saxifraga*, *Tellima*, *Tiarella*, *Veratrum nigrum*, *Viola* and *Xanthosoma*. Add *Quercus* which offer intense reddish, purple hues, the dark holly *Ilex x merservae* and *Fagus sylvatica* 'Purpurea' and dark leaved *Rhododendron* offering a huge selection of plants to employ before we even think about contrasts. Take care when positioning plants, as although purple-leaved *Corylus* and *Fagus* will tolerate partial shade, best foliage colour is seen when grown in full sun.

Adorable aroids. There is nothing quite excites me like a black aroid. They are the most fascinating plants. If aroids were men, they would be the dark, tall handsome types, the irresistible ones. There are some ravenous black spathes out there, unfortunately some can be very variable and unless you have seen the spathe, you might be surprised with a green one. I suppose they should come with a health warning, some of them are strong-smelling, but usually only noticeable if you stick your nose right in there.

Enjoying moist woodland and rocky wasteland, aroids have unusual spathes with enough dark ones to satisfy any black enthusiast. Green leaves are attractive too, lobed or palmate. *Arisaema* are wonderful, the spathes often brownish-purple and white striped but

The shady garden is tranquil and serene

some plain dark purple. Dark, but never sinister, always a statement of simple elegance. These are sleek plants. Plants you see and want immediately. Essential plants to use in the black garden, so immensely handsome. Each one is trying to be better than the last, and succeeds admirably. These are plants to get to know better. My favourites include *A. engleri* and *A. speciosum*. Superb foliage, mottled stems and interesting ripening fruits do not detract from the magnet of the spathe (hood-like) and the spadix (tail-like). Flowers are found at the base of the spadix. *Arisaema* can change sexuality. Flowers on young plants tend to be male, with older plants having female flowers or both sexes present. Under stress, such as in cases of severe drought, female plants can revert. Like sex between silky black sheets in sexy black underwear, *Arisaema* are the plantification of sex. The spathes look like they have been unzipped to reveal the spadix. I'll say no more.

Intriguing little *Arisarum* with their dark spathes, scurrying to hide amongst green foliage, are useful in a woodland setting too.

Beguiling *Arum* are curious yet so very interesting. Attractively shaped and marked leaves are a feature of many species in addition to deliciously dark spathes and spadices. Many species have spathes flushed purple, but some are outstandingly dark. *A. nigrum* has a dark purple-brown spathe and spadix and *A. palaestinum* takes first place, stealing the limelight from other membes of the genus. Its near-black spathes are an incredible sight in combination with the outer pale greenish white spathe. The spadix is also near-black. The provenance of this plant has particular significance, from some areas this species has a horsey smell; from others it is sweet-smelling.

Pinellia have more modest spathes than *Arisaema;* their contribution is one of foliage rather than flower. The heart-shaped foliage of *P. cordata* is glossy dark green above, dark purple with white veins on the underside. Spathes are greenish-yellow tinged purple. This species appreciates heat and humidity to be at its best, so it is not suited to every garden, but does tolerate other conditions and fairs well in most areas.

There is also a purple-spathed form of *P. tripartita*.

The leaves of *Asarum* are attractive enough in themselves, a welcome addition to any garden, often amazingly marbled and glossy green, making excellent groundcover or edging. Often quite rare, they are worth seeking. *A. maximum* has no offputting scent and has absolutely amazing dark owl-eyed flowers. *A. magnificum* has superb flowers of black and white in spring with equally magnificent foliage.

Aristolochia display large and extremely showy flowers, again, not always pleasant smelling, but I forgive them this small fault because they are dark and fascinating, though never black. The usual purple or maroon flowers, often marked with cream offer contrast to darker flowers. A little malodour need not bother us. Keep the fly spray handy. The woody vines of *Aristolochia* will certainly cause comment for other reasons. They enjoy a shady site in moist woodland.

Excellent in a woodland wonderland too are the fabulously fascinating *Fritillaria*, well worth the trial and effort to get the darkest. *F. obliqua* is suited to the woodland garden or edge of woodland, but is not normally seen in cultivation. *F. camschatcensis*, the black sarana, black queen of fritillaries will appreciate light shade, in humus-rich soil which is always moist, even after flowering. This is an easy fritillary to obtain and to grow and very popular owing to the depth of colour, dusky very near-black. Not all dark fritillaries enjoy these conditions.

Helleborus orientalis, the blacks go from strength to strength. The undertones are just as sumptuous as the main colour. Some good purples are found in *H. orientalis* 'Purpurascens'. All these are variable, see them in flower before you buy, many nurseries have Hellebore weekends at flowering time in February, these are an eye-opener. The colours are truly amazing. I picked up a near perfect black at Heronswood in the Northwest Pacific. My American friend still has custody of this, one day... Hand-pollinated blacks are becoming easier to find, a must have on everyone's black list.

Terrific *Trillium*, American toad lilies are perfect

Black does not hide amongst shadows, but steps into the limelight

partners to so many of the above woodland plants. Do not encroach too much on their space, they like to keep to themselves a little. *T. chloropetalum* has superb leaves marked with silvery marbling and superbly deep dark red-black flowers, the darkest I have seen. *Trillium* which give good contrasting flower colour are the pink of *T. grandiflorum roseum*, the yellow of *T. luteum* which has superb leaves, and the delightful greenish-yellow of *T. viridescens*.

Scoliopus is allied to *Trillium*, but this, along with Sauromatum is not a plant I desire. Seductive *Scopolia* is more to my taste. The fascinating dark pendent bells on the hardy *S. carniolica* are fabulous, those on *S. carniolica* 'Zwanenburg' even darker with flowers set against a contrasting green calyx. It resembles Atropa in flower and chemically, for which it has been used as a substitute, and is another source of tropane alkaloids. An alkaloid from *Scopolia* and *Papaver somniferum* was the source of 'twilight', used as a pre-anaesthetic. The plant is no longer used in this way in Britain *Scopolia* combine well with other open woodland plants. At the risk of sounding like one who is planning one of those classic British murders, allow me to describe another two poisonous beauties. The bells of *Atropa belladonna*, deadly nightshade are intriguing but not as dark, and this is not normally found used as an ornamental. All parts are toxic if eaten. Another deadly, but beautiful flower with purple-black veined cream flowers and a black throat is *Hyoscyamus niger*. Often found on sandy soil near the coast, henbanes are interesting plants for dry areas, but seldom seen in cultivation, and then usually as part of a herb garden, but should only be used medicinally as with all these three plants by qualified practitioners. They are subject to strict regulations in some countries.

Digitalis is another poisonous plant suited to light shade and found at the edge of woodland. *D. parviflora* is the darkest I have seen, chocolatey brown. *D. purpurea f alba* provides a perfect compliment, expect some purple flowers among this white strain which appears like luminous candles arising from a dark sea of black plants.

For light shade or the edge of woodland, try adorable *Anemone* with bronzed foliage include *A x lipsiensis* with its finely cut bronzed leaves and sulphur yellow flowers and *A. ranunculoides* 'Superba' with lobed, deeply divided bronzed leaves. Both prefer mosit soil in partial shade.

Beguiling Bergenia add winter interest with their large, often glossy foliage and flowers in shades of white to deep rose pink. Admirable plants for easy ground cover, especially in light soils. The best foliage colour is found in *B. purpurascens* in winter which offers deep purple or beetroot red colouring, especially in frost, stems are reddish brown enhancing the effect. *B.* 'Bressingham Ruby' is one of the best with neat, spoon-shaped leaves having serrated edges which turn a polished burgundy to contrast with the lighter crimson undersides. Deep rose flowers blossom in spring, offering a good contrast to the darker flowers of its woodland companions. *B.* 'Eroica' is a good new cultivar with foliage colouring well in autumn and displaying maroon undersides. *B.* 'Oeschberg' has blackish purple leaves in winter and is a handsome plant at this time of year. Some like it cold, all Bergenia colour better on poor soils exposed to cold.

To my eye, *Actaea (Cimicifuga)* has foliage of an exquisite colour in some forms and I do admire those bottlebrush-like, whitish flowers on long stems which sway on the wind. The species *C. simplex* is the one where we find the dark foliaged cultivars of the bugbane, preferable to the mainly seed grown *C. simplex Atropurpurea* Group which can be variable and at best takes a few years for the deep colouring to show through.

Corydalis flexuosa first caught my eye owing to its extraordinary blue flowers with striking hints of purple, which are so exquisite. The leaves of *C. flexuosa* 'Purple Leaf' emerge in spring, blotched deep purple, an added attraction to an admirable plant.Superb in partial shade in moderately fertile, humus-rich, moist but well-drained soil. These cool climate lovers are summer dormant. For dark flowers, try *Corydalis popovii* which is best in an alpine house.

Dramatic *Dracunculus vulgaris* is a striking plant, suitable for partial shade or full sun. A little off putting very close-up, since as the flowers open, they attract blow-flies with an aroma of rotting meat, this subsides after the first day, the flowers then being sweeter for the remaining two days. After flowering in July, the plant dies down and you will need to make use of the space as it will leave a good sized gap.

Epimedium are superb shade plants offering bronzed foliage in early spring. Their increasing popularity is easily understood, as they offer attractive leaves and flowers. Markings are amazingly varied from blotches, staining, blush and edging usually in bronze-red. They make good ground cover and edging to a woodland setting. *E. acuminatum* often shows good red-bronzing tones in its handsome foliage, lovely flowers, sometimes with deep purple. *E. alpinum* is appealing with striking flowers and almost black edged foliage. However, *E.* 'Black Sea' steals the show here, no other *Epimedium* is as dark, the foliage turning blackish-purple in autumn.

Dark hardy *Geranium* can be grown for their foliage effect alone or for their flowers. A quick cut over the flowering stems when flowering has finished, rewards the gardener with fresh foliage towards the end of the season when it is much appreciated. Dark *Geranuim* thrive in almost dry shade once established, although they appreciate a good soil.

Heuchera give an excellent display in moist soil in a partially shaded site. An easy subject to grow which will reward you with a mound of dark foliage for very little effort on your behalf. An ideal garden plant for a dark accent, the effect much enhanced by underplanting with *Lysimachia* 'Goldilocks' or other golden foliage.

Liriope is one of my permissible purples. The fine-textured, dark green foliage of *L.* 'Miniature National Arboretum' is accompanied by large berries. *Liriope muscari* is a welcome addition too.

Tender *Maranta*, often grown as houseplants in cold areas, are superb shade plants. They work well as houseplants with other tender subjects such as *Calathea* which have dark undersides. *Calathea*

'Dottie' has round, shiny leaves, an ideal blend of black and purple with a vibrant burgundy zigzag on each leaf, making it very distinguished. *Maranta* can be used outdoors in warm climates.

Podophyllum are not widely grown but are beginning to become more easily available, deservedly so. The distinctive foliage and attractive flowers renders them well worth getting to know. Emerging foliage is striking, often heavily suffused blackish purple and often with a rough surface. Excellent companions to *Trillium*, that fabulous white flowered *Sanguinaria canadensis* which I admire so much, and *Dicentra cucullaria* amongst other shade lovers which include *Berberis*.

Saxifraga are useful plants in either moist or dry shade, depending on the plant you choose and make handsome groundcover. Hardy, herbaceous *Tellima* offer good ground cover in shade, never deeper than reddish-purple, the lighter colour serving as a contrast to darker plants. *Tiarella* are useful for tolerating a wide variety of conditions, but dislike extreme wet. New breeding has produced many similar looking cultivars, all bearing dark brown-black markings. *T. wherryi* 'Bronze Beauty' is an older, compact perennial, a much admired variety. Imposing in shade are the spires of *Veratrum nigrum* making an interesting vertical statement of starry black flowers.

Viola are suitable for partial shade or full sun in moist but well-drained soil and can make a handsome floral effect at the entrance to a woodland garden. *Viola* are short-lived and need to be replaced regularly. Often seeding themselves to death, they require dead-heading regularly to prolong flowering. As soil can also become pansy sick, they are best planted in different areas of the garden. Black *Viola* and pansies are many and vary from the cheeky-faced to sultry, sexy black plants. *Xanthorhiza simplissima* is a relatively little-grown shrub, suitable for moist woodland. Green leaves turn bronze at first, then red-purple in autumn. White flowers are borne in pendent racemes in spring as the leaves emerge.

Xanthosoma violaceum, the blue taro is a frost tender perennial suitable for fertile, humus-rich soil in partial shade. I admire the elegance of this plant with its deep violet stems and highly attractive arrow-shaped, pale purple-green leaves. Edible tubers are pink inside. Grow it if you have the right conditions.

Highlight dark woodland gardens with strong groups of shade-loving white lilies which glow against dark plants. Illuminate the woodland floor in spring with extended patches of white daffodils, which glow ever stronger in the low sunlight at the end of the day, appearing luminous against a cloud of dark foliage.

The shaded garden, by its very nature, evokes a tranquil, serene area. One in which to avoid the over bright glare of the sun and of strong colours. Shade determines the plants used. Dark red tree *Paeonia* are superb with *Arisarum europaeum* and the deep dark spathes of *Arisaema*, all plants here offer good foliage as a bonus. Add *Epimedium*, black *Helleborus orientalis*, young *Fagus sylvatica* in its dark forms and *Prunus*, both pruned to shape to form a background with *Clematis montana* working its way through in summer and *Ilex x meservae* adding interest. *Bergenia* and *Leucothoe fontanesiana* 'Scarletta' (acid soil only) have a stake in the foreground planting.

Hyoscyamus niger

LONG BORDER

Associated in my mind with Gertrude Jekyll and the superb idea of gradating colour, not that she did it with black. The longest herbaceous borders are found at Arley Hall in Chesire in the U.K, and there are a few dark plants integrated there, *Berberis* being used to unite the planting.

The best effect is achieved when the colouring of the plants is graded from one end to the other, or from one end to the middle and then repeated in reverse. Starting light and working towards dark is just as effective as the other way around. It is important not to work on one level, the scheme needs to flow, the eye needs to be taken up at regular intervals. Achieve a natural effect by allowing the odd plant to rise in the middle of the border or towards the front. In this kind of border, plants are best in groups of threes or fives. Repeat planting brings unity to the whole. Try not to be too rigid and regimented, have a few surprises as well. Vertical interest is of importance in a border of such great length. Clothe the walls. Use your contrasts in a long border, they will serve their purpose well. Work your way from blacks, to purples to lilacs, or from pinks to reds to maroon-blacks then black. Use black, purple and gold, I am not averse to the odd lemon in here, I believe it works excellently. The combination of black, white and silver is also a favourite for this planting. Keep the interest going all season long by using plants which have more than one season of interest where possible, underplant with bulbs, add annuals, keep pots ready for any gaps.

Plants with stature are needed in a long border to provide the full stops. Use a purple *Cordyline* or *Canna,* or a small shrub such as *Ilex x meservae.*

Black plants are suitable for any spot in the garden

CONTAINERS

Container gardening is pure enjoyment. Making recipes for containers is such a pleasure and I never tire of thinking up different combinations of plants. The beauty of containers is that you can change the main focus of the planting easily, and you can move pots in and out of eyesight as they come into their best or fade from the scene. This is gardening as versatile as it can get. The adaptability of this kind of gardening has immense appeal. A superb way to grow bulbs too, avoiding the eyesore of foliage in the border after the bulbs have finished flowering.

Finding suitable containers is a challenge. I like large containers, urns, stone troughs as well as hanging baskets. Unusual objects cajoled into the role of plant containers can be fun. Choose colours and textures which fit in well with your garden. Dark containers can be used for dark plants, but work best when a gold contrast is used in the planting.

Allow containers to overflow, brimful is best. Let plants cascade over the edge to soften the look of the scheme. Remember also that plants dry out easily and quickly, especially on hot days.

Cordyline, Phormium, Ipomoea, Solenostemon (Coleus) and regal *Pelargonium* make wonderful container subjects. Choose contrasting colours and foliage to achieve a striking display. Specimen plants such as *Colocasia* 'Black Magic', and *Alocasia* are perfect in large containers.

Containers are ideal for many tender plants and can easily be moved under cover for winter. Combine a *Cordyline* with a dark Regal *Pelargonium*, a black *Viola*, a dark *Hedera* (ivy), *Cosmos atrosanguineus*, a dark *Heuchera* and the contrasting foliage of *Senecio cineraria* and *Helichrysum petiolare.*

Another favourite planting of mine is *Colocasia* and *Ophiopogon* with the excellent dark *Solenostemon* 'Merlot' and golden foliage.

For pots on the patio, you can simply do no better than an elegant display of succulents. *Aeonium,*

Echeveria, Sedum, Saxifraga and *Sempervivum* look just right on their own, add a dark leaved red *Pelargonium* for a welcome splash of colour.

Aeschyanthus is a good hanging basket plant, easily grown in cultivation. A minimum 10°C (50°F) and an occasional misting in summer will keep them happy. *A.* Black Pagoda Group bears mottled leaves, green on the surface, purple beneath, the deep orange flowers are a glowing contrast.

Centradenia inaequilateralis 'Cascade' is a trailing tender perennial, suitable for a pot or hanging basket. Its bronze-pink leaves and small violet-purple tibouchina like flowers appear in May and June and sometimes again in August to November. High humidity is needed and in warm areas this is useful in the shrub border.

Elatostema (syn. Pellionia) is also a candidate for the hanging basket with its dark greenish leaves which can appear black. *E. repens* has wavy-margined leaves which are attractively marked grey and pale green and are often bronze-flushed on the upper surface, but pinkish beneath. *E. repens v pulchrum* from Vietnam has dark purple-green leaves with a mosaic of very dark midribs and veins and is tinged purple on the underside. Both of these have pinkish stems and are also suitable for ground cover in warmer areas.

Fittonia species have dark leaves with paler markings, making them appear darker still. *F. albivenis Argyroneura Group* appears so dark as to be near black with superb silvery white veins. In temperatures below 15°C (59°F) grow in a terrarium or under cover in a hanging basket.

Haloragis erecta is usually promoted for use in baskets and containers. A half-hardy branching perennial from New Zealand, grown mainly for its foliage. Bronzed leaves have attractively serrated margins. A *Gunnera* relative, enjoying the same conditions of constant moisture.

Impatiens are superb for containers, and pots can be brought indoors in cooler weather. The New Guinea types have very dark foliage which contrasts well with the bright flowers.

Small leaved *Peperomia* can make good specimens for terrariums and bottle gardens. Never black but leaves are interestingly dark. *P. caperata* 'Burgundy' has rich, dusky purple, deeply corrugated leaves. *P.* 'Inca Princess' has dark green-black leaves with a light central stripe, burgundy stems and undersides. *P. caperata* 'Luna Red' has reddish stems and heart-shaped leaves, wondrously silvered, deeply corrugated and veined. *P. obtusifolia* 'Columbiana' bears fleshy leaves of a rich purple.

Pilea involucrata is a trailing perennial suitable for hanging baskets. The cultivar 'Moon Valley' is upright and open, producing toothed leaves which are flushed black-brown.

A window box by Proven Winners, Ipomoea 'Black Heart' Lysimachia and Symphytum 'Axminster Gold'

PAST, PRESENT AND FUTURE

Black plants have long appeared in myth and symbolism, paintings and tapestries, and yet we still stop and stare.

In the past, black plants have commanded huge sums of money. Tulipomania took Holland by storm in the 1600's. A single bulb could change hands for several thousand dollars or be as valuable as a mansion house. One of the rarest was a cream and deepest purple striped tulip. The darkest tulips came along much later, even though Alexandre Dumas wrote about them in his romantic novel 'The Black Tulip' in 1850. The elusive black was always top of the hybridizers list. Tulipomania craze may have only lasted four years and ended with many in financial ruin, but the quest to breed a black tulip continues to this day. Hybridizers have come very close to creating the black tulip, it is one of the darkest plants.

Also testifying to the popularity of black plants in the past, is the garden book, written by Sir Thomas Hamner and completed in 1659, but not published until 1933, in which he describes the black auricula of his time. In the mid-seventeenth century, Sir Thomas Hamner was successful in raising new auricula varieties including one named 'Black Imperial'. Even at this time, the darker the flower, the more desirable. Breeding work on auricula continues to this day, and many dark ones are currently available.

A century later, in 1756, Count Grigorijj Demidov, the owner of gardens in Western Siberia, sent to Peter Collinson a 'lily as near to black as any flower'. In 1776, a certain flora nigra (black flower), was offered for sale at £21 in the catalogue of one Robert Edmeades. Black *Primula auricula* as well as *Ranunculus* (buttercups) were also on offer in combinations of black and coffee, black and violet, black-brown and dark olive. *Ranunculus* of similar colouring are available today. *Auricula* reached their

peak in popularity in the 18th and 19th centuries and were especially beloved by Lancashire weavers in England, often housed in an Auricula theatre.

The elusive black rose is another hybridizers' dream. Redoute painted and described several dark roses. *Rosa rubrifolia* with its wine-coloured foliage, particularly on the underside of the leaves. *R. pimpinellifolia Mariaeburgensis* with its unusual black hips. *R. gallica purpurea velutina parva* which Redoute also noted as being called 'Van Eeden's Rose'. This is described as having brilliant purple flowers, an admirable violet on opening with a velvety look. The petals of this desirable plant finally blacken before falling and perhaps gave rise to the existence of the elusive black rose. *Rosa gallica purpureoviolacea magna*, 'Bishop's Rose' is featured as a fine purple-violet flowered plant with reddish stems. *Rosa gallica mahaka flore subsimplici*, 'Near single Maheka', also known as 'The Fair Sultana' was a magnificent gallica with very deep, dark red velvet flowers. The fine violet rose, *Rosa gallica gueriniana*, 'Guerin's rose' is also mentioned. The gallicas themselves are occasionally velvet red, but more often in the cultivars. The first detailed account of the velvet roses was given by Roessig in his Beschreibung (1799, 1803) and some were portrayed in his Die Rosen. All had dark purple petals, either with a violet sheen or with a blackish sheen. In both hues, there were single, semi-double and double forms, making six different roses in all. Velvet roses had been grown since the 1600's. Roessig named the semi-double violet form *R. violacea* and the rose still cultivated as *R.* 'Violacea' complies with his description, the parentage is thought to be *R. gallica*, but coming from the East where the species is thought to attain taller growth than it does in Europe. In the 1930's, Nancy Lindsay collected a rose in Iran which she described as the 'crested red cabbage', with leafy sepals and roundish leaflets as in *R.* 'Violacea', but with very double, purple-red flowers. Towards the end of the eighteenth century, these velvet roses were used in breeding the gallicas which became so popular in gardens. *R.* 'Tuscany', is one example still available today. The darkest roses owe their origin to *R. gallica* and are admired not just for their colouring, but also for their inherited scent. Many so-called *gallicas* are of nineteenth century origin from seed of open-pollinated flowers. Many of the darkest roses are bred for cut flowers with long stems, but there are dark patio varieties and handsome climbers too.

Black plants have been favourites with illustrators and botanical artists in the past. In the Art of Botanical Illustration by Wilfred Blunt and the late W.T.Stearn, there are a number of illustrations of dark plants, testimony to their popularity in years gone by. The admirable *Iris susiana*, the mourning iris is depicted in gouache by G.D.Ehret in 1745, labelled *Iris susiana, flore maximo, ex albo nigricante.* The almost black-grey striped petals are wonderful. In the same book, there is a fabulous, stylised figure of the dragon arum, *Dracunculus vulgaris* taken from the manuscript Herbal of Apuleis of the seventh century. Almost black *Viola tricolor* is shown from the Camerarius Florilegium of c.1590. Whilst in The Flowering of Kew by Richard Mabey dark plants are also in evidence. Again, the sensuous Turkish species, *Iris susiana* is shown here, but this is Redoute's superb engraving, from his Les Lilacees in 1802. *Stapelia asterias, S. grandiflora* and *Trichocaulon piliferum* were executed as hand-coloured engravings by D. Mackenzie in the 1700's and reproduced in Francis Mason's Stapeliae Novae in 1797. Matilda Smith (1854-1926) illustrated *Amorphophallus titanum* in a superb watercolour.

The Garden at Eichstatt, Basilius Besler's magnificent florilegium, also amply demonstrates the popularity of dark flowers in times gone by. Besler was a Nuremburg apothecary. *Paeonia polyanthus flore rubro* is shown from an original colouring copperplate made in 1636. There are superb illustrations of *Muscari neglectum, Rosa gallica, Paeonia peregrina,* an *Iris* species, then known as *I. calcedonica latifolia,* a combination of near black standards, and deep red falls. *Veratrum nigrum, Dianthus caryophyllus, Pulsatilla vulgaris* are other dark flowers depicted.

Although many 'black' plants are hundreds of years old, it is only today that we include so many dark plants in our gardens. Tastes change and gardens change likewise and with today's modern breeding technology, new plants reach the market quicker than they ever have before. Programmes tend to be concentrated on certain genera or species. With regard to dark flowers, we find many amongst *Primula auricula; Iris*, particularly bearded types; *Pelargonium* and *Hemerocallis.* With dark foliage, we have seen a concentration on *Geranium, Heuchera* and *Solenostemon.* Newly bred *Heuchera* have near black foliage as well as excellent purple foliage too following breeding programmes by Dan Heims in the U.S. Dan is also breeding wonderful new x *Heucherella* and *Tiarella.* The breeding of dark foliaged *Geranium* in the purple to blackish purple category continues.

A recent breeding programme of *Sambucus* by the Horticultural Research Institute in the U.K. brought to light the dark-leaved *S.* 'Black Beauty' and *S.* 'Black Lace'. It is inevitable that black plants will continue to be launched onto the market. I await with bated breath more wonderful new dark plants. Compare new with old 'black' ones that existed before, and there is little doubt that plants are getting darker. Purple was named the plant colour of the Millenium, black is the plant colour of the future.

Geranium pratense 'Midnight Reiter'

THE COMPLETE
A-Z OF DARK
PLANT PROFILES

ACAENA

Mat forming perennials from New Zealand with year round foliage make useful ground cover.

HOW TO GROW
Suitable for a rock garden or wall in sun or partial shade, dislikes being overshadowed. Hardy to -12°C, 10°F. Z 6.
Separate rooted stems or take softwood cuttings in late spring.

A. inermis 'Purpurea' bears purple toothed leaves and insignificant flowers armed with red spines.
A. microphylla 'Kupfurteppich' usually sold as 'Copper Carpet' makes a neat, creeping carpet of ground hugging bronze leaves with bright red burrs. 3cm (1"+).

PLEASE NOTE: Where hardiness and USDA Zones are given they refer only to the specific plants described. Hardiness can vary.

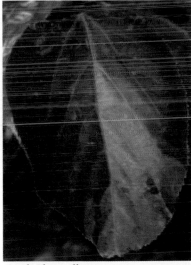

Acalypha wilkesiana

ACALYPHA

Rarely seen Pacific spreading shrubs with wonderfully coloured foliage, speckled and splashed.

HOW TO GROW
Under glass, grow in loamless compost in full or filtered light. Water freely when in growth, applying a balanced feed monthly during summer. Reduce watering in winter. Pot on or top dress in early spring or autumn. Outdoors, grow in fertile, humus-rich, moist well-drained soil in full sun for the best colour. Eventually 2-3m tall (7-10ft). Frost tender. 10°C (50°F).
Root softwood cuttings in early spring or semi-ripe cuttings in late summer with bottom heat.

A. 'Choco Thunder' bears fiery foliage speckled and splashed in bronze and rose.
A. wilkesiana 'Haleakala' has large, furled, solid copper-purple leaves with a filigree edge.
A. wilkesiana 'Macafeeana' has the combination of red blotched leaves splashed with bronze crimson. Introduced in 1877.
A. wilkesiana 'Macrophylla' is much darker overall, reddish-brown. Introduced in 1876.
A. wilkesiana 'Marginata' bears bronze-green leaves edged with crimson or orange. Introduced from Fiji in 1875.
A. wilkesiana 'Mooreana' has most attractive, deep bronze leaves growing in fan-shaped whorls.

ACER

Impressive, elegant form and foliage and spectacular colour have made Japanese maples highly suitable specimen plants or small shrubs. Good for large containers.

HOW TO GROW
Sow in fertile, moist but always well-drained soil in full sun or partial shade. Autumn colour is better if grown in neutral to acid soil. Protect from strong winds and mulch roots in temperatures below freezing. Prune to retain a healthy framework in late autumn to midwinter. Late spring frosts can kill foliage. Older trees resent disturbance. Hardy to -29°C (-20°F). Z 5-9.
Sow species seed in autumn. Cultivars should be grafted. Seedlings from cultivars cannot bear the cultivar name.

A. campestre 'Royal Ruby' is a splendid purple-leaved form which retains its colour well.
A. negundo v violaceum only reaches about half the size of the large wild green *A. negundo*. Purplish new shoots and twigs, mature to brownish green-purple. Male flower tassels are purplish.
A. palmatum f atropurpureum has compact form suitable for small gardens, making good container subjects. The dark purple, deeply lobed spring foliage gives way to a paler olive-purple in summer followed by deeper scarlet tones.
A. palmatum 'Akegarasu' is an

Acer palmatum 'Atrolineare'

Acer palmatum 'Bloodgood'

Acer palmatum 'Fireglow'

Acer palmatum 'Garnet'

Acer palmatum 'Koriba'

Acer palmatum 'Sunset'

upright grower with dark purple-red foliage. 3-4m (12-15ft).

A. palmatum 'Atrolineare' is a foliage aristocrat bearing ribbon-leaves of purple-red.

A. palmatum 'Beni-kagami' has pendent branches and a bushy habit with 5-lobed red-purple leaves which turn bronzy to wine-red with distinctive red seedheads in autumn. A strong grower. Height and spread 8m (30ft).

A. palmatum 'Beni-otake' is a dwarfish form with deeply dissected foliage of reddish purple.

A. palmatum 'Bloodgood' is a striking cultivar, smaller than 'Beni-kagami' also having deeply cut 5-lobed leaves of a darker red-purple turning red in autumn. The best of the purple cultivars, a real thoroughbred. Dramatic in spring, darker than 'Atropurpureum' in summer and offering good autumn colour. 5m (18ft).

A. palmatum 'Brandt's Dwarf' is a sport of *A.p.* 'Atropurpureum' and just half the size.

A. palmatum 'Burgundy Lace' with similar colouring is smaller still. It has fringed foliage at the margins, deep burgundy by midsummer. Graceful and cascading. 3m (12ft).

A. palmatum 'Fireglow' has dark purple leaves turning scarlet in autumn. 3m (10ft).

A. palmatum 'Garnet' retains the red-purple colour of its finely cut lobes into autumn in sun, a strong growing shrub with an open, spreading habit. 4m (12ft).

A. palmatum 'Hessei' is a superb cultivar with dark crimson deeply divided foliage. Ht 5m (15ft), spread 6m (20 ft).

A. palmatum 'Inazuma' the Thunder Maple has rich purple-red serrated leaves turning bronze-green in summer, then crimson in autumn. Makes a tall, rounded pendulous shrub. 3-4m (10-12ft).

A. palmatum 'Koriba' shows a variation of colour in leaves of differing maturity.

A. palmatum 'Linearilobum Atropurpureum' has deeply cut red purple foliage. Ht 5m (16ft), spread 4m (13ft).

A. palmatum 'Moonfire' *(below)* bears splendid dark purple-red foliage on dark red stems to complement any planting scheme. An erect, fast growing plant when young. 4-5m (14-18ft)

A. palmatun 'Nuresagi' bears spring foliage tinged red and purple, maintaining the colour into late summer. 5-6m (18-22ft).

A. palmatum 'O-kagami' has leaves which open purplish-red in spring, darkening in summer, finally turning red and scarlet in autumn. Up to 4m (13ft).

A. palmatum 'Oshu shidare' is beautiful with deep purple leaves on pendent branches descending to the ground. 3m (10ft).

A. palmatum 'Red Dragon' is a cultivar offering very deep purple-red foliage, retaining its excellent colouring into autumn.

A. palmatum 'Red Pygmy' is a dwarf form growing to around 1.5m (5ft) with young, dark red-maroon, finger-like leaves turning green with age.

A. palmatum 'Shaina' is a good

Acer palmatum 'Moonfire'

51

upright growing, compact and dense, shrubby form with bright red new foliage which matures to a deep maroon.

A. palmatum 'Sherwood Flame' has deep reddish purple foliage well into summer with red seedheads. Slender, upright form. 3m (10ft).

A. palmatum 'Sunset' brings flame colours to the garden.

A. palmatum 'Tamukeyama' is attractive for its deep crimson red leaves accented by a white-silvery wax on stems. Spring colour is followed by scarlet tones in autumn. 3m (10ft).

A. palmatum 'Trompenberg' bears deep purple-red foliage with leaves rolled over at the edge. Good autumn colour. 3-4m (10-12ft).

A. palmatum 'Tsukushigata' features rich purple-red leaves, looking black in sun, on green stems, holding its colour well all autumn. 3m (10ft).

A. palmatum 'Umegae' bears delicate purple red leaves, with a bright green main vein, turning crimson in autumn. A semi-dwarf,

spreading form. 2m (7ft).

A. palmatum 'Yezo-nishiki' features reddish-purple leaves becoming deeper purple in summer with glorious autumn tints of scarlet and carmine. Mature trees form a broad top. 4-6m (14-20ft).

A. palmatum v dissectum Dissectum Atropurpureum Group. Diminutive lacy foliage with red-purple leaves which are deeply divided. Height 2m (7ft), spread 3m (10ft). Z6.

A. palmatum v dissectum 'Crimson Queen' has red-purple leaves throughout the summer and fiery autumn tones. Deeply and finely divided foliage. Slightly larger than the above.

A. palmatum v dissectum 'Dissectum Nigrum' has dark bronze-purple leaves, silvery beneath when young. It is odd that one of the palest bears the name 'Nigrum'. 1-2m (4-7ft).

A. palmatum v dissectum 'Inaba-shidare' has deeply cut bronze-red leaves with vigorous new growth, holding its colour well. 2m (7ft).

A. palmatum v dissectum 'Pendulum Julian' bears deep purple-red leaves on pendent branches, turning bright crimson in autumn. 3m (10ft).

A. palmatum v dissectum 'Stella Rossa' has attractive red foliage.

A. platanoides 'Crimson King' is a stunning cultivar of the slow-growing Norway Maple with deep crimson-purple leaves, maturing slightly darker and having bright rich, red autumn colour. Greater wind-tolerance than other maples. 18m (60ft), spread 15m (50ft). Z3.

A. platanoides 'Crimson Sentry' is narrowly upright and has dark red-purple foliage, but not as dark as the above. 12m (40ft), spread 5m (15ft).

A. platanoides 'Faassen's Black' is similar to but darker than 'Crimson King'. Leaves turn up at the margins.

A. platanoides 'Goldsworth Purple' is a lighter shade with wrinkled young leaves.

Acer palmatum v dissectum 'Crimson Queen'

Acer palmatum v dissectum 'Dissectum Nigrum'

Acer palmatum v dissectum 'Iniba shidare'

ACTAEA

Known as *Cimicifuga* until recently reclassified.
Clump-forming perennials found in moist, shady areas in temperate regions and are suitable for woodland. Handsome, compound leaves are divided into leaflets with racemes or panicles of bottlebrush-type flowers.

HOW TO GROW

Grow in moist, humus-rich soil in partial shade, rich in organic matter. Hardy to -29°C (-20°F). Z 5. Divide cultivars in spring.

A. simplex 'Hillside Black Beauty' bears stunning, coppery purple foliage with creamy bottlebrushes swaying on 1.5m (5ft) stems. Strong fragrance. 60cm (2ft).

A. simplex Atropurpurea Group does well in an open situation in rich, retentive soil, and, unlike other *Actaea*, its leaves will not scorch. The deeply cut leaves and stems become dark purple, topped in autumn with slender spires of small, sweetly-scented cream flowers. 180cm (6ft).

A. simplex 'Brunette' has very deep purple foliage, dark stems and contrasting compact racemes of white flowers. 120cm (4ft).

A. simplex 'Elstead' has purple stems and buds opening to white.

A. 'James Compton' is a superbly dark form, performing well in an open situation. Named after the gentleman who reclassified the genus.

Actaea simplex Atropurpurea Group

AECHMEA

Rosette-forming bromeliads, mainly from rainforests bear attractive, arching leaves which are often marked in bands. Spike-like inflorescences with long-lasting flowers and brightly coloured bracts appear in summer and can be followed by fruits. Architectural black leaves and stunning flowers.

HOW TO GROW

Epiphytic bromeliad compost with bright filtered light in low humidity. Water freely when in growth and apply a low nitrogen fertiliser once a month. Water by filling the central plant vase.
Outdoors grow as epiphytes, or in the ground in moist epiphytic or gritty humus-rich soil. Grow as houseplants where temperatures fall below 10°C (50 °F).
Root offsets in early summer.

A. orlandiana bears rosettes of strap-like leaves in mid-green up to 30cm, banded dark purple with purple marginal spines. (1 ft) long.

In summer, red stems bear inflorescences to 10cm (4") long with spikes of 4-6 red-bracted, yellowish white flowers, followed by ovoid pale green fruit. Used along with *A. chantinii* as a parent.

A. 'Black' bears almost black and silver striped stiff leaves.

A. 'Black Bands' is an amazing camouflage of black and silver markings. Simply wonderful.

A. 'Black Chantinii' has extraordinary black-grey striped leaves and red flowers. 20cm (8").

A. 'Black Ebony' has black-green stiff leaves with silver markings and long-lasting red and yellow flowers.

A. 'Black Goddess' bears dark foliage with bright red and yellow flower spikes.

A. 'Black Ice' is another *chantinii* offspring, very similar to 'Black'.

A. 'Black Jack' (M. Foster) has strap black leaves with small red flowers. In a basket the leaves hang down, reminiscent of a large, hanging *Ophiopogon planiscapus*.

A. 'Black on Black' (J. Anderson) has superb long leaves, strap like and loose with almost no stripes.

A. 'Black Panther' (Hummel) bears upright, erect black leaves with very few stripes and bears yellow flowers.

A. 'Black Prince' (Hummel) has purple-black stiff leaves with faint grey stripes.

A. 'Blackie' has narrow, black-green strap leaves, erect but not very stiff.

A. 'Nigre' is brownish-black on the reverse of the leaf with marginal spines, having bright red and yellow flowers.

AEONIUM

Well-known dark succulents act as plant architecture in containers or in the garden border. These Mediterranean plants colour best in sun.

HOW TO GROW

Where temperatures fall below 10°C (50°F) grow under glass using a cactus compost. Water freely during the growing season, allowing the compost to dry out between waterings. Apply a balanced feed every 6 weeks when in growth. Keep dry when dormant. Outdoors, where temperatures permit, choose a site in partial shade or full sun in a moderately fertile, well-drained soil. Z9b-10. Hardy to -2°C (28°F). Take rosette cuttings in early summer. Allow a callus to form, insert into cactus cuttings compost at 18°C (64°F). Keep barely moist until roots have formed.

A. arboreum 'Atropurpureum' is an erect succulent. Its branches bear tight rosettes of spoon-shaped, dark purple-black leaves which turn green in winter.

A. 'Zwartkop' is one of the most wonderful black plants and one every enthusiast should choose to grow. Its rich purple-black leaves retain their colour year-round in good light. Flowers are yellow and appear in late spring. Reaches 2m (7ft) height and spread in its native Turkey and northern Africa, much smaller in Great Britain.
A superb plant, like a horticultural statue and one plant I shall always grow. An excellent container plant, kept well-drained and never overwatered. Housed under cover over winter in cooler areas. In warmer areas it can be planted out where it makes an amazing addition to the border. This slow-growing succulent has a tendency to shoot up like a tree with just one single stem, but it is superb when branched. To encourage branching cut off the stem and replant.

54

Ajuga reptans 'Braunherz'

Ajuga reptans 'Catlin's Giant'

AJUGA

Offering excellent bronze to black foliage, Ajuga make eye-catching dark carpets for underplanting. Easy shade lovers from temperate Europe and Asia which spread freely in moist soil.

HOW TO GROW

Leaves can scorch in full sun. Hardy to -29°C (-20°F). Z 5.
Divide plants at any time. Separate rooted stems or take softwood cuttings in summer.

A. reptans 'Atropurpurea' gives a good contrast of deep blue flowers to the lush, burnished purple foliage, retaining its colour throughout the year. 20cm (8").

A. reptans 'Black Mary' has near black leaves. 20cm (8").

A. reptans 'Braunherz' (Mahogany) is darkest when kept cool and on the dry side, contrasting beautifully with lighter tones and the usual blue flowers. 20cm (8").

A. reptans 'Bronze Beauty' bears crowded, crinkly, glossy leaves of a rich metallic purple with blue flowers in spring.

A. reptans 'Burgundy Glow' has silvery green leaves which are suffused a deep wine-red providing a vivid carpet all winter. 15cm (6").

A. reptans 'Catlin's Giant' ('Macrophylla') has tall flower stems to 30cm (1ft), bearing rich blue flowers to complement new rosettes of large glossy bronze-purple leaves to 15cm (6").

A. reptans "Ebony" is one of the darkest, a superb near-black form.

A. reptans 'Loie's Lavender' has masses of unusual lavender-grey flowers over a winter mat of purple shiny, small leaves.

A. reptans 'Pink Surprise' offers pink flowers in April and impressive dark purple foliage.

A. reptans 'Purple Torch' bears clear pink flowers over bronze foliage. 8cm (3").

A. reptans 'Royalty' spreads its prostrate rosettes of wavy, ruffled dark purple foliage.

A. reptans 'Valfredda' ('Chocolate Chip') is near black with small foliage and blue flowers. A mini spreader. Sun to shade. 7cm (3").

ALCEA

Short-lived perennials or biennials from temperate parts of Europe and Asia. Attractive to butterflies and bees, these tall plants make an excellent dark accent grown along a wall or in a mixed border.

HOW TO GROW

Grow in well-drained soil, moderately fertile in full sun. Often need staking, especially in exposed sites where they are best pinched out to form a bush. To control Hollyhock rust grow as biennials sowing in July, not as perennials. Hardy. Z. 2-10.
Grow from seed and select the best 'black' to sow the following year.

A. rosea 'Black Beauty' is maroon-black, shining and glistening with yellow anthers. 2m (6ft)
A. rosea 'Nigra' is remarkable for its single, deep chocolate-maroon flowers with yellow anthers speckling the dark flowers with their fairy dust. Can be variable, but at its best is a stunning black, silky, with just a slight hint of purplish red as the blooms age. Sold under different names, such as 'Watchman'. **A. 'Arabian Nights'** is a selection offering single and double flowers. 2m (6ft).
Some colour mixtures such as **A. rosea East Coast Hybrids** contain near black Hollyhocks. 2m (6ft).

Alcea rosea 'Nigra'

ALOCASIA

Large-leaved, evergreen, mainly rhizomatous, sometimes tuberous-rooted perennials that demand attention. Their natural habitat is tropical forest and sunny, usually damp sites by streams and marshes in south and south-east Asia. Striking, large, arrow-shaped leaves are often astonishingly well-marked with black, dark violet or bronze. Relatively insignificant spathes can be borne at any time of year followed by clusters of red or orange fruits.

HOW TO GROW

In frost-prone areas grow under glass in filtered light. A mix of bark, sand and loam is a suitable medium. In growth, provide high humidity and water freely, more moderately in winter. Feed every 2-3 weeks with a balanced fertiliser. Moist, humus rich soil outdoors in partial shade. 15-18°C (59-64°F). Seed should be obtained ripe and sown immediately at 23°C (73°F). Divide rhizomes or separate offsets in spring or summer. Stem cuttings can be rooted in early spring.

A. amazonica 'Nobilis' has tinted black foliage with white-green veins. Dramatic. 90cm (3ft).
A. 'Black Velvet' is a compact plant with rounded blackish-green leaves to 20cm (8") with exotically veloured surfaces emboldened by irridescent creamy white veins, light green undersides and stems. Loving humidity it is slow to grow.

A. 'Corozon' bears wide waxy pewter arrow-shaped leaves with dark veins on a dwarf plant. 'Elaine' and 'Aquino' are similar.

A. cuprea, the copper Taro, is a rhizomatous perennial with distinct oblong-ovate leaf blades, 45cm (18") long and leaf stalks 60cm (24") long. Upper leaf surfaces are strikingly marked with dark green metallic zones and midribs with copper coloured areas in between. Undersides distinctly reddish-violet. Purple spathes are 15cm (6") long. 1m (3ft).

A. cuprea 'Blackie' can be difficult to overwinter in the U.K. Its heart-shaped deep purple-black leaves are stunning. 1m (3ft).

A. 'Elaine' is a rare variety with thick, leathery deep blue-grey leaves. The undersides are reddish purple highlighted with darker veins. Slow to reach 45cm (18").

A. 'Fantasy' is the best dwarf with glossy, purple leaves and the stunning contrast of ivory veins.

A. 'Frydek' has delicate white veins on large, matt green leaves shaded black. 90-120cm (3-4ft).

A. indica v metallica bears purple leaves with a metallic sheen.

A. 'Mark Campbell' (David Fell) bears impressive near black leaves.

A. plumbea 'Nigra' produces purple or dark olive-green stems and similarly coloured elegant, polished ovate leaves with the stunning combination of wavy margins, purple veins and metallic purple colouring on the undersides of the leaves. Each leaf blade and leaf stalk is a gigantic 1m (3ft) long. White-ivory hood-shaped spathes 15cm (6") long contrast beautifully with the dark foliage. 1.5m (4-5ft). This exquisitely handsome plant is hardier and easier than A. cuprea.

A. 'Purple Prince' (Davidf Fell) has short, waxy arrowhead leaves with striking, iridescent purple veins.

The leaves of A. sanderiana would not disappoint either, with its excellent combination of very dark bottle-green leaves with a pale green margin and raised veins. Undersides are maroon.

A. wentii (A.discolor) has peltate leaves with bronzy shades.

ALTERNANTHERA

Tropical plants which can give dark accents in bedding or containers.

HOW TO GROW
Under glass, grow in full light, well ventilated. Outdoors grow in moist, but well-drained soil in full sun for best leaf colour. 5°C (41°F). Z 8-11.

Divide in spring, take softwood or greenwood cuttings in summer.

The best I have seen by far is A. dentata rubiginosa (Ruby), also known as Christmas clover or false globe amaranth, not at all like the *ficoidea* types. Fabulous foliage with truly dark leaves and masses of contrasting, long-lasting, ivory button flowerheads all winter.

A. ficoidea is a mat-forming perennial with long, pointed leaves and inconspicuous flowers which can be found in shades of burgundy bronze or near black, all 20-30cm (8-12") high.

A. 'Purple Knight' is available as seed, dark leaves give good accent to flowering plants.

Alocasia sanderiana (far left)
Alternanthera dentata rubiginosa

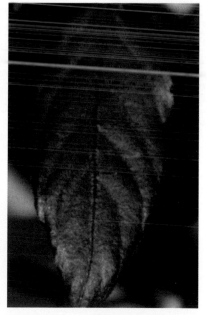

AMARANTHUS

Spreading tropical annuals or short-lived perennials offer deep red or purple leaves, making useful accent plants in summer bedding schemes in frost-prone areas.

Amaranthus lividus ssp lividus

HOW TO GROW
Under glass grow in full light. Water freely in summer and provide high humidity. Outdoors protect from strong winds in full sun. Grow in a moderately fertile, humus-rich soil, watering freely during summer, especially in dry periods. *A. caudatus* tolerates poor soil. Half-hardy.
Sow seed under glass or *in situ* for *A. caudatus*.

A. caudatus (Love-lies-bleeding) has many cultivars with purple foliage. Unusual, deep red tassel-like pendent flowers appear freely from summer to early autumn. 90-150cm (3-5ft).
A. cruentus bears purplish green leaves but nothing to compare with the cultivars of the above species.
A. 'Early Splendour' bears crimson flowers above bronze-red foliage.

A. hypochondriacus leaves are heavily suffused with purple. Those of **'Pigmy Torch'** are so dark-purple as to almost appear black, bearing deep reddish purple tassels. Has been grown at Levens Hall in Cumbria with purple-leaved *Canna* having brilliant scarlet red flowers and a dark *Lobelia*. A superb all dark combination. 1.5m.
A. lividus ssp lividus is delicately suffused purple.
A. tricolor cultivars sometimes bear dark hues.

AMORPHOPHALLUS

Devil's tongue is a genus of over 90 species. Found in moist shaded habitats in tropical Africa and Asia. Often large, magnificent spathes are usually unpleasantly scented to attract pollinators, but often only noticeable close-up, and the odour disappears with pollination. Frost tender but can be placed outdoors once danger of frost is passed.

HOW TO GROW
Dormant tubers should be planted in late winter or early spring at a depth of 10cm (4"). The corm-like rhizomes can be 50cm (20") across. Position in filtered light. Water freely when in growth, applying a balanced liquid fertiliser once a month. Reduce watering as the foliage dies down. Tubers can be overwintered in warm, barely moist conditions.

A humus-rich soil is required outdoors in partial shade. Some flower only every three years.
Sow seed in autumn or early spring. Separate offsets when dormant.

A. cirrifer has a purplish spathe with a brownish spadix at near ground level.
A. eichleri bears a purple-rimmed, ruffled spathe reminiscent of an Elizabethan ruff, with a mouldy-looking grey spadix.
A. henryi has a superb blackish spathe, the inner is a good purple, lies almost flat thereby exposing the spadix.
A. konjac has the darkest, intense blackish-purple spathes with a dark brown-crimson spadix, up to 90cm (3ft long) atop a 60cm (2ft) stem. Massive, divided leaf can reach up to 1.25m across (5ft) and is heavily mottled with dark purple. Corms can eventually weigh 8 kilos (17 pounds). The easiest one to grow. Colours better in bright light, but does emit a strong, unpleasant odour. A giant of the plant world, used as a food source in Indonesia and Japan. 13°C (55°F), reported as hardy in London, emerging from dormancy later than other species, in July and August.
A. paeoniiflorus has a spathe which sits like a swollen, ruffled, deformed purple male limb on top of a short stem. Something to get people talking!
A. pendulus has incredible dark leaves with a white central line.
A. rivieri is native to the forests of

Thailand, Vietnam and SE China and widely used in herbal medicine. Another giant with huge silver and green mottled stems and large leaves. On mature plants the inflorescence is a magnificent dark red-purple spathe, incredibly ruffled, and enveloping the fat red spadix.

A. swynnertonii has an inner dark spathe, outer creamy, with a purple spadix.

A. tenuistylis has a purple inner spathe with a mottled cream-grey outer and a purple spadix.

A. titanum bears reddish-purple spathes to 1.5m (5ft) long, each with a white protruding spadix on 1m (3ft) long stalks.

ANGELICA

Excellent large leaved ornamentals with architectural value in the garden. Happiest by a stream or in damp woodland.

HOW TO GROW
Grow in deep, moist, fertile loamy soil in full or partial shade. Hardy. Z4.
Sow fresh seed in a cold frame, needs exposure to light to germinate. Transplant seedlings when small, to flower in 2-3 years.

A. atropurpurea is an interesting foliage plant, a good addition to the border. New growth appears with eye-catching red stems and rich claret and green foliage. Leaves mature to mid-green with red

veining. Clusters of white-pink umbellifer flowers appear in summer. A biennial, although often a short-lived perennial which does not seed as much as many of its relatives. 1.2 to 2m (4-6ft).

A. gigas is a dramatic biennial producing domed umbellifer flower heads of an astonishing deep beetroot from mid to late summer on thick branching, blackish stems above enormous, divided leaves. The flower heads emerge like a monster unfurling to materialise into a ravishing beauty that will turn heads. Save seed and sow immediately it is ripe. Not for limy soils. 2m (6ft).

A. sylvestris 'Purpurea' is an impressive plant with leaves, stems and flowers suffused purple, seeds freely so select the best blackish foliage. Flowers from June through to September. 2m (6ft).

A. 'Vicar's Mead' is similar to the above but not quite as architectural, producing its darkest, glossiest foliage early in the year, with pink flowers.

Anthriscus sylvestris 'Ravenswing'

ANTHRISCUS

This cow parsley makes an attractive spread of dark leaves at its best in spring.

HOW TO GROW
Any well-drained soil will suit in sun or partial shade. Hardy. Z5. Sow fresh seed *in situ* in spring or autumn. Select dark foliage.

A. sylvestris 'Ravenswing' makes wonderful dark chocolate mounds of finely divided foliage. Small white flowers are produced in late spring to summer. Self-seeding may become a nuisance if not dead-headed. Discard green seedlings. 1m (3ft).

ANTHURIUM

Wonderful aroids from wet mountain forests in tropical and subtropical N. and S. America. Long lasting spathes, excellent for use as cut flowers, so glossy they have the appearance of being plastic. The added attraction of interesting dark zoned leaves.

HOW TO GROW
Plant crowns just above soil surface and cover with a layer of sphagnum moss. Roots must never dry out. Indoors, grow in epiphytic compost. Water freely in growth, reducing in winter. Need medium-high humidity and relatively low light levels. Sensitive to cold and temperature fluctuations.

Apply a balanced feed when in growth every 2-3 weeks. Top dress annually, pot on every two years. Min 18°C.
Seed may take several months to germinate. Divide in winter. Root stem cuttings or offsets in spring and summer.

A. 'Ace of Spades' is a dwarf variety with very dark green leaves which appear a translucent black.
A. 'Arizona' is a very dark red, with a green tipped white spadix.
A. 'Black' is one to die for, an *andreanum* type, with deep chocolate black spathes.
A. 'Choco' is dark brown with a green tipped white spadix.
A. 'Cognac' bears brown spathes, greenish in winter with a green tipped white spadix.
A. 'Negrito' has coppery black spathes and purple spadices with dark green, arrow-shaped leaves to 30cm (1ft).
A. 'Rapido' bears purple spathes and spadices.
A. 'Safari' is quite unusual with deep burgundy spathes with white veins and a burgundy spadix.
A. 'Violet Tapers' bears a bright violet spadix against a small pearl spathe stained violet, and dark leathery compact foliage.
A. red leaf bears reddish-purple leaves, possibly **A. 'Red Beauty'** which bears heart-shaped leaves of red-burgundy with a shimmery velvet surface. Similar to **'Black Valentine'** but easier to grow.
A. atropurpureum bears green, heavily tinged spathes, a purple spadix and dark purple berries.
A. dressleri and **A. papillilaminum** have dark shading on the velvety leaves, but very slight in the ones I have seen. *A. dressleri* can be difficult to cultivate, needing a cool climate. Hybrids are usually easier in cultivation than species.
A. purpureospathum (A jenmanii) is a bird's nest type, with thick, cardboard-like leaves with heavy veining and attractive purple-red new growth.
A. wilfordii, the chocolate bird's nest bears new leaves of claret, maturing into succulent mahogany cocoa tones.
The following are really dark-green leaved varieties, but absolutely amazing and so dark green as to be permissible, **A. crystallinum, A. crystallinum x magnificum, A. warocqueanum** and **A. veitschii. A. xanthosomafolium** is an incredible 2.10 m (7 foot giant) with black shading on its green leaves highlighted by light green veins.

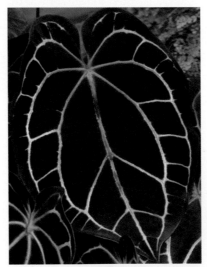

Anthurium crystallinum

ANTIRRHINUM

The Snapdragons include annuals, perennials and sub-shrubs from mainly rocky sites in Europe, USA and N. Africa. Grown for their lovely tubular, lipped flowers which are produced from early summer to autumn.

HOW TO GROW
Grow *A. majus* in fertile soil in full sun in a sharply drained site. Usually grown as a bedding annual even though it is a short-lived perennial. Prolong flowering by dead-heading. Hardy.
Sow seed of *A. majus* in autumn or spring. Sow tiny seed thinly as seedlings often damp off.

A. majus 'Black Prince' has long been a favourite of mine, with that all too rare combination of good dark foliage and appealing dark flowers. In a good form the linear foliage approaches black, with a maroon underside and the flowers are a very dark, deep red. Eye-catching when planted en masse. If you only grow one *Antirrhinum*, make it this one. Not normally prone to rust. Keep green seedlings as colour develops in the leaves near flowering time. I have found the best coloured leaves to appear in the second year.
A. 'Night and Day' bears contrasting deep red and white flowers over dark foliage.
There is also a new seed strain of dark-leaved *Antirrhinum* with a mix of coloured flowers.

AQUILEGIA

Distinctive dark, nodding flowers and attractive foliage are the qualities of these perennials. Found in meadow, woodland and mountainous areas of the northern hemisphere, they produce basal rosettes of mainly lobed leaves. The many forms of *A. vulgaris* are good in light woodland and effective in the herbaceous border. Cross-pollinate readily.

HOW TO GROW
Grow in fertile, moist but well-drained soil in full sun or partial shade. Hardy. *A. vulgaris* Z3. Preferably obtain seed as soon as ripe and sow immediately in a cold frame. Sown in spring a period of cold stratification may help. Cultivars can be divided, but do resent disturbance.

A. atrata (nigricans) has deep reddish-purple, almost black flowers from May-July. Easy in moist or slightly dry soil in partial shade. More top hat than Granny's Bonnet. Distinguished.

A. grata is a beautiful species from Yugoslavia with deep inky-violet flowers in spring. 40cm (16").

A. karelinii is a wonderful, dainty plant from the Pamir Mountains bearing numerous very dark violet flowers that make an immediate impression. 60cm (2ft).

A. secundiflora bears small violet flowers with spurs above delicate lacy foliage. 30cm (12").

A. 'Mobius' has tall, sturdy stems and blackcurrant flowers, the tepals having a glistening sheen. 80-100cm (32-36").

A. 'Roman Bronze' bears foliage opening yellow, darkening to an orange-bronze with deep violet flowers. Discard any seedlings with paler foliage. 60cm (2ft).

A. vulgaris v flore pleno black bears near black double-flowers.

A. vulgaris v stellata 'Black Barlow' is a double, purple-black version of the better-known and curiously fascinating *A.vulgaris v stellata* 'Nora Barlow'. 90cm (3ft).

A. vulgaris 'William Guiness' ('Magpie') bears dense clouds of puckered deepest blue-black and white flowers. For impact plant in small groups of 3-5 plants. 60-90cm (2-3ft). The frilly, double black and white, **A. vulgaris 'William Guiness Doubles'** stands at 60-90cm (2-3ft). Not as dark nor as attractive to my eye.

A. viridiflora ('Chocolate Soldier') is a choice and unusual plant from Siberia producing delicate sprays of sweetly perfumed green skirted flowers with intriguing maroon-brown centres forming a perfect contrast to the yellow anthers. 30cm (12").

Aquilegia vulgaris 'William Guiness'

ARISAEMA

Kings of the aroid family, tuberous or rhizomatous perennials from moist woodland and rocky wasteland. The unusual, interesting dark spathes have more than a hint of mystery, more than a touch of magic and more than a mere suggestion of sensual pleasure. Wonderful lobed or palmate green leaves being an added bonus. Some of the most exciting plants in horticulture.

HOW TO GROW
Plant tubers or rhizomes at a depth of 15-25cm (6-10") in winter or spring in humus-rich soil. Under glass, grow in deep pots in leaf mould, grit and loam in bright, indirect light. Mulch in winter and protect from late spring frosts. Cold hardiness is untested on newly introduced species. Never allow dormant tubers to dry out completely. Fully to half hardy and when grown outside are best in partial shade, full shade will make them leggy. Some will not appear above ground until early summer, so mark their position carefully. Sow seed in containers in autumn or spring in a cold frame. Offsets can be removed and potted up in late summer.

A. amurense usually bears a solitary, divided leaf. Hooded spathes appear on purple stems 8-12cm (3-5") long, each strikingly striped in dark purple and white in spring. 45cm (18"). Z6.

A. asaroides bears beautifully marked leaves and large, brown spathes. Z 6-9.

A. asperum is similar to the above and often seen in the Temple Gardens of Kyoto, Japan. Z 6-9.

A. ciliatum is a most attractive Chinese species which can bear clean purple-brown and whitish-green striped spathes ending in a 10cm tail with a curl from June to July. The spadix is small and whitish. Enormous, dissected parasol leaves appear later and get bigger every year. Sun to light shade. 80-90cm (32" -36"). Z6-7.

A. ciliatum v liubaense is from China, classified as *A. ciliatum* until recently. A striped maroon and white, hooded spathe has a long prominent whip and sunshade leaves comprising narrow leaflets. Stoloniferous. Hardy and accommodating. 80cm (32").

Deep violet spathes are not

Arisaema consanguineum

unknown on the delightful Indian species, **A. concinnum.**

A. consanguineum is an alluring, seductive beauty with a perfectly shaped deep purple and whitish striped spathe, and a smallish white spadix.

A. cordatum bears a palish spathe but well spotted with dark maroon and a dark purple spadix coupled with handsome leaves.

A. costatum bears deep purple-brown spathes with white stripes10-15cm (4-6") long, the tip is down-turned, the purple spadix tail is 30cm (12") long all this to some extent hidden beneath the single, wax-like, trifoliate, red-margined leaf. 40cm (16"), or larger. Easy outdoors.

A. elephas has a large, trifoliate green leaf, flushed purple and edged in red. Spathes are 15cm (6") long, deep purple with white stripes at the base. The spadix develops a long, curved purple appendage which extends to the ground. A delightful Chinese species, reasonably easy as far north as Edinburgh.

A. engleri can be found as a fantastic purple spathed form, deepening to the curled hood which is almost black. Contrasts superbly with the white spadix peeping from the cream, striped throat. The base of the spathe is covered in a blue-black bloom. Heavy, serrated leaves unfurl after the flower. What a show off, this plant knows how handsome it is!

A. fargesii is an excellent garden species from China with broad, glossy leaves and bold striped spathes of rich red-brown and white. Hardy and reliable. Deserves to be widely grown.

A. franchetianum has a deep maroon spathe, striped white and a large, glossy tripartite leaf. 35-40cm (14-16"). Z 6. Superb.

A. griffithii, is one of the most unusual and largest of the *Arisaema*, it has to be seen to be believed. In April-May large dark purple spathes appear, veined delicately with white, almost like a purple and creamy white snakeskin, fluted at the edge and curled in on itself with a charm all of its own. The spathe is produced near ground level, emerging in summer. No-one could call such a showy plant shy, but the habit of the curled over spathe, leaves you guessing at just what it has to hide within its depths. The trifoliate leaves are heavily veined and textured, breathtaking in themselves. Even though this tuberous perennial is not hardy, it is easy to cultivate. Exceptionally striking. Up to 60cm (2ft).

Arisaema ciliatum

Arisaema griffithii

A. iyoanum nakaianum bears a superb black spathe with a rolled back edge. A very rare Japanese species which is well worth seeking. One much divided leaf sits beneath the spathe. Z 6-9.

A. kelung-insulare has a long, thin black spathe. Z 6.

A. kishidae is a hardy species of the *serratum* group, with two divided leaves and a rusty-reddish-brown flower, a long-extended spathe tip and a club-like spadix. A rare selection features a central splash of silver to each leaf. An absolute gem and little charmer. Z 5-9.

A. kiuohianum bears a single leaf to 30cm (12") tall with 7-13 leaflets. Dark purple spathes are curved with white markings on the inner and outer, appearing in late spring on a short stalk near ground level. The mouse tail spadix is to 15cm (6") long. 20cm (8"). Z 6-9.

A. limbatum has a superb dark spathe. A sino-Japanese species.

A. lobatum has only recently been introduced into the U.K. Spathes are a lightish brown, with white, and the shiny green leaves appear

after flowering. Not the darkest, but superb. 30cm (12").

A. maximowiczii has a dark purple stem, the spathe being green sometimes purple when the fancy takes it, striped white. Rare. Z 5-9.

A. nepenthoides is a startling sight. The mottled petioles rise to almost 1.5m (5ft), bearing a deep purple and white striped spathe, from the base of which the leaves unfold.

A. ochresia has a knock-out purple striped spathe with a purple netted white limb and a threadlike spadix 8-20cm long (4-8"). 70cm (28").

A. propinquum is a native of the Himalaya, producing stunning striped purple spathes from May to June. The purple spadix hangs tongue-like almost to the ground. Hardy if well mulched.

A. purpureogealatum occasionally appears in nursery or seed listings, it displays a deep purple-black hood with a slender tail almost 30cm (12") long.

A. rhizomatum bears an ochre spathe, densely covered in purple and black spots, the thick spadix is red with dark purple spots. The leaf sheath is purple with brown and white spots. A rare species from the forests of Guangxi and Guizhou. Needs extra drainage.

A. rhombiforme seems well suited to U.K. gardens. Bears a slim, rich brown spathe, striped white.

A. ringens, the true species from S. Korea and Japan (it is also a synonym for *A. robustum* which has green spathes) bears a large hooded and curled green and purple-striped, purple-lipped

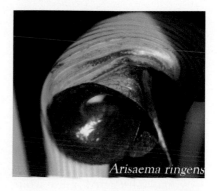

Arisaema ringens

spathe 10-15cm (4-6") long. So tantalisingly dark within as it sits beneath its umbrella of a green leaf in pure, undisguised temptation. Fairly hardy in leafy soil in shade, keep moist in summer. Early into flower, easy and deservedly popular. 30cm (12"). Z5-9.

A. ringens f sieboldii bears a plain purplish spathe.

A. sahyadrium is an unbelievable, knock your socks off tropical species. So dark! So desirable!

A. sazensoo is often wrongly listed as a synonym of *A.sikokianum*, but it blooms later and does not have a bulbous spadix. The purple spathe hood drops way down over the tube, appearing like a monk in meditation, from the Buddhist name, *Zazen*. Z 6-9. There is a superb variegated form too.

A. serratum (japonicum) black form has to be seen to be believed, a great choice from this genus. A sumptuous, very desirable, black sexy, silky spathe has real wow impact. Opulently rich, very dark, near-black spathes can be produced on this northeast Asian species. A startling, golf-ball like spadix is displayed against the truly magnificent spathe. The species can be variable and produce green spathes, or ones spotted or striped purple. Ultimately desirable and breathtakingly beautiful. Tender, needs protection. 1m (3ft). Z 5-9.

The Japanese species, **A. sikokianum** has a deep purple outer spathe, the inner being green shading to white, surrounding a striking club-shaped pure white spadix to give perfect contrast. The elegant form commands attention, this is a classic. An easy tuberous perennial, borderline hardy, worth testing with a good mulch in loose, leafy soil in shade. 30-50cm (12-20"). Z 5-9.

A. speciosum, a Himalayan species, is one of the most attractive, if not the easiest Arisaema to grow, it is well worth the challenge. Its long, slender spathes are purple, almost black with white stripes deep into the throat, slightly recurved margins, held well above the foliage. The most alluring and dark, mysterious yet theatrical of the species. Say wow three times! Its spathe curls over slightly at the end, hiding the delights within. The spadix is white at the base with an incredibly long dark purple tail over 30cm (12"). The petiole is spotted purple. A single 3-palmate leaf is borne at the same time of flowering in late spring to summer. Thriving best in humus-rich soil which is gritty and well-drained. Needs frost protection. 60cm (24").

A. taiwanense bears a fabulous black spathe with a white inner and white golf ball spadix. Z 6.

A. takedae x sikokianum is a superb near black cross having a black and white inner spathe.

A. ternatipartitum is a dimunitive and very rare species with 3-parted leaves, and 'ears' on the brown spathe which appears in midseason. Easy in a trough and forms colonies. Z 5-9.

A. thunbergii has a spectacular, deliciously purple, striped white on the outer with a magnificently contrasting darker inner spathe. The curved spathe ends in a long tail. Z 6-9.

A. thunbergii ssp urashima also bears purple spathes. Z 6-9.

A. triphyllum, commonly known as Jack-in-the-pulpit, produces stately spathes of green on the outside with purplish-brown inside. A hardy native of eastern North America, found in moist woods and bogs and appreciative of moist, leafy soil in partial shade. Flowering in mid-May to early July. Although blackish spathes and purple striped spathes can be produced, spathe colour is extremely variable. Most attractive leaves, sometimes with black markings. 15-60cm (6-24"). Z4.

A. undulatifolium v limbatum has a wonderful striped spathe with a black and white hood.

A. utile (verrucosum vutile) is a dark purplish-brown sino-Himalayan species with the hood dropping over the spathe to end in a long tail. Quite enchanting.

Arisaema ternatipaticum (far left)
Arisaema thunbergii (left)
Arisaema utile (below)

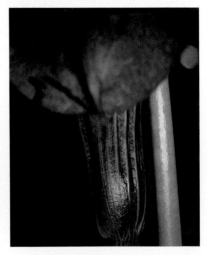

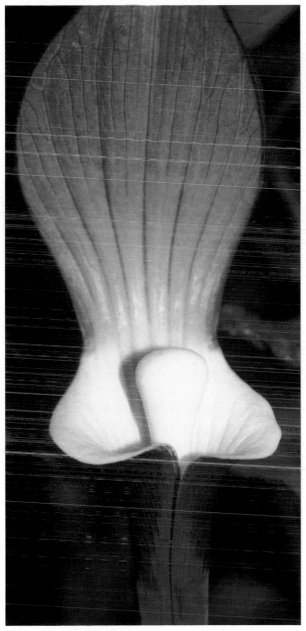

Arisaema sikokianum

Arisaema engleri

Arisaema serratum

Arisaema fargesii

66

ARISARUM

Small members of the aroid family, with bulbous dark spathes, almost hidden beneath foliage.

HOW TO GROW
Plant tubers 8cm (3") deep in autumn. Under glass, grow in humus-rich, gritty compost in filtered light.
Sow seed in a cold frame in spring.
Divide in autumn or winter.

A. proboscideum is the easiest species to obtain. A native of the woodlands of south-west Spain and southern Italy. Mats of attractive arrow-shaped, glossy green leaves, approximately 10cm (4") long almost hide the blackish maroon spathes with long, thin curled tips like whips which are commonly referred to as mousetails. They give the appearance of mice scurrying away to hide. An easy rhizomatous perennial, flowering from February to March. Capable of forming large colonies of low carpets which provide attractive edging for a woodland setting. Easy in shade. Hardy.15cm (6"). Z7.

A. simmorhinum is rarely seen, bearing cobra-hood spathes of dark-red brown, shading to cream at the base, with a large, swollen spadix. Native to North Africa and Spain. Reputedly tender, but hardy in London to -7°C.

A. vulgare, native of the Mediterranean, is a tuberous perennial with arrow-shaped leaves of mid to yellowish green appearing in autumn, smaller than the above, but sometimes attractively mottled purple. In winter or spring, small green hooded spathes are produced which are striped brown, with blackish-brown spadices. More suited to the alpine house, grow outside in an open site in full sun, keep dry in summer. 10cm (4"). Survives -5°C (23°F) for short spells if well mulched.

ARISTOLOCHIA

Mainly evergreen and deciduous climbers found in moist woodland in temperate and tropical regions of both hemispheres provide attractive, often heart-shaped leaves and petalless flowers in shades of white, purple or maroon, veined or mottled with dark hues. Some have unpleasant aromas, usually only noticeable at close quarters. Don't sniff just admire!

HOW TO GROW
A loamless compost will suit them under glass in bright filtered light. Water freely when in growth and apply a balanced feed every month. Little water is needed in winter. Outdoors grow in fertile soil in sun or partial shade. Hardy species overwinter best in dry soils. Climbers need strong support. Prune after flowering in spring, pruning back to 2 or 3 nodes. Fully to frost hardy.
Sow seed as soon as ripe or in spring. Divide perennials in spring or take root cuttings in winter. Root softwood cuttings of climbing or scandent species grown under glass in early spring, and of hardy species in midsummer.

A. californica is a tender, deciduous, climber which can reach 4.5m (15ft) or more. It bears heart-shaped leaves and small, dull purple flowers with the upper lip divided into 2 lobes.

A. chilensis bears funnel-shaped, deepest purple flowers with marbled, cup-shaped grey-green leaves. Half hardy trailer.

A. gigantea is a tender evergreen twiner with dark green heart-shaped leaves. Solitary flowers, to 15cm (6") across, are purple with white veins or maroon and are borne in summer. 10°C (50°F). 10m (30ft).

A. gigantea 'Brazilensis' is superb with a surprising lemon scent.
The large flowered, **A. grandiflora** bears purple and green flowers emitting a strong odour to attract pollinating flies but only noticeable when close. Tender. 10m (30ft) or more.

A. hirta is a native of parts of Turkey, flowering from March-May in rocky places. Long, narrowish green leaves and large, hairy purplish-red flowers with the distinguished odour of rotting meat. Well-drained, stony soil, kept dry in winter. Hardy to -10°C.

A. labiata has veined, purple and cream flowers, 20-30cm (8-12") long appearing in late summer. 10m (30ft) or more. 3°C.

A. littoralis (Calico flower) is a fast-growing creeper native to Brazil, needing high humidity and frost protection. Highly attractive purple flowers are veined white, similar in colouring to *A. gigantea*, but having stronger markings and a purple band deep in the throat of the flower which is of a different shape to the latter species. Grown as an annual in cool climates. 5-8m (15-25ft). 7°C (54°F).

A. macrophylla is a strong grower, crowding out other plants, so be careful where this one makes its home! Dark green heart-shaped leaves tend to cover the pipe-shaped flowers which are green, mottled purple or brown 8-10m (25-30ft). Borderline hardy.

A. trilobata has tubular creamy flowers flushed purple-maroon ending in a magnificent dark purple which trails into a long tail. Combined with wonderful passionflower like veined leaves. 3m (10ft) or more. 10°C.

Aristolochia grandiflora

ARUM

Curious and interesting describe this genus which adds drama to the garden. These tuberous perennials are found in partially shaded habitats in S. Europe. Attractively shaped and marked leaves are a feature of many species.

HOW TO GROW
Plant tubers at a depth of 10-15cm (4-6") in autumn or spring. Choose a position in partial shade or full sun in well-drained, humus-rich soil. Under glass grow in loamless compost with added grit, in full or filtered light. In growth, water freely and apply a balanced feed monthly. Reduce watering as the leaves wither and keep almost dry when dormant. Hardiness varies.
Sow seed in autumn in a cold frame, first removing the pulp from the berries, wearing gloves. Divide after flowering.

The little known **A. apulum**, native to southern Italy, bears erect green spathes with a dark purple inner and a purple spadix. Easy.

A. byzantium bears brownish-purple spathes with a greenish white inner and a purple spadix. Easy in a damp, shady spot given plenty of room. Quite hardy. Often seen as *A. concinnatum*.

A. canariense (A. italicum ssp italicum) is notable for its purple inner spathe and dull purple petioles. Flowers in April to May on grassy banks in shade.

A. conophalloides v caudatum, a native of Turkey, growing in woods and among rocks, bears purplish spathes, 34-38mm long (14") and spadices from May to June.

A. conophalloides v syriacum is deepest, dark purple. A Turkish native, flowering in May to June.
Both **A. dioscoridis** and its numerous varieties and **A. hygrophilum** have spathes marked or flushed dark purple, the spathes of the former being green or maroon purple, but can be almost totally near-black and of the latter green. **A. dioscoridis** is easy in a warm, dry site. Usually hardy but strong-smelling.

A. dioscoridis v liepoldtii grows in hedges and rocky places in southern Turkey to Syria. Leaves emerge in winter, and creamish-yellow, spotted black spathes, which can sometimes be almost all black, appear from April to May, and cannot be described as sweet-smelling. Easy to cultivate at the base of a south-facing wall.

A. dioscoridis v smithii has deep maroon markings on flat, open creamy spathes in April to May.

A. dioscoridis v spectabile is purple on the lower half of the spathe, changing colour through large purple blotches to a greenish tipped spathe in March to May and is endemic to Turkey. (Peter Boyce says it does not differ from the species). 25-35cm (10-14").

A. elongatum, the real thing, bears pale green spathes, stained purple inside and a maroon spadix in late spring over unmarked leaves. Bright red fruits. 10-15cm

(4-6") tall on flowering, then 30-40cm (12-16"). Native to the almost inaccessible area around the Black Sea. Hardy in a moist sunny position. Handsome. Z 4-5.

A. idaeum from Crete has purple spathes and spadices. Deep green sagittate leaves. 20-30cm (8-12"). Hardy but intolerant of wet. Z 3-4. There is also a very rare black spotted leaf form of **A. italicum**.

A. italicum ssp italicum has variable but very attractive purple-black spotted leaf markings. Z6.

A. maculatum 'Pleddel' bears dark maroon spotted leaves and pale green spathes marked maroon. The dark green glossy leaves of this highly variable species can be spotted, very rarely wholly purple.

A. nigrum is one of the best, having a dark, deep black-purple spathe 12-20.5 cm long (5-8") with a superb sheen and dark purple spadix. Native of former Yugoslavia and northern Greece, the large, glossy black-green leaves emerge in early spring, followed by the magnificent spathes in April to May, far darker than *A. orientale*, but also stronger smelling. Exotic looking, but easily grown in the garden, providing a rich, free-draining soil in light shade, out of early morning winter sun. Vigorous and hardy, capable of surviving harsh European winters. Water and feed well.

A. orientale from the Crimea has dark purplish brown spathes, a dark purple spadix, deep green floppy leaves and bright orange fruits. Makes a good garden plant

in the U.K. Wide distribution with a wide variation, the best are very desirable for their dark colouring. Very hardy. 25-30cm (10-12"). Z5.

A. palaestinum steals the limelight with its near-black spathes and spadix in April. The outer spathe is greenish white. It can have a musty smell or be sweetly scented depending on provenance. One of the darkest of Arums, uniform in colour, is found in Lebanon, Syria and Israel, by shady walls and amongst rocks and is best in dry shade. Give protection from extremes of wet and cold, good drainage is essential. Foliage is not frost hardy. Superb. 45cm (18").

A. pictum has a maroon-purple spathe sheltering the purple spadix within. Superb leaves are a dark, lustrous green highlighted by pale veins, flushed purple on opening, the colour is usually retained on the margins of mature leaves. Autumn flowering and successful outdoors in many parts of the U.K. Try it in a large pot.

A. purpureospathum, discovered in southwestern Crete, and not named until 1987, bears glistening, dark purple spathes and small spadices, being seemingly very easy in cultivation. Leaves emerge in autumn (fall) and spathes appear in spring. One of the most attractive Arums. Vigorous and hardy, not seeming to mind winter wet. Will struggle to survive frost in pots, but much hardier out in the garden. Bears orange-red berries. I grew mine from seed. 25-30cm (10-12").

A. rupicola and its varieties are native to the eastern Mediterranean with long, slender spathes often flushed purple. An added bonus of being odourless.

A. sintenisii is not as dark as *A. nigrum*, but this is still superb with a near black spadix, darker than the deep purple-black inner spathe with a paler outer.

ASARUM

Wild gingers are prized for their beautifully marked leaves, often large, marbled and silver-marked which conceal out-of-this world, pitcher-shaped flowers, being mostly brownish-purple. Natives of the forest floor, they make good ground cover and edging and are often grown in pots in Japan.

HOW TO GROW
Grow in partial to full shade in moderately fertile, humus-rich, moist but well-drained neutral to acid soil. Susceptible in dry conditions. Hardy but may be found to shed their leaves at temperatures below -15°C (5°F). Sow fresh seed in a cold frame. Divide in early spring.

A. arifolium is a variable American species with large, elongated, heart-shaped leaves up to 15cm (6") long, marked with lighter green. The deep purple, globular flowers are borne at ground level. Z 5-9.

A. asaroides has large, tubby brown flowers. Grey-green leaves have cloudy silver patterns which take on a rose blush in winter. Z 6-9.

A. campaniforme is a Chinese species with outward-facing, bell-shaped flowers of cream edged in black, with a black band around the red throat.

A. canadense is known as wild ginger. Green, hairy, heart-shaped leaves and urn-shaped purple-brown flowers are borne near ground level in spring. 8cm (3").

A. caudatum from the coastal mountains of western U.S.A. is a ground-hugging, evergreen species, spreading in patches with large, kidney-shaped leaves rising to 20cm (8") above the ground on stems covered in white fur, hiding the purplish-brown flowers.

A. caulescens is a Japanese species with unmarked, blackish-green, heart-shaped leaves, brown flowers arch open, like a ram's head, with a cream inner and dark throat.

A. celsum is a very rare, clump-forming evergreen species with variable leaves, usually unmarked, and purple-brown flowers with rings and ridges. Z 8-9.

A. chinense bears pubescent foliage often silvered, with small, hairy dark purple-brown flowers.

A. debile bears small leaves and small brown-purple and white flowers beneath the foliage.

A. delavayi is one of the largest species, with elongated, heart-shaped leaves 12-15cm (4-6") long, often well-silvered, and large flowers with a black edge and throat having a cream inner with an amazing textured surface.

Asarum maximum

A. dimidiatum is a rarely seen deciduous Japanese species with bright green leaves and dark purple flowers. Z 4-8.

A. dissitum has handsome foliage, almost glossy or velvety often with white spots and bears small, brownish tubular flowers.

A. europaeum, asarabacca, has small, narrowly bell-shaped greenish purple or brown flowers. One of the easiest to obtain. Z 8-9.

A. epigynum is a rare creeping Taiwanese evergreen species with narrow, pointed leaves and fuzzy brown pouch like flowers. Z 9-10.

A. forbesii has superb foliage, long arrowhead leaves beautifully veined in pewter. Exquisite. Chunky flowers are dark chocolate purple with a white centre.

A. hartwegii has the added advantage of dark green-bronze leaves with broadly tubular brownish-purple flowers.

A. hatsusimae has white-tipped brownish flowers perched on stems unusually held above the ground and slightly succulent leaves. Z 8-9.

A. heterotropoides forma mandschuricum is a north China species with urn-shaped, purple-brown flowers. Very hardy.

A. infrapurpureum has heart-shaped foliage which is dark purple on the underside, visible from above owing to the undulating leaf. It bears small, purple flowers.

A. kiusianum is a clump-forming evergreen species with leaves to 7.5cm (3") long, usually patterned. Bears brownish-purple flowers. Z 7.

A. kiusianum v tubulosum bears cafe au lait to white flowers for the chocolate garden. Z 7-9.

A. maculatum is a deciduous species from Korea with beautifully patterned leaves and dark purple, near black flowers. Z4-8.

A. magnificum has dramatic, large white and brownish-black flowers, prominently three-lobed with a heavily ridged white throat, tinted violet in spring. Large leaves are heavily marked with silver. Z 7b.

A. maximum has velvet, black throated, white centred, black tri-lobed, flaring bell-shaped flowers to 6cm wide. Lush, glossy, evergreen leaves to 18cm (7") are usually silvered above, purple beneath. Suitable for a cold greenhouse. Z 7b-9.

A. megacalyx has glossy dark evergreen leaves to 7.5cm (3") long, often patterned. Bears large, bell-shaped, nearly black flowers. Does well in rich, loose soil. Z 5-8.

A. nipponicum is now rare in the wild, bearing leathery oval green leaves, usually patterned to 10cm (4") long. Brown flowers in winter.

A. nobilissimum makes large clumps with leaves to 20cm (8") and bears brownish flowers to 7cm (3") across. Z 7b-9.

A. shuttleworthii 'Velvet Queen' is a small creeping form from southeastern U.S., with round, silver-marked leaves and large dark flowers in mid spring. 12cm (5").

A. simile bears oval-triangular leaves of a velvety dark green, usually plain. Brownish flowers have undulate lobes. Z 8-9.

A. splendens is a fine species with dark black-green leaves, often flushed purple and well-patterned in silver and pale green. Large, bell-shaped grey flowers have a cream internal ring, spotted purple with an intense violet throat.

A. wulingense from China bears superb narrow foliage up to 25cm (10") long, well marked in silver. Flowers are purple, covered in short yellow hairs, darker into the red throat.

ASTER

Flowers when most wanted, late in the season, but the following *Aster* are grown primarily for their superb dark foliage.

HOW TO GROW
Well-drained, open, moderately fertile soil in full sun. Open site. Divide in spring or autumn.

A. laevis 'Calliope' bears superb dark leaves, making an impressive clump of straight, tall black stems topped with lavender daisy flowers in late summer. This has earned a place in my garden. 90cm (3ft).

A. lateriflorus has foliage which turns copper in autumn, but the cultivars are much darker.

A. lateriflorus 'Lady in Black', selected by Coen Jansen, has stunning near black foliage making a feature throughout summer before the small white flowers with raspberry centres appear in late autumn. A more open form than the one below. 120cm (4ft).

A. lateriflorus 'Prince' selected by Eric Smith for deep bronze to black foliage and stems. White and pink flowers in autumn. Good contrast with pink flowered plants, making an excellent contribution to the dark garden. Effective used as a hedge. 60cm. (2ft).

Aster lateriflorus 'Prince'

71

ATRIPLEX

Easy to grow, easy to seed, spikes of purplish ruby red foliage make quick filler plants for gaps left early in summer.

HOW TO GROW

Enjoys fertile, moist soil, well-drained in full sun. Water well in dry periods to reduce the tendency to bolt.

Sow seed in situ in succession from spring to early summer.

A. hortensis v rubra is the darkest, much used at Great Dixter, a strong annual and good dot plant. Decorative as well as edible, this useful and easily grown foliage plant comes true from seed. A rapid grower which can be used in the border, or in summer bedding schemes contrasting well with darker plants. Seeds around freely. 60cm -1.2m (2-4ft).

Atriplex hortensis v rubra

BEGONIA

A large genus of over 900 species from warm areas. A large number have deeply bronze or purple foliage nearing black. Newer cultivars are bred to tolerate lower humidity than before.

HOW TO GROW

Keep just moist, allowing **B. rex** to dry out a little between watering, rhizome rot can be a problem if they are too wet. Superb in shade. **B. rex** are mainly rhizomatous perennials cultivated for their foliage, bright light enhances the darker colours, whilst lower light brings out the metallic sheen often found on the attractive, evergreen leaves. Maintain a temperature of 21-24°C (70-75°F). Direct sunlight will scorch leaves. Avoid splashing leaves when watering.

B. semperflorens are fibrous-rooted evergreen perennials. Bushy and fairly compact, they enjoy a little shade. Normally used as annuals in summer bedding schemes, overwinter them indoors or under glass in cold areas. Hybrids have been developed with deep bronze leaves which contrast beautifully with the flowers in shades of white, pink, salmon and red. Overwinter at a minimum of 10°C (50°F).

Seed is very fine and high temperatures are needed for germination. *B. rex* can also be propagated by rhizome sections and by leaf cuttings. *B. semperflorens* can be propagated by basal cuttings.

BEGONIA CANE TYPES

Compact types are suitable for baskets.

B. 'Anna Christine' bears black-green leaves with lovely coral flowers year round. Low growing.

B. 'Arabian Nights' (Brad Thompson (hereafter abbreviated to B.T. 1990) Mallet. Bears dark leaves with red overtones. Flowers of rose and white. Lowish growth.

B. 'Arabian Sunset' (B.T. 1990) has dark green leaves with a reddish cast from the red reverse. Flowers are rose and white.

B. 'Baby Beth' (B.T. 1992) bears small, serrated dark bronze leaves, red backed with medium pink flowers. Compact.

B. 'Baby Ruth' (B.T. 1992) bears black cut leaves with silver spots and dark pink flowers on a compact plant.

B. 'Babylon' (B.T. 1990) Mallet. The black leaf is set off by pinkish spots having a red reverse. Flowers with red ovaries and pink petals are the perfect complement.

B. 'Black Gold' (B.T. 1990) Dark serrated medium leaves with large pink flowers on this naturally branching, heavy bloomer.

B. 'Black Satin' (B.T. 1990) bears extremely dark black, medium sized leaves with large pale pink flowers in profusion. Pinch to branch well.

B. 'Dangling Pearls' (B.T. 1990) possesses very small black leaves, with some spots and a red reverse. Pure white flowers dangle like pearls, almost continually and prolifically. Low growing.

Begonia 'Arabian Sunset' (above)
Begonia 'Dragon Wing' (below)

Begonia 'Burgundy Star (above)
Begonia 'Midnight Twister' (below)

B. 'De Cups' (B.T. 1990) has large, black cupped leaves with a red back with large white spots on new growth. Dark pink flowers are held well above the foliage. Upright.

B. 'Down Home' (Stewart) bears dark green, near black foliage with heavy silver steaking and a red reverse. Pendent clusters of large light red flowers.

B. 'Eddie Sakamoto' (B.T.) has red-black leaves with red undersides and dark pink flowers. A medium, upright growing type.

B. 'Flo' Belle Moseley' bears dark angel wing leaves speckled pale pink and deep rose-pink flowers.

B. 'Guy Savard' is an upright growing variety with large, up to 25cm (10") leaves of dark purple with silvery pink spots and currant red flowers to complete the show.

B. 'Irene Nuss' (Nuss) is a superba type with bronze-green leaves and a red reverse complimenting the fragrant coral-pink flowers.

B. 'Jeanne Jones' (B.T. 1992) has satiny black cut superba leaves with silver spots atop and red beneath. Large pink flowers in clusters.

B. 'Jumbo Jet' bears purple stems (eggplant) and black-maroon leaves with a slow growing habit.

B. 'Lady in Red' (B.T. 1992) bears medium pointed black leaves with a serrated edge and a red back. Dark red flowers in profusion.

B. 'Lady Olivia' (B.T. 1992) has small plain black leaves with a red reverse, complimented by pale pink and white flowers. Compact.

B. 'Little Miss Mary' (B.T. 1992) bears black leaves with pink splashes and red undersides contrasting with dark red flowers.

B. 'Little Miss Mummy' (B.T. 1992) has small black serrated leaves with raised white dots and large, stunning cream-white flowers on long petioles. Resistant to mildew although sometimes shy to bloom.

B. 'Long Heart' (B.T. 1990) has black serrated leaves with a red reverse and large pale pink flowers. Low growing upright.

B. 'Low Hangers' (B.T. 1990) displays black leaves and red undersides with delicious pink-salmon flowers on long petioles.

B. 'Madame Coulat' (B.T. 1996) bears small, very black leaves with a red reverse. Profuse, small dark red contrasting flowers are carried in large clusters. Compact.

B. 'Maria Holmes' (B.T. 1992) offers medium black leaves with some spots and a red underside. Flowers are pale reddish orange. This low grower is everblooming.

B. 'Mariposa Rojo' (B.T. 1990) Mallet. Reddish black leaves with pink spots and rose and white flowers on a full growing upright which is compact.

B. 'Meredith Grenier' (B.T. 1992) bears black cut, pointed leaves with unusual lavender pink spots and a red reverse. Pink flowers are borne on this compact low grower.

B. 'Merwin Amerman' (B.T. 1992) has almost black leaves with silver spots and a red reverse. Dark pink and white flowers on this upright grower, usually needs staking.

B. 'Naugahyde' (B.T. 1992) has large, thick black serrated leaves with a red back, accompanied by large cherry red flowers.

B. 'Ossie Williams' (B.T. 1992) has black cut superba leaf with silver splashes and contrasting red undersides. Large, mid-pink flowers. Medium, upright growth.

B. 'Palos Verdes' (B.T. 1990) has bronze-black serrated, medium-sized leaves with red backs. Large, mid-pink flowers.

B. 'Passing Storm' (Worley) bears heart-shaped bronze foliage with a rose metallic overlay.

B. 'Pink Taffeta' (B.T. 1990) bears near black leaves with a silver shimmer and red backs. Large-

Begonia 'Flo Belle Moseley'

medium pink flowers contrast perfectly. Retains leaves in winter.

B. 'Prodigy' (B.T. 1992) possesses black leaves with a red reverse and dark red flowers held above the foliage. Low, upright growth.

B. 'Ruby's' (B.T. 1992) has medium, serrated black leaves with a red reverse. Very bright clusters of small red flowers on medium compact growth.

B. 'Russian Sabers' (B.T. 1990) features black, pointed leaves with red backs on a low growing variety with profuse dark pink flowers.

B. 'Sands of Arabia' (B.T. 1990) Mallet. Black leaf with pinkish spots and a red back. Flowers bear red ovaries and pink petals.

B. 'Sharon Seelert' (B.T. 1992) has black narrow leaves with silver spots and red backs and flowers of white and pink.

B. 'Shatoyant' (B.T. 1990) carries puckered and wavy, large, dark bronze-black leaves to contrast with large medium-pink flowers.

B. 'Sophie's Choice' (B.T. 1992) Very large satiny black cut superba leaf, at least 30cm (12"), with silver spots and red reverse. Large mid-pink flowers on a tall variety.

B. 'S. Thompson' (B.T. 1990) has rounded, dark reddish-black leaves with silver spots and large, bright pink flowers.

B. 'Tingley Mallet' has hairy maroon leaves and pink flowers with upright growth.

B. 'Vivian Hill' (B.T. 1992) has black, narrow pointed cupped leaves with silver spots and dark red flowers on an upright plant.

Begonia 'Benitochiba' (top)
Begonia 'Tingley Mallet' (above)

BEGONIA RHIZOMATOUS

60°F minimum temperature. The bigger these get, the better they look, young leaves can change quite dramatically when mature.

B. 'Anaconda' (B.T. 1993) bears very large green star-type leaves with black markings. Abundant pink flowers on tall stems.

B. 'Baby Douk' is similar to *B.* 'Bokit', but with white flowers.

B. 'Beatrice Haddrell' (Merryfield 1955) has star-shaped almost black leaves with chartreuse veins. Pink flowers are freely produced in winter to spring. A real favourite!

B. 'Bedford Velvet' is a delightful specimen plant of darkest leaves.

B. 'Benitochiba' (rex) is a newish cultivar with cut, shimmering metallic leaves, veined black.

B. 'Ben Lexcen' is hairy with largish dark leaves marked in green, resembling *B.* 'Black Falcon' and bearing pink flowers.

B. 'Bethlehem Star' (Wagner 1975) has small dark bronze leaves, with a light chartreuse central circle and white marginal hairs. Profuse pink flowers from late winter-spring.

B. 'Black Ace' is vigorous, with almost black leaves, needing no resting period.

B. 'Black Coffee' has deep green star shaped leaves with lots of black overtones, eyelash-fringed, maroon undersides. Pink flowers in spring.

DARK BEGONIA

B. 'Comtessa de Montesquieu'

B. 'Bedfod Velvet'

B. 'Fireworks'

B. 'Midnight Magic'

B. 'Black Prince'

B. 'Red Robin'

B. 'Elaine Wilkerson'

B. 'Contessa Rizare de Plata'

B. 'Vesuvius'

B. 'Clifton'

B. 'Beatrice Haddrell'

B. 'Texas Star'

Begonia 'Boston Cherries and Chocolate'

B. 'Black Mamba' (B. T. 1993) has large, black spiral, star-type leaves with plentiful pink flowers on tall stems. Upright leaves on mature plants reach large dimensions.

B. 'Black Prince' combines dark colour with interesting leaf shape.

B. 'Black Velvet' (Stanford 1967) Small, dull black-green velvet leaves are star-shaped and shallowly lobed with marginal eyelash hairs. Pink flowers on long spikes in late winter- spring. Spectacular in heat.

B. 'Bokit' has medium, rich green leaves with black markings and light pink flowers in winter.

B. 'Boston Cherries and Chocolate' is an excellent example of a dark chocolate spotted red, it almost looks edible. Excellent form.

B. 'Bowkit x Rex' has purple and black leaves with a reddish underside flowering in late winter. 15-20cm (6-8").

B. bowerae v nigramarga, is the darkest of the eyelash begonias which are so unfussy and easy to grow. Bronze-black star shaped leaves with broad light green markings along veins and blush pink flowers in late winter.

B. 'Brown Satin' has large sharkskin black-brown leaves with green banding.

B. 'Brown Twist' (Woodriff 1997) bears dark bronze-green leaves, medium spiralled with white tinged, pink flowers in spring to early summer. An attractive, small-leaved variety.

B. 'Burgundy Velvet' bears deep burgundy leaves, green spotted and completely green at the leaf margin. Central veins form a yellow star.

B. 'Burmese Python' (B.T. 1993) has large star-shaped dark green leaves with black markings and pink flowers.

B. 'Bushmaster' (B.T. 1993) bears large double spiralled dark green leaves with black markings. Pink flowers are held aloft on stems up to 60cm (2ft) long. Leaves can reach immense proportions.

B. 'Butterfly' has 3-pointed star-shaped leaves, dark to medium green patterning with some black shading. Light pink flowers in spring. A good grower.

B. 'Caribbean Corsair' (Anderson). Deep, puckered olive green leaves with black overtones, are enormous to 30cm (10") with slightly wavy edges. Pink flowers in spring.

B. 'Cathedral' has very unusual folded and cut leaves with pale green centres, and dark green edges blushed red. Most unusual, but not very dark.

B. 'Chicago Fire' has outstanding red and black colouring.

B. 'Clifton' bears small green leaves marked with near black.

B. 'Comtessa de Montesquieu' bears elegant textured dark leaves.

B. 'Contessa Rizare de Plata' is a mesmerizing kaleidoscope of wondrous colouring, almost black to silver green. An instant captivating favourite.

B. 'Curly Stormy Night' (B.T. 1993) is an extremely dark, near black, spiral-leaved plant with a velvet appearance. Flowers are almost red. Very compact with leaves reaching large dimensions.

B. 'Daisy' (Paul Lowe) has small dark leaves with abundant light pink flowers.

Begonia 'Helen Teupel'

B. **'Dollar Down'** bears bright red tiny leaves edged in black.

B. **'Dragon Wing'** this is not the plant you will find under this name at the garden centre with green leaves, but a stunning deep brown, near black and chartreuse green leaf in a pattern giving a stained-glass window effect.

B. **'Earl-ee-bee'** (Budd 1964) has large divided, near black leaves with a chartreuse centre and greenish white flowers profusely borne in spring.

B. **'Ebony'** has dark green leaves with mahogany undersides.

B. **'Elaine's Wilkerson'** has deep green-black leaves with large green blotches on younger leaves.

B. **'Fireworks'** (rex) makes an excellent specimen with large leaves having near black veins pulsing through the silver and pink rings to the outer edges.

B. **'Filigree'** is pink on satin black.

B. **'Happy New Year'** is similar to 'Merry Christmas' but with spots on the bright green ridge.

B. **'Helen Lewis'** has silver-banded dark wine-red leaves.

B. **'Helen Teupel'** (rex) has long, jagged dark purple-black leaves splashed with metallic silver and pink. Excellent large leaves with a classic colour combination. Great.

B. **'Hocking Billiken'** bears chocolate spiralled leaves sprinkled with green having a white eye.

B. **'Hocking Bravura'** has chocolate furled leaves highlighted by a parchment of white veins.

B. **'Hocking Shockwave'** has dramatic, big chocolate leaves edged and freckled in green. Pink flowers are borne in January.

B. **'Humerous'** (B.T. 1995) has reddish-black satiny medium-sized leaves. A low-growing yet full and compact variety.

B. **'Jester'** (B.T. 1995) has small cut, double-spiralled, brownish-black leaves. Bears pink flowers on a compact, full growing plant.

B. **'Little Star'** has dark green, near black leaves with paler centres and veins bearing pink flowers.

B. **'Makezza'** bears medium lobed leaves of green and black with white flowers, superb in a basket.

B. **'Marion Palmer'** (T.Anderson) Large, plum star-shaped leaves with a burgundy reverse. Spikes of pink flowers late winter to early spring. Great outdoors in Z. 10.

B. **'Marmion'** has small leaves of greenish-yellow and black. Superb.

B. **'Merry Christmas'** (rex) has stunning leaf colour, with a black centre surrounded by almost white, tinged pinkish-purple, a green ridge and a black edge.

B. **'Midnight Magic'** has good almost black leaves. Oustanding.

B. **'Midnight Twister'** bears spiralled leaves, circling from black to green with a striking red underside. Very desirable. Height 25-30cm (10-12").

B. **'Night Crossing'** (B.T. 1992) bears large, black star-shaped leaves with pink flowers. Reaches a good size whilst maintaining a full appearance. As Brad Thompson describes it, 'Mature leaves appear like black parasols'.

B. **'Norma Pfrunder'** (B.T. 1992) has black, serrated leaves with red undersides. Dark red flowers complement the colouring. Low, upright grower.

B. **'Oh No'** shows its *elsoniae x listada* parentage in its slenderish leaves which are dark with paler veins. Bears pinkish white flowers.

B. **'Omaha Beefsteak'** has scintillating red and black leaves.

B. **'Orient'** has truly dark smallish leaves on a compact plant.

B. **'Python'** (B.T. 1993) features star-shaped black leaves with green diamond markings. Dark pink flowers. Medium growth.

B. **'Raquel Wood'** is a superb must-have plant bearing hairy stems, with glossy green leaves blotched black, which mature silky black, like taffeta. Deep rose flowers are borne in winter on this plant which makes quick growth.

B. **'Raven'** (B.T. 1993) Medium fuzzy black star-shaped leaves on long petioles with red hairs. Light pink flowers contrast well. An easy, compact grower.

Begonia 'Raquel Wood'

B. 'Razzamatazz' (rex) is a medium-sized plant with spiral leaves, satiny red with black centre and margins.

B. 'Red Heart' has shiny, bright red leaves with black centres and edges Very showy.

B. 'Red Robin' (rex) is compact with heart-shaped red leaves with a contrasting matt black centre and edge. Striking, a firm favourite.

B. 'Red Planet' is an adorable, tiny plant with glossy maroon leaves zig-zagged in chocolate brown.

B. 'Rosy Boa' (B.T. 1993) Medium black leaves with light pink flowers.

B. 'Satin Shirley' (B.T. 1990) bears small, satiny black leaves with pink flowers. Compact.

B. 'Shamus' bears deep emerald, spiralled leaves with reddish black on the surface and edges.

B. 'Stormy Night' (B.T. 1993) has medium sized satiny black star-shaped leaves with green sinuses and green petioles. Compact.

B. 'Tar Baby' a miniature delight is this tiny, burgundy maple leaved sweetie with black veins and black edging to the leaf.

B. 'Texas Star' bears black-green leaves, deeply and attractively lobed, around 10cm (4") wide. A strong grower.

B. 'Tiger Kitten' has soft, velvety dark brown olive leaves with small light green patches.

B. 'Tempest' has deep lobed and spiralled leaves marked with metallic red and black.

B. 'Tiny Bright' has small leaves of shimmering red, green and bronze bands like satin.

B. 'Venetian Red' is a shimmering pink on a dark coal background with very velvety leaves.

B. 'Vesuvius' is a medium-sized plant with almost fluorescent, puckered lava spots on leaves of black and green. Quite remarkable and very eye-catching.

B. 'Vista' is a small grower with satiny black leaves splashed with bright rose.

BEGONIA SHRUB-LIKE
Superb specimen plants, often with large leaves, sometimes with eyelash margin hairs.

B. foliosa is a fern leaf type with burgundy foliage arching and trailing, having small, starry white flowers. Needs higher humidity than most. 60cm (2ft)

B. 'Murray Morrison' (1975) is a cross between *B. listada* x *paranaensis*. Bears dark green, pale veined leaves.

BEGONIA SPECIES
Superb species, with dark leaves, all needing a minimum 10°C (50°F).

B. goegoensis was discovered in Goego in Sumatra in 1881. Distinctive egg-shaped leaves are dark with paler veining with red undersides. Needs high humidity. Rhizomatous type with tiny white flowers.

B. kingiana is a superb Malaysian species forming a low rosette of leaves from a basal rhizome. Smooth, shiny leaves with a lattice of light green over near black. Not an easy subject.

B. listada is a superb very dark green species with lighter veins giving the appearance of black in certain light.

Begonia solimutata

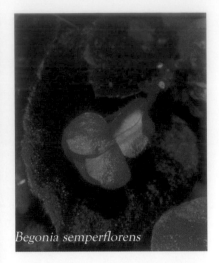

Begonia semperflorens

B. masoniana is well known as the 'Iron Cross' owing to the distinctive black-brown marking on the green leaf. I find this so susceptible to botrytis that I have given up growing it.

B. mazae is one of my favourite species which I first came across at Kew gardens, a superb small-leaved plant with darkish green leaves, blushed black.

B. paranaensis bears green leaves with beautiful dark shading. A vigorous species, fast growing.

B. pearcei has interesting dark leaves, quite silky.

B. sharpeana is a native of New Guinea found growing on moist forest margins, the mid green leaves are veined black.

B. solimutata from Brazil bears bullate leaves black-brown with broadish green veins, reddish beneath. A very attractive species, producing small white flowers.

BEGONIA SEMPERFLORENS
Doublet Series has bronze foliage. Available with pink, red or double white flowers.

From seed try **Victory Series, 'Coco'** and F1 **'Cocktail'** , F1 **'Expresso'** and F1 **'Partydress'** all offer a mix of flower colour with bronze foliage. The F1 **'Whisky'** also offers bronze foliage with the striking contrast of white flowers, as does F1 **'Ambra'**. There are also mixes of green and bronze foliage.

TUBEROUS BEGONIAS
'Midnight Beauty Orange' has dark chocolate, almost black foliage crowned by masses of fully double, rich orange blooms. 25cm (10").

Begonia listada

BERBERIS

Evergreen or deciduous shrubs found throughout the northern hemisphere, offer some good purple foliage which can be used as a backdrop for smaller plants. Often used as hedging.

HOW TO GROW

Any well-drained soil in full sun for fruiting and autumn colour. Purple-leaved cultivars can turn green in the shade. All those below are hardy to -29°C (-20°F) Z 5-10. Sow seed in a seedbed in early spring. Garden seed will probably result in hybrids. Take semi-ripe cuttings in summer.

B. thunbergii f atropurpurea has dark-red purple or purplish bronze foliage turning a metallic bronze-black in autumn. 1m (3ft) or more.

B. thunbergii 'Atropurpurea Nana' is a dwarfer, neat, rounded form of the above, with some greenish tints in the foliage. Try it in a rock garden. 45cm (18").

B. thunbergii 'Bagatelle' is a very compact form with shiny deep purple foliage which turns red in autumn. 30cm (12").

B. thunbergii 'Bailone' (Ruby Carousel TM) is reddish-purple, forming a low bush of 90cm (3ft).

B. thunbergii 'Bailtwo' (Burgundy Carousel TM) has slightly larger foliage than 'Bailone' and makes a larger shrub 90 x 150cm (3 x 5ft).

B. thunbergii 'Concorde' is a dwarf type with deep purple foliage. 45cm (18").

B. thunbergii 'Crimson Pygmy' is usually referred to as *atropurpurea* in the U.K., but is listed as a separate cultivar in the U.S. Retains its purple colour all season. 60 x 60cm (2ft).

B. thunbergii 'Dart's Red Lady' has very dark purplish red foliage which turns brighter red in autumn. 80cm (32").

B. thunbergii 'Golden Ring' is a little different in that its light purple foliage is very narrowly margined with golden yellow, turning rich red in autumn.

B. thunbergii 'Helmond Pillar' is a narrowly upright form and therefore a good choice for restricted space. It has dark red-purple foliage. Admirable and a favourite with me. 1m (3ft).

B. thunbergii 'Marshall Red' is an upright form with purple leaves, retaining their colour all season.

B. thunbergii 'Red Chief' is a taller form with shiny dark purple leaves, with contrasting yellow flowers in spring. 1.5m (4.5ft).

B. thunbergii 'Red Pillar' is an upright, deciduous shrub with reddish-purple foliage which turns crimson in autumn. 1-1.3m (3-4ft).

B. thunbergii 'Rose Glow' has good rich purple leaves with pinkish-whitish variegation coming through in the second year, giving a rose effect. Best hard-pruned each March. 1.5m (4.5ft).

B. thunbergii 'Royal Burgundy' (Gentry's Cultivar) bears velvet like, rich burgundy leaves that hold their colour in full sun, becoming even darker in autumn. Bears

bright red berries on bare branches in winter. A tidy and compact form good for containers. 60cm (2ft) tall and 90 cm (3ft) wide.

B. thunbergii 'Royal Cloak' has large purple leaves enhanced by its arching habit.

B. thunbergii 'Sparkle' has glossy green foliage, valued in the garden for its reddish-purple fall colour.

B. vulgaris 'Atropurpurea' is a purple-leaved form of the common hedgerow species.

Berberis x ottawensis f purpurea is a vigorous form with red-purple foliage.

B. x ottawensis 'Silver Miles' bears silver variegation, turning red in autumn.

B. x ottawensis f purpurea 'Superba' is a clonal selection with purple-red foliage turning crimson in autumn. A deciduous shrub

Berberis thunbergii 'Red Pillar'

Berberis x ottawensis f purpurea 'Superba'

with densely massed stems useful for hedging and prized by flower arrangers. It is similar to, but taller than *B. thunbergii f atropurpurea* and more vigorous. New growth is bronze red and it bears yellow flowers. Superb as a standard. 1.8m (6ft).

BETULA

Deciduous trees from the northern hemisphere, known for their wonderful ornamental bark, but there are two surprise birches with purple foliage. Hardy, tolerant of exposed sites and suitable for small gardens.

Betula 'Crimson Frost'

HOW TO GROW

Moderately fertile, moist but well-drained soil in full sun or light dappled shade.

Seed may produce hybrids as they cross easily. It is far better to obtain seed of specified wild origin. Sow in a seedbed in autumn. Root softwood cuttings in summer. Graft under protection in winter.

B. 'Crimson Frost' has wonderful dark purple, glossy leaves on a graceful plant.

B. lenta has dark red bark.

B. nigra, (River Birch) is named after the shaggy red-brown bark, peeling in layers when young and most attractive. On older specimens, the bark becomes blackish or greyish white and fissured. Mature trees fork into several limbs. Enjoys moist soil. 18m (60ft).

B. pendula 'Purpurea' fits the bill a little better with its purple-tinged bark and the coveted rich dark-purple leaves. Slow growing. 10m (30ft).

BIARUM

An unusual genus of 15 species of tuberous perennials mainly from the Mediterranean and W. Asia. Spathes, which can be malodorous, are produced in autumn. The species described need to be grown in a bulb frame, with the exception of *B. tenuifolium*. Both seed and plants can be difficult to obtain.

HOW TO GROW

Plant dormant tubers at a depth of 5cm (2"). They will do well in equal parts of loam, leaf mould and grit in full light. Keep warm and dry when dormant, water sparingly in growth.

Sow seed at 13°C (55°F) in autumn or spring. Prick out as soon as possible. Divide tubers in summer.

B. arundanum is the name given to the variable *B. tenuifolium* found in Spain. Dark chocolate, velvety spathes with black-purple spadices appear near the ground, before the narrow leaves emerge in autumn.

B. carratracense is the most amazing of this confusing genus of aroids. Huge maroon-black spathes open on the ground in early autumn.

B. dispar bears dark purple-brown spathes with a purple spadix.

B. eximium is a tuberous perennial bearing large, dark purple spathes and near-black spadices at ground level in autumn. Spathes are followed by the leaves. 8-10cm (4").

B. ochridense bears small purple brown and green spathes from September to October. 8cm (3").

B. tenuifolium is perhaps somewhat easier to grow as it is hardy and can be grown outside at the base of a sunny wall, although it may still be at its best in an alpine house or bulb frame. Narrow, often twisted, sometimes pale green spathes flushed purple or maroon-black spathes and nearly black spadices in autumn before the leaves. 10-20cm (4-8").

CANNA

Native to the Americas and grown in England at least since the late 1500's. Once beloved by Victorians for their sheer flamboyance, they are now used in 'hot' schemes by many gardeners where they combine so well with other dark foliage plants such as *Ricinus*, *Amaranthus* or *Phormium* and contrast perfectly with green foliage and hot flower colours. Glorious tender perennials grown for their bold, paddle shaped leaves which are often purple and for their equally attractive flowers.

HOW TO GROW

Grow in loamless potting compost with shade from hot sun under glass. Water freely when in growth and apply a phosphate-rich liquid fertiliser monthly.

Outdoors grow in a sheltered site in full sun in fertile soil, watering freely in dry spells. In frost-prone areas lift the rhizomes when frost has blackened the foliage. Store frost-free in barely moist peat or leaf mould. In frost-free areas leave in the ground applying a good winter mulch. Hardy to 0°C (32°F). Z 8-11.

Sow chipped or pre-soaked seed in spring or autumn. Divide rhizomes into short sections, in early spring.

C. 'Ambassador' has purple foliage and clear red flowers, may well be 'Black Knight'.

C. 'America' has purple foliage with dark scarlet flowers.

C. 'Aphrodite' has dusky pink flowers over bronze foliage maturing green.

C. 'Assaut' (Vilmorin-Andrieux 1920) has purple-brown leaves with bronze veins and dark buds, opening into gladiolus-like orange-scarlet flowers. Distinct from 'Black Knight' in its rounded petals and paler flowers, but appears identical to 'Hercule' and 'Vainquer'. 1.8m (6ft).

C. 'Australia' is a superb form. Very dark black-red spear shaped leaves with a satin-like sheen rise like spires towards the sky, holding their colour well even in intense heat, topped by shocking red-orange flowers. Good in containers and as a bog plant or as a semi aquatic. Maintains colour even in shade. 1.2m (4ft).

C. 'Biarritz' has red-purple foliage and yellow flowers.

C. 'Black Knight' makes an impressive statement with its tall bronze foliage with very dark red flowers with long, velvety petals. 1.8m (6ft).

C. 'Black Magic' bears golden flowers, bronze foliage. 1.8m (6ft).

C. 'Brighton Orange' has dark bronze, narrow lance-shaped leaves and small, delicate orange flowers. 1.5m (5ft).

C. 'Caliente' has large bronze leaves which set off the large 15cm (6") red flowers. 1.5m (5ft).

C. 'Centenaire de Rozain-Boucharlat' (Melanie) has pink flowers, bronze foliage. 1m (3ft).

C. 'Champigny' is of medium height with deep bronze foliage and fuchsia pink flowers.

C. 'Champion' has soft pink flowers over bronze foliage.

C. 'China Lady' has orchid pink flowers over bronze-purple foliage. 1m (36").

C. 'Cleopatra' bears yellow and red flowers over green-bronze foliage. 120cm (4ft).

C. 'Cleopatra Ty Ty Red' has reddish leaves and red flowers.

C. 'Constitution' bears purple narrow foliage with rich, creamy light pink flowers. Delicate aura and slow to multiply. 1.5m (5ft).

C. 'Dawn Pink' has dark burgundy foliage and large pink flowers.

C. 'Delibab' raised in Hungary in 1996 makes a stout patio plant. Large coral flowers and fleshy, leathery, matt pewter leaves. In flower before it reaches 1m (3ft).

C. 'Di Bartolo' is tall with deep pink flowers and purple leaves.

Canna 'Pink Futurity'. Many, but not all of the Futurity Series produce dark leaves.

C. 'Durban' bears purple-maroon leaves with red and yellow stripes which fade on maturity and shocking red flowers. Introduced into the U.K. under this name in 1994. 1-2m (3-6ft).

C. 'E. Neubert' bears pale bronze, narrowish foliage and flame coloured flowers with a touch of yellow on the lip. Like 'Verdi'.

C. edulis is a tall species bearing large fleshy green leaves, edged and veined purple. Stems are purple too. 3m (10ft).

C. 'Embleme' (H. Cayeux 1927) has vermilion flowers ablaze over bronze foliage. Tall.

C. 'Etoile de Feu' has fiery, large red flowers with a yellow throat aflame over bronze foliage. Tall.

C. 'Felix Roux' is a short plant with turkey-red flowers over the bronze foliage.

C. 'Feuerzauber' has brown leaves and dull scarlet flowers.

C. 'Futurity Red' has outstanding medium-red flowers over deep burgundy-bronze leathery leaves. 60cm (2ft).

C. 'Futurity Rose' bears pink flowers and pale bronze leaves. 120cm (4ft).

C. 'General Eisenhower' has chocolate-coloured leaves, well-shaped and tapered. Flowers are large, orange and yellow. A tall, stunning variety. 1.8m (6ft).

C. 'Grand Duc' bears smallish orange flowers over bronze-purple foliage. Medium height.

C. 'Hercule' (Vilmorin-Andrieux) Bronze foliage sets off the scarlet flowers. 2m (8ft).

C. indica 'Purpurea' produces broad, dark purple leaves with small, bright red or soft orange flowers. Easily propagated from seed, which leads to much variation. 1.5-3m (5-10ft).

C. 'Ingeborg' has loose light orange flowers over matt pewter-bronze foliage.

C. 'Intrigue' displays upright and narrow, distinctive black-purplish red foliage with small, apricot-peach flowers. No other Canna is like this. Provides an excellent vertical accent. 2.2m (8ft).

C. 'Jim Ronger' bears fascinating dark leaves and exotic orange flowers.

C. 'King Humbert' (1902) is a fine old cultivar with vivid purple leaves and orchid-like bright red flowers. 2m (8ft).

C. 'La Fayette' (1925) is worthy for its good, deep bronze foliage and floriferous bright orange flowers, similar to 'Assaut'. Tall.

C. 'La Gloire' (1920) bears bronze leaves and pale apricot flowers.

C. 'Liberte' is a tall variety with orange flowers and bronze foliage.

C. 'Louis Cottin' bears dark purple foliage, (there is a green one in circulation) with burnt copper-yellow, large, well-shaped flowers. Eye-catching patio type.

C. 'Madame Angele Martin' (Vilmorin-Andrieux 1915) bears brown-bronze leaves beneath pale salmon-pink flowers. 1m (3ft).

C. 'Madame Paul Casaneuve' (Crozy 1902) bears large, pure apricot flowers to combine perfectly with bronze foliage. Tall.

C. 'Maggie' is a patio type with true pink flowers over contrasting shiny, deep bronze leaves.

C. 'Mystique' bears good bronze dark foliage.

C. 'Paprika' bears red-orange flowers over purplish foliage. 1.5m (5ft).

C. 'Plantaganet' has bronze foliage with strong red flowers. Medium.

C. 'President Carnot' (Crozy 1889) has deep red flowers, yellowish in the centre over bronze foliage. 1.7m (5.5ft).

C. 'Professor Lorentz' bears streaky bronze foliage and large orange flowers. Like 'Wyoming'.

C. 'Red Wine' has luscious red flowers and deep red-wine foliage. Excellent in flower and foliage.

C. 'Russian Red' has red flowers and bronze leaves. 2m (7ft).

C. 'Saladin' bears large, deep pink flowers with a satin sheen over bronze foliage. 2m (8ft).

C. 'Saumur' is similar to 'Verdi' with tangerine flowers.

Canna 'Semaphore'

84

C. 'Semaphore' (Vilmorin-Andrieux 1895) (Pacific Beauty) is a superb old French cultivar with stately, bluish-bronze leaves and delicate, narrow-petalled saffron and orange flowers. 180cm (6ft).

C. 'Shenandoah' (Wintzer 1894) bears large pale pink flowers over bronze foliage. 1.5m (5ft).

C. 'Shining Pink' bears watermelon pink flowers and purplish foliage. 65cm (26").

C. 'Soudan' is a tall variety with large soft orange flowers.

C. 'Sudfunk' is a short growing, early variety. Bronze leaves are set off by the deep orange-red flowers. 80cm (32").

C. 'Tashkent Red' bears rich scarlet red flowers over huge dark purple leaves. A superb choice for the hot border. 2m (7ft).

C. 'Tchad' (Turc) has the pleasing combination of bronze foliage and deep glowing red flowers.

C. 'Tirol' (Pfitzer 1930) bears green leaves tinged purple with salmon-pink flowers. 1m (3ft).

C. 'Tropicanna' (l'haison), a sport of Wyoming, has good dark foliage and yellowish-orange flowers.

C. 'Vainqueur' bears vermilion flowers over bronze foliage. Tall.

C. 'Verdi' (Kapiteyn) bears narrow, pale bronze foliage contrasting with tangerine flowers.

C. 'Wine N' Roses' has purple flushed foliage and rose flowers.

C. 'Wyoming' (Wintzer 1906) has brown-purple foliage with dark purple veins and frilled orange flowers, with apricot feathering. 2m (7ft).

CENTAUREA

Cornflowers are an easy addition to the garden, associating well with cottage garden plants.

HOW TO GROW
Full sun and well-drained soil. Seed sown *in situ*.

C. cyanus 'Black Boy' has been re-introduced with its double dark maroon flowers. Easy from seed. Superb with silver foliage. Looks good with *Scabiosa*.1m (3ft).

C. nigra enhances pink shades with its black buds opening to purple. A native flower which grows to 60cm (2ft). Worthy of inclusion in a wild meadow.

C. nigra ssp rivularis has browner buds and is very free-flowering.

CERCIS

From North America, Eastern Redbud is one small tree or large shrub that would surely not disappoint on the colour of its foliage. Grow young shrubs in the border or trained against a wall. Older trees make good specimens.

HOW TO GROW
Grow in fertile, deep, moist but well-drained soil in sun or partial shade. Older plants resent transplanting. Pollard in spring for large foliage on established plants. Hardy, but protect young plants from frost. Z4.
Root semi-ripe cuttings in summer.

C. canadensis 'Forest Pansy' (1947 Forest Nursery, McMinnville, U.S.) has pleasantly attractive heart-shaped leaves of deep red-purple, producing a myriad of shades with the sun shining behind from mid-May to November. Bears rose-pink flowers from spring to summer, not always freely in temperate climates. Shelter from the worst winds in any reasonable soil. 3.5m (12ft).

C. canadensis, C. occidentalis and C. siliquastrum (Judas tree) also have bronze-purple young foliage.

CIMICIFUGA see ACTAEA

CLEMATIS

The darkest flowering hybrid Clematis clothe a large shrub or wall gracefully and the shrubby *C. recta* is a valuable addition to the herbaceous border whilst *C. montana* vigorously covers a strong pergola. Roses and Clematis are the classic romantic combination.

HOW TO GROW
Grow in fertile, humus-rich, well-drained soil in sun or partial shade. Roots need a cool run. Feed well. Mulch in late winter. Plant 6-8cm (3-4") below soil level.
Layer in late winter or spring.

C. montana v rubens 'Warwickshire Rose' bears very dark burgundy leaves especially from summer onwards and pink flowers in April to June. 5m (16ft).

Clematis recta 'Purpurea'

Also consider the bronze leaves of **C. montana v rubens 'Tetrarose'** which has deep colouring.

C. recta 'Lime Close' has non-vining stems emerging a deep midnight purple in mid-spring gradually fading to green overtones but retaining its colour well. 120cm (4ft).

C. recta 'Purpurea' bears a mass of white scented flowers in June-August. New foliage is deep purple, turning green as it matures, needing support. Tolerates sun or semi-shade. 2m (6ft). -25°C.

C. recta 'Velvet Night' retains the purple colouring much longer.

C. 'Black Madonna' has large deep violet-purple flowers with red stamens in May-June. Sun or semi-shade. 3m (10ft).

C. 'Black Prince' is deepest purple, fading to reddish purple, in flower from July-September. Tolerates sun or shade. This is a chance seedling raised by Alister Keay of New Zealand in 1990 and introduced into the U.K. in 1994. Prune group 3. 3m (10ft).

C. 'Negritjanka' originated in USSR,Ukraine in 1964. The name means 'African Girl'. One of the darkest purples with reddish-purple anthers flowering from July to September. Prune group 3. 3m.

Clematis 'Romantika'

C. 'Romantika' (Uno Kivistik 1983) has almost black flowers on opening, becoming deepest purple in July to September with contrasting anthers. Any aspect. Grow with pale colours for the best effect. Prune group 3. 3m (10ft).

C. 'Rooguchi' is a smaller flowered clematis of near black colouring.

CODIAEUM

The variegated leaves commonly known as Croton, come in many enticing dark hues. Grown in frost-prone areas as houseplants, these plants from Malaysia and the E. Pacific islands can reach 1.5m (5ft) in tropical climates, grown in shrub borders or as hedges.

HOW TO GROW
Grow in loamless compost in full light with shade from hot sun under glass. Apply a balanced feed every 2 weeks and water freely when in growth, sparingly in winter and using tepid water. Top dress or pot on in spring.

Outdoors grow in fertile, humus-rich, moist but well-drained soil in sun or partial shade.

Leggy plants can be cut back. Root softwood cuttings in summer. Air layer in spring.

C. 'Banana' has elongated, spiralled foliage of deep purple splashed orange and red with a bright yellow band.

C. 'Flamingo' has mid-green leaves with cream veins, turning yellow and maturing red or purple.

C. 'Evening Embers' is dense and strong growing with oval, shallowly lobed leaves of bluish-black 15-25cm (6-10") long, suffused with red and green.

C. 'Mume' matures to magenta and purple with emerald green.

C. 'Mortimer' the piecrust croton has cream-splotched leaves turning crimson-purple as they mature. Crimped, frilly-edged foliage.

C. 'Purple Bell' bears strap-like black leaves with contrasting orange spots.

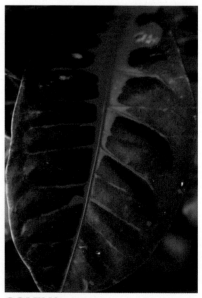

COLEUS see
SOLENOSTEMON.

COLOCASIA

Swamp or moist areas of tropical Asia is where you would find the 6 species of these large-leaved deciduous or evergreen perennials. The immense and incredibly opulent leaves are attractively arrow-shaped with prominent veins. Delicately fragrant flowers appear at any time, rarely in cultivation. At least 2 species are grown for their edible fruits. In Hawaii, you could try the glutinous poi or a taro burger. The former might take some getting used to, but the latter is delicious. Majestic.

HOW TO GROW

Under glass, pot up tubers into loamless potting compost in spring at 18°C (64°F). Need bright, filtered light and high humidity. When in growth, water freely and apply a balanced feed monthly. Keep tubers dry and frost-free when dormant. Outdoors, grow in fertile, humus-rich, moist or even wet, slightly acid soil in partial shade. Frost tender.

Divide in winter or early spring.

C. affinis 'Jenningsii' has green leaves veined with a green centre and black markings. Superb.

C. 'Black Marble' bears green leaves with black-purple speckling and marbling.

C. 'Burgundy Stem' has green leaves, flushed black along veins, very pale almost white undersides on amazingly tall purple stems. Z 7b-10. 2m (6ft).

C. esculenta 'Black Magic' (C. 'Jet Black Wonder', C. 'Cranberry', C. jankensii 'Uahiapele') is fantastic. Huge arrow-shaped leaves to 30cm (1ft) or more long are a uniformly dark purple-black on deep purple stems. 2m (7ft). Excellent for bold, tropical plantings, perfect by an ornamental pond, easy in shallow

Colocasia esculenta 'Illustris'

water, incredible in a large pot. A real centre stage plant. Has been overwintered in the U.S. to 0°C (32°F). Z 7b-10.

C. esculenta 'Chicago Harlequin' is blushed purple.

C. esculenta 'Fontanesii' is a spectacular giant, grown since 1865 with black stems and 90cm (3ft) long heart-shaped leaves with a black cast. Hold your breath for the 30cm (12") long yellow flowers with the delicious fragrance of papaya. 2. 3m (7ft).

C. esculenta 'Illustris', (antiquorum) the Imperial taro, named by William Bull in 1902, has glorious dark purple brushed, soft shimmery leaves with pale veining. Mature plants produce leaves on 90-120cm (3-4ft) petioles. Superb semi-aquatic. 1m (3ft). Z 8.

C. esculenta 'Nigrescens' has lighter leaves with deep purple veining and a leathery leaf texture.

C. 'Heterochroma' is superb with black markings.

C. multiflora 'Midnight' is very similar to 'Black Magic'.

Colocasia esculenta 'Black Magic'

COPROSMA

Coprosma bear bronze, purple or brown glossy, leathery leaves. Mainly from Australasia and S.Pacific. Berries will be produced where plants of both sexes are grown together.

HOW TO GROW
Under glass, grow in loam-based potting compost with added grit. Prefer bright-filtered light with good ventilation. When in growth, water freely and apply a balanced liquid fertiliser monthly. Outdoors, grow in neutral to slightly acid, moderately fertile soil, moist but well-drained. Suited to coastal areas in sun or partial shade. Frost hardy to half hardy.
Sow seed in a cold-frame in spring. Root semi-ripe cuttings in summer.

C. 'Black Cloud' bears black-brown leaves.

C. brunnera forms good ground cover with chocolate-brown leaves on wiry stems. 45cm (18").

C. 'Black Beauty' has almost black, glossy leaves in winter.

C. 'Chocolate Soldier' has glossy, chocolate-brown to dark green leaves, marginally larger than the species, *C. brunnera*. 1m (3ft).

C. 'Coppershine' has narrowly, glossy dark-green to purple leaves suffused rich copper all season. 1m (3ft). Half hardy.

C. x cunninghamii 'Purpurea' bears purple winter leaves on a vigorous shrub.

C. 'Karo Red' has deep green

leaves which turn purple-black in colder months. 1.5-2m (5-7ft).

C. repens 'County Park Purple' bears dark leaves.

C. repens 'Yvonne' is compact, displaying dark bronze-black leaves.

CORDYLINE

Palm-like shrubs and small trees from S.E. Asia, the Pacific and Australasia. Wonderful specimen plants which are highly desirable for their bold, structural form.

HOW TO GROW
Water moderately in growth under glass in bright, or filtered light. Apply a balanced feed once a month. Water sparingly in winter. Top dress or pot on in spring. Outdoors, grow in fertile, well-drained soil in sun or partial shade. Wrap in hessian in winter for protection in frost-prone areas. Half hardy to frost tender.
Sow seed in spring. Remove well-rooted suckers in spring.

C. australis 'Atropurpurea' has foliage flushed purple at the base and on the main veins beneath.

C. australis 'Black Tower' is a striking deep reddish-purple, slightly darker than *C. australis* 'Purple Tower'.

C. australis 'Purple Tower' has broad leaves heavily flushed plum-purple.

C. australis Purpurea Group has slightly paler, browner leaves than the above. Vigorous, almost hardy.

CORYLUS

From northern temperate woodland regions, the ornamental purple filberts offer some of the best dark foliage.

HOW TO GROW
Grow in fertile, well-drained soil in sun for the best colour. Good on chalky soils. Remove any suckers. Coppice in spring for large leaves. Hardy to -29°C (-20°F) Z 5-10.
Sow fresh seed. Layer cultivars in autumn, graft in winter.

C. maxima 'Purpurea' has textured, deep purple foliage especially in full sun, with purple-tinged catkins in late winter and purple fruit husks. Its habit is vase-shaped when young, spreading later. Vigorous and good for difficult, dry sites. 6m (20ft).
C. maxima 'Red Filbert' ('Rote Zeller'/ Zellernut) bears rich, purple leaves throughout summer, catkins are pink.
C. fusco-rubra is very rare, but also bears purple leaves. 4.5m (15ft).

Corylus maxima 'Purpurea'

COSMOS

This tuberous-rooted perennial from Mexico should be known to everyone who loves dark plants. Commonly known as Black or Chocolate Cosmos.

HOW TO GROW
In mild areas mulch in winter, or lift like a dahlia and keep tubers frost free. Grow in full sun and moist but well-drained soil. Z8.
Does not come true from seed, root basal cuttings with bottom heat in early spring.

Cosmos atrosanguineus is an essential component of the dark garden. Never black but dark chocolate red with a velvet sheen, darker on first opening. An admirable plant and one I always enjoy growing. The dark buds come into flower easily, opening into dark maroon spoon-shaped flowers and if you stick your nose right in there, nearer, nearer, you might just get that sniff of chocolate scent, aided by warm evenings, that has earned the plant its common name of chocolate cosmos. This plant appears to hold a secret, it has a mystery and is very desirable. The pinnate, dark green leaves are a bonus. Tubers, being small, are not easy to overwinter and tend to shrivel easily.
Flowers midsummer to autumn. Plant in a container and enjoy. 75cm (30").

Cosmos atrosanguineus

COTINUS

Essential purple foliage, eye catching when backlit by the sun. Deciduous trees and shrubs make a good backdrop for smaller plants of contrasting colour. Fuzzy plumes of smokey inflorescences have earned the name of smoke bush. Newer cultivars retain their colouring better.

HOW TO GROW
Moderately fertile, moist but well-drained soil in full sun for purple leaved forms. Hardy to -18°C (0°F) Z 7-10.
Layer in spring. Root softwood cuttings in summer.

C. coggygria 'Black Velvet' has claims as the darkest one yet. Selected by Steve Campbell, Sebastopol, CA from a block of purple-leaved seedlings for better growth habit, heavy flower production, and exceptionally dark, black-purple leaves.

C. coggygria 'Grace' is a tree-like hybrid with large, soft purplish foliage which becomes reddish in autumn. Bears fruiting panicles of purple-pink. 6m (20ft).
C. coggygria 'Nordine' originated at the Morton Arboretum in the U.S. and is considered to be the hardiest of the purple-leaved cultivars, retaining good colour.
C. coggygria 'Notcutt's Variety' bears dark maroon-purple leaves.
C. coggygria 'Royal Purple' has dark red-purple foliage, translucent in sunshine, reddening towards autumn. Cut back hard in spring to enjoy larger leaves. A first class shrub with bold shape and colour. Retains its colour brilliantly for me. Excellent with good yellow shrubs such as *Berberis thunbergii* 'Aurea'. 4m (12ft).
C. coggygria Rubrifolius Group (Foliis Purpureis) has purplish foliage when young which later turns purplish-green or green. An old form and parent of many of the modern purple-leaved forms.

C. coggygria Purpureus Group (f purpureus) is purplish only in its inflorescence. Foliage is green, with good autumn colour.
C. coggygria 'Velvet Cloak' has purple foliage which turns vivid reddish purple in autumn.
C. Dummer hybrid No. 5 makes a superb small tree of very good purple tones, found at Wisley.
C. obovatus is a small tree with leaves to 12cm (5"), pinkish bronze when young turning to brilliant orange, red and purple in autumn. Pinkish-grey fruiting panicles persist into autumn. 10m (30ft).

CRINUM

A rare breath-taking Crinum quite unlike any other. Well worth seeking.

HOW TO GROW
Plant in spring with the neck of the bulb just above soil level. Under glass, grow in loam-based potting compost with sharp sand and well-rotted manure in full or bright filtered light. Water freely when in growth, keep moist after flowering. Outdoors, grow in deep, fertile, humus-rich, moist but well-drained soil in full sun. Frost tender.
Difficult to divide. Sow fresh seed under glass and be very patient.

C. purpureum has great presence. A lovely deep shade of purple on this architectural beauty with erect leaves so unusual for *Crinum*. Makes a statement in any garden.

Continus coggygria 'Royal Purple'

Continus coggygria 'Grace'

DAHLIA

New bronze foliage Dahlia take the black garden by storm with a riot of different flower colours. Best foliage colour is usually found in full sun. Darkest *Dahlia* flowers are equally exciting and useful late in the season when many other plants are past their best. Many feature in the top 50 rated by the ADS bulletin. I have a preference for the semi-cactus type, but dark flowers feature in almost all categories.

HOW TO GROW

Grow in fertile, humus-rich, well-drained soil in full sun. Feed with a high-nitrogen feed once a week in early summer, then a high-potash feed once a week to promote flowering from midsummer to early autumn. Stake and dead-head as required. Cut back stems after foliage has been blackened by frosts, and lift the tubers, hang upside down to dry. Store frost-free in peat or dry sand in a well-ventilated place. In frost-free areas leave in the ground and protect with a mulch. Frost tender. 0°C (32°F). Z10-11.

Sow seed of bedding types in early spring, hardening off before planting out after the last frosts. Take basal shoot cuttings from tubers started into growth under glass in late winter or early spring. Tubers can be divided, each with an eye.

Dahlia 'Bishop of Llandaff' (right)

Dahlia 'Black Barbara' (far right)

D. **'Akita no Hikari'** bears almost frilled petals of deep dark red.

D. **'Arabian Night'** (Weljers 1951) has deep maroon-black flowers, to 10cm (4") across, fading as they age over green foliage. 90cm (3ft).

D. **'Attila'** is a very dark purple, black towards the centre.

D. **'Aurora's Kiss'** is deepest wine crimson, almost black. Miniature ball type. 105cm (3.5ft).

D. **'Barbarossa'** bears huge dark red flowers, dinner plate size to 20cm (8") across. 90cm (3ft).

D. **'Bednall Beauty'** is like the 'Bishop' but with crimson flowers.

D. **'Belinda Black'** makes an excellent cut flower with its red-black blooms 9cm (almost 4") across. 90cm (3ft).

D. **'Bishop of Llandaff'** (I. Treseder 1928) has stood the test of time with its purple dissected foliage and scarlet flowers. 1.m (3ft).

D. **'Black Barbara'** is a fine dark flower in black-red with mahogany tints 8cm (3") across. A good performer in heat. 90cm (3ft).

D. **'Black Bat'** (Takeuchi 1983) the black red petals of this decorative type are offset by yellow stamens.

D. **'Black Beauty'** (1993) is outstanding with long stems topped with velvet black, cactus type flowers.

D. **'Black Diamond'** is a giant ball-flowered, with very dark deep maroon quilled flowers having some black shading. Long flowering in a sunny spot. 1m (3ft).

D. **'Black Embers'** is a waterlily type with central black fading to deep crimson at petal tips.

D. **'Black Fire'** is a small flowered decorative.

D. **'Black Monarch'** is a decorative giant type with oxblood-red blooms around 25cm (10") across with some black hints, shading to crimson. 1.2m (4ft).

D. **'Black Narcissus'** (1956) is an outstanding dark, one with claims to be the darkest. Its laciniated dark petals on flowers 15-20cm (6-8") across are mesmerizing. A vigorous semi-cactus. 1.2m (4ft).

D. **'Black Pom'** is a deep dark purple pompon type.

D. **'Black Tucker'** (1981) from Holland is a superb miniature ball type with very dark, near black flowers, superb form and a multi-award winner.

Dahlia 'Arabian Night'

D. 'Blackie' is an outstanding double black-red. 1.1m (3.5ft).

B. 'Burma Gem' is valued for its burgundy-purple double flowers to 10cm (4") across. 1.5m (5ft).

C. 'Canyon Midnight' (Corning 79) has black-red flowers.

D. 'Chat Noir' (1985) ('Black Cat') is the finest I have grown. Sumptuous large, velvet red-black flowers in profusion over mid green foliage. Superb and an excellent performer, in prolific flower all season. Semi-cactus type.

D. 'Chocolate Orange' bears large peachy single flowers over blackish leaves. 60cm (2ft).

D. 'Clarion' bears a clear single yellow flower over very dark foliage.

D. 'Copper Queen' is a new introduction from New Zealand having deep crimson flowers over deep beetroot foliage. 1.1m (3.5ft).

D. 'Crossfield Ebony' is a tiny pompon form with black-red flowers. At least 1m.

D. 'Danjo Doc' has impressive deep wine crimson blooms. 1.3m (4ft).

D. 'Dark Delight' (Connell 1979) is fairly dark.

D. 'Dark Deliouse' bears medium, semi-double deep magenta flowers over dark foliage. 75cm (30").

Dahlia 'Chat Noir'

D. 'Dark Desire' is very dark and attractive, bearing unusual single chocolate flowers with petals that seem to dance and contrasting yellow stamens supported on dark, wiry stems. 90cm (3ft).

D. 'Dark Secret' bears single, near black flowers with yellow centres over lacy cut foliage.

D. 'David's Choice' is like the one below but with yellow flowers.

D. 'David Howard' (David Howard 1965) is a decorative type with dark purplish foliage and glowing, double orange flowers all summer which contrast well. 90cm (3ft).

D. 'Deep Delight' bears deep red-purple, semi-double flowers on black stems above blackish foliage. 70cm (28").

D. 'Diablo' bears dark brown-purple leaves contrasting with lovely single primrose flowers. 30cm (12").

D. 'East Court' is a dwarf orange-red with dark foliage.

D. 'Ellen Huston' (Earle Huston 1975) is a superb double flowering orange with contrasting dark purple foliage. Looks good with D. 'David Howard'. 30cm (12").

Dahlia 'Dark Desire'

D. 'E. Matador' has dark blackish foliage and large lavender flowers, similar to its parent D. 'Suffolk Punch'. 1m (3ft).

D. 'Fascination' (Elsdon 1964) has light semi-double pinkish-purple flowers against dark bronze-black foliage. Peony-flowered. 60cm (2ft).

D. 'Fidalgo Blacky' (Matthies 1993) is a superb deep purple-black. Sensational. Winner of over 170 awards. 1.2m (4ft).

D. 'Fire Mountain' (Walter Jack 1985) has fire red blooms over almost black foliage. Miniature-flowered decorative. 1.1m (3.5ft).

D. 'Fusion' (1993) has dark leaves and white flowers with a slight pink blush to the petals.

D. 'Glenplac' is a pompom type with small deep dark wine red flowers, very attractive.

D. 'Grenadier' is an old variety with double scarlet peony flowers and dark blackish foliage. 1m (3ft).

D. 'Haresbrook' bears large semi-double deep purple flowers over blackish foliage. 60cm (2ft).

D. 'Heatseeker Flame' bears orange-red single flowers over dark foliage. 45cm (18").

D. 'Hy Halo' (Holland) has a lilac flower with a dark centre and yellow stamens over dark foliage.

D. 'Japanese Bishop' is an orange-pink flowered Bishop of Llandaff.

D. 'Jessie G' (Connell) bears a tight head of dark petals, a ball type with flowers 7cm (3") across. 1.2 m(4ft).

D. 'Juanita' (1951) is a cactus type with velvety ruby flowers, keeping its colour. Prolific with flowers 15cm (6") across. 1.3m (4ft).

D. 'Kensington Gore Bright' bears orange small cactus type flowers over dark foliage. 45cm (18").

D. 'Lessandra' is a dark seedling from D. 'Suffolk Punch'.

D. 'Lost Angel' is a sport of D. 'Suffolk Punch' exhibiting similar dark foliage.

D. 'Magenta Magic' has bright red stamens surrounded by dark magenta petals, tipped and edged light pink. Attractive purplish-black foliage. 50cm (20").

D. 'Martinique' is a dark red with 10-15cm (4-6") semi-cactus blooms.

D. 'Midnight Dancer' flat purple petals on a 10-15cm (4-6") bloom.

D. 'Midnight Magic' (Connell 1981) is a U.S. bred dark red.

D. 'Midnight Sun' from N.Z. with deep yellow flowers over almost black foliage. 1.1m (3-5ft).

D. 'Moonfire' (Walter Jack 1997) has dark purple foliage with soft yellow-orange and glowing, vermilion flowers. Quite distinctive, superb en masse. Excellent, single, dwarf bedding dahlia. 60cm (2ft).

D. 'Moor Place' is an oustanding wine-red pompon type, verging on black in some situations, good for exhibition. 1.1m (3.5ft).

D. 'Mount Noddy' bears single dark red flowers with very good dark foliage, bred in the U.K.

D. 'Night Queen' is a dark red cultivar grown at JC Raulston Arboretum in the U.S, flowers are 7cm (3") across. 1.2m (4ft).

D. 'Offenham Strain' are black-leaved plants with strong coloured flowers. 60cm (2ft).

D. 'Old Boy' has medium dark foliage. 60cm (2ft).

D. 'Olympic Fire' is a dwarf single, somewhat lighter than D. 'Japanese Bishop'.

D. 'Pot Black' (1994) is a deep red-black miniature ball.

D. 'Preston Park' has single scarlet flowers and almost black foliage. 45cm (18").

D. 'Quantam Leap' has weakish stems and yellow flowers.

D. 'Rip City' (Gitts 1992) has black-red double blooms 15cm (6") across. Semi-cactus type. 1.2-1.8m.

D. 'Roxy' bears dark foliage with startling single magenta flowers from June to the first frosts. Floriferous. 40cm (16").

D. 'Royal Blood' is a newish cultivar with near black foliage and single, scarlet flowers.

D. 'Shadow Cat' (Connell 1986) is a dark red with blackish shading. A strong grower. 1.2m (5ft).

D. 'Sisa' bears yellow flowers above blackish leaves.

D. 'Spartacus' is a good dark red, the colour and form of this plant are excellent. Vigorous grower.

D. 'Suffolk Punch' (1975) is an older variety with very dark leaves, often used to breed new dark-leaved varieties.

D. 'Summer Night' (Nuit d'ete) is a very dark blackish-crimson flower on a semi-cactus-type. A favourite. 1m (3ft).

D. 'Tally-Ho' bears desirable purple-black foliage and single flowers of rich vermilion. An American look-alike 'Bishop of Llandaff'. 90cm (3ft).

D. 'Taylor Nelson' is a dark red semi-cactus type, with flowers 10-15cm (4-6") across.

Dahlia 'Summer Night'

D. 'Teddy Dahl' is a dwarf red with dark leaves.

D. 'Tesapore' bears red flowers over dark foliage

D. 'Velvet Night' (K.Hammett 1985) is an absolute stunner in dark red shading to black.

D. 'Yellow Hammer' has yellow flowers with an orange disc over dark, almost black foliage.

D. 'Zeno' (Connell 1988) bears black petals fading to deep red at the tips with a bright yellow centre.

D. 'Zorro' is a very dark purple, an informal decorative type with blooms over 5cm (10") across. Prolific flowerer on strong stems, consistent and good for cutting. In the ADS top fifty. 1m (4ft).

Bedding *Dahlia* from seed include D. 'Diablo' bears bright-coloured blooms above deep bronze foliage. D. 'Redskin' has double flowers, with maroon to bronze-green foliage. D. Classic Series has bronze foliage and peony flowers. There is also a range of D. 'Bishop's Children' offspring of *D.* 'Bishop of Llandaff'.

DIANTHUS

Dark flowers amongst carnations, pinks and sweet williams from seed. Select the darkest.

HOW TO GROW

Fully hardy *Dianthus* species and cultivars prefer well-drained, neutral to alkaline soil in full sun. Young border carnations and pinks appreciate soil enriched with well-rotted manure or garden compost. Do not plant too deep. Sow seed of annuals and biennials under glass in early spring, or biennials in situ in autumn. Take cuttings from Dianthus perennials in summer. Layer border carnations after flowering.

D. barbatus Nigrescens Group offers darkest flowers on green or mahogany foliage, possessing a wonderful fragrance too. Z4.

D. barbatus 'Sooty' is a selection of the above with that rare and stunning combination of darkest maroon-red, almost black flowers and deepest mahogany foliage to match, darkening as the season progresses. Best vigorously rogued out. 30cm. Z4.

D. Black and White Minstrels Group is a half hardy annual pink. A striking contrast of deep purple, bordering on black and white double flowers, blooming from June to the first frosts with a light fragrance. 30cm (12"). Z3.

D. 'Charcoal' is a border carnation with unbelievable charcoal-grey purple flowers with crimson slashes from July-August. Poor shape but an unusual colour.

D. 'King of the Blacks' bears flowers of the very darkest velvety purple-crimson on a hardy perennial carnation to 60cm (2ft).

Dahlia 'Tally-Ho'

Dianthus Black and White Minstrels

DODONAEA

In this genus of 50-60 evergreen shrubs and small trees from tropical and subtropical areas there is a gem of purple foliage.

HOW TO GROW
Under glass, grow in loam-based potting compost in full light. When in growth, water freely and apply a balanced feed monthly. Reduce watering in winter. Top dress or pot on each spring. Outdoors grow in moderately fertile, moist but well-drained soil in full sun. Pinch out tips of young shoots to encourage bushy growth. Sow seed in spring. Root semi-ripe cuttings in summer.

D. viscosa 'Purpurea' is a vigorous, erect to spreading shrub with foliage strongly suffused purple. Bears pink to reddish brown, or purple capsules from summer to autumn. Tolerates drought and exposure to wind in coastal areas. 1-5m (3-15ft).

Dodonaea viscosa 'Purpurea'

DRACUNCULUS

Dramatic as you have never seen it before. Large spathes, superbly dark and hardy in all but the coldest areas.

HOW TO GROW
Plant the frost hardy tubers at a depth of 15cm (6"). Grow in full sun or partial shade, easy at the base of a south-facing wall and protect with mulch. Not reliably hardy in cold winters. Safest in a bulb frame in cold areas. Z9.

D. muscivorus, whilst not as dark as *D. vulgaris*, is interestingly spotted. Native to the Balearics, Corsica and Sardinia, found growing in scrub and grassy places near the sea. Spathes are not as attractive or dramatic as *D. vulgaris* and are produced in April to May. Hardy to -5°C.

Dracunculus vulgaris

D. vulgaris, native of the Mediterranean and found in scrub and rocky places. Grown in the U.K. since 1200 and known in Boston, Massachusetts since 1866. Perfectly hardy in Oregon, U.S. and in the south of England. The purple spathe and purple, shining, almost black spadix rise in April from basal leaves of dark green, marked purple-brown. Stems are attractively marked too. This is the drama queen of dark plants. On the first day the flowers open, you might detect a strong odour which then fades. Flowers only last another 2 or 3 days. A spectacular form from Crete with pedately divided foliage and huge, fleshy brown-purple spathes on maroon spotted stems. The large leaves are often marked with spectacular silver splashes. 1.5m (5ft).
The spectacular white Cretan form, the spathe drooping to reveal the purple-black spadix to perfection is quite rare. Well-drained soil in a dry spot. Min -3°C for short periods only.
D. canariensis found in the Canaries and Madeira bears pure white spathes and a cream spadix, an excellent contrast to its dark cousin.

ECHEVERIA

Attractive, mainly evergreen succulents make up this genus of around 150 species. Leaves are often tinged red or black, the softer side of dark is exquisite.

HOW TO GROW
Under glass, grow in cactus compost in full light. Water moderately when in growth, applying a balanced feed monthly. In winter, keep barely moist. Place outdoors in summer, in moderately fertile to poor soil in full sun. Frost tender.
Sow fresh seed under glass. Root stem or leaf cuttings in late spring, or separate offsets in spring.

E. affinis has almost black foliage.
E. agavoides 'Metallica' has grey-flushed, purple fleshy rosettes.
E. 'Baron Bold' has unusual, crinkled leaves flushed purple, particularly in cold weather.
E. 'Black Knight' has thick, glossy green leaves flushed black-purple with dusky red flowers in August to November. 20cm (8").
E. 'Black Prince' is a black-leaved form with red flowers which is very choice. 15cm (6").
E. 'Delight' is flushed pinkish-purple especially at the edges of its charming, crinkled leaves.
E. 'Harry Butterfield' has pink and grey crisped succulent leaves and reddish flowers in August to October. Exquisite.
E. 'Mahogany' is a good dark.
E. 'Mauna Loa' bears large succulent, crinkle-edged volcanic pink-bronze evergreen rosettes.
E. nodulosa has erect stems with whitish rosettes which are heavily marked with purple-red margins.
E. secunda v glauca flushed in soft shades of purple, quite sensuous.

EMINIUM

Rare members of the aroid family, native to Turkey and the Syrian desert, offering some sumptuous and incredibly dark spathes.

HOW TO GROW
Treat as for Arum.

E. albertii is pale reddish-brown with a reflexed spathe in April to June. Needs cover, keep dry in summer.
E. intortum has black spathes very close to the ground, with largish green leaves. Survives in a bulb frame, but does not really thrive.
E. rauwolfii has black inner, velvet textured spathes surrounding the thickened spadix on short stems appearing in March to May above green lobed leaves with prominent veining, sometimes spotted white. Stunning in a hot, well drained spot.
E. regelii bears a deep black spathe.
E. spiculatum is an incredible plant with a deep black inner spathe and a greyish cream outer, having a black spadix. Well veined leaves. Cultivated at the Basel Botanic Garden, Switzerland.

Echeveria secunda v glauca

ENSETE

Superb tropical foliage in non-windy areas.

Ensete ventricosum 'Maurelii' ('Rubrum'), the Abyssinian black banana bears black-red leaves, mahogany midribs and margins and reveals the purple-carmine undersides as the leaves unfurl. This superb large plant has great stature and presence and is a good subject for a large container. Hardy to 0°C (32°F).

Ensete ventricosum 'Maurelii'

EPISCIA

Flame Violets are evergreen, dwarf perennials of creeping habit from tropical forests. Leaves are often puckered and many are bronze or chocolate coloured beneath attractive, bright flowers produced from spring to autumn.

HOW TO GROW

Under glass grow in loamless compost with added vermiculite. Best in bright, filtered light with high humidity. In growth, water moderately, apply a quarter-strength balanced feed at each watering. Never overwater, keep only just moist in winter. Outdoors, grow in fertile, humus-rich, moist but well-drained soil in partial shade. Ideal in hanging baskets, a warm greenhouse or conservatory. 15°C (59°F).

Surface sow fresh seed under glass in early spring. Divide or separate plantlets or root stem cuttings with bottom heat in summer.

E. 'Blackfoot' is a black-green form with silver-green veins with a hint of raspberry. Red-orange flowers.

E. 'Chocolate Cream' has dark chocolate-brown leaves with silvery rose netting and red flowers. Easy.

E. 'Chocolate Velour' has purple-brown leaves like velvet plush topped by large lilac-blue flowers. Superb and a favourite with me.

E. 'Coco' has dark metallic rose foliage with silver veins, blushed silver overall and surrounded by heavy bands of dark black-brown.

E. 'Country Cowgirl' has deep green-bronze velvet leaves with silvery stripes and pink veins.

E. cupreata is variable but its darkest forms are superb. Blistered surfaces of leaves appear blackish, veined in silver. A mat-forming perennial usually bearing red or yellow flowers, sometimes spotted purple in the throats. 15cm (6").

E. cupreata 'Acajou' has dark tan leaves especially at the edge, netted with silvery green. Orange flowers.

E. cupreata 'Chocolate Soldier' has dark leaves veined silver.

E. cupreata 'La Solidad' bears bronze, erect stems and soft, coppery leaves with a silver midrib.

E. cupreata 'Mosaica' has almost black leaves with a sheen.

E. 'Fanny Hague' has dark chocolate, near black leaves with an intriguing central green arrow-pointed repeating pattern.

E. lilacina has copper-green leaves with purple undersides, bears white flowers with lavender-blue throats. **E. lilacina 'Cuprea'** has lavender-blue flowers with white centres.

E. 'My Black Beauty' (McKhee) has black-green foliage with metallic rose or green veins.

E. 'Pink Panther' bears light green and dark bronze foliage and is almost always in bloom, bearing large deep pink flowers.

E. 'Ronnie' is a very easy variety with coral red flowers over chocolate brown foliage, having prominent silver-green veins.

E. 'Star of Bethlehem' has very dark chocolate leaves with striking cream blooms striped pink.

E. 'Tiger Stripe' has silver-green veins on a chocolate background.

E. 'War Paint' bears near black foliage with a deep scintillating metallic ruby-rose overlay and dark silvery green edges. Red flowers.

EUCOMIS

Good dark foliage on strap like leaves are visible in the garden.

HOW TO GROW
Well-drained, fertile soil in sun. In cooler climates, grow in a container and give protection in winter. Z8.
Separate offsets in spring.

E. 'Avon Avarice' is by far the darkest and best *Eucomis*, keeping its colour well on fairly stiff strap leaves to 30cm (12").
E. 'Sparkling Burgundy' is a selected form with dramatic, strap-like purple foliage forming dark burgundy rosettes to 60cm (2ft) wide, best in full sun. A tall stalk arises in late summer, carrying miniature purple pineapples.
E. 'Zeal Bronze' is not as dark but has maroon and green leaves with red and green pineapple flowers. Hardy. 45cm (18").
The dwarf species **E. schijffii** is purplish and glaucous. Hardy. 3°C.

Eucomis 'Avon Avarice'

EUPATORIUM

The herbaceous Eupatoriums can look coarse if not well sited. Best suited to a large pondside or a large border in retentive soil where they associate well with larger grasses in late season. Until recently they offered purple tinged foliage, but newer introductions offer that little bit extra.

HOW TO GROW
Grow in retentive soil in full sun or partial shade. Z4.
Sow seed in a cold frame in spring. Divide in spring.

E. purpureum subspecies maculatum 'Atropurpureum' is an herbaceous, clump-forming perennial which has darker stems than the species and bright rose-purple flowers on slightly shorter stems. Slightly lime shy. 150cm (4.5ft).
E. album 'Braunlaub' bears brown-flushed young leaves and flowers.
E. rugosum 'Chocolate' has gained popularity with its lovely dark chocolate foliage and white plates of blooms late in the year. Colours best in sun, although will tolerate dry shade. Has been sold as 'Brunette'. 120-150cm (4-5ft).
The species **E. purpureum** also offers variable purple-tinged foliage, and stems marked and blotched with purple, having purple-pink flowers.

EUPHORBIA

A varied and large genus of over 2000 species which offers some valuable herbaceous plants with very interesting dark foliage and intriguing flower structure.

HOW TO GROW
Moist, humus-rich soil in dappled shade or full sun. *E. dulcis* will tolerate drier soil. Hardy.
Sow fresh seed of hardy perennials in a cold frame, or sow in spring. Divide in early spring, or take basal cuttings in spring or early summer. Cut surfaces can be dipped in charcoal or lukewarm water to prevent bleeding.
CAUTION! irritant sap.

The *amygdaloides* types are flushed in tones of purple early in the year.
E. amygdaloides 'Efanthia' bears burgundy foliage in cool weather and greenish gold bracts in spring. Z 4-11. 25-35cm (10-14"). Z6.
E. amygdaloides 'Purpurea' ('Rubra') is a very attractive, superb form of the native Wood Spurge. Maroon stems carry dark evergreen leaves, while the new shoots are vividly tinted beetroot-red, followed by bright yellow-green flower bracts. Easy in moist soil, full sun or partial shade. 80cm (32"). -23°C, -10°F. Z 6-9.
E. amygdaloides 'Craigieburn' is similar to the above, but much smaller, struggles in my good moist soil in sun. In a pot it increases slowly. 37cm (15"). Z6.

Euphorbia amygdaloides

E. amygdaloides 'Welsh Dragon' has dark evergreen leaves with a pewter and red flush as well as red stems. Green flowers are also flushed red in March to May. Z6.

E. characias ssp characias 'Perry's Winter Blusher' has flowers and stems flushed red. 1-1.5m (3ft). Z8.

E. characias ssp wulfenii 'Purple and Gold' turns purple in cold weather and is a good form. Z8.

E. cotinifolia 'Atropurpurea' is a superb dark leaved *Euphorbia* with the appearance of *Cotinus*.

E. denticulata is noteworthy, strongly dislikes wet conditions.

E. dulcis 'Chameleon' bears deep purple foliage retained in full sun. Purple-tinted yellow flowers in spring. Floppy. 30cm (1ft). Z4.

E. 'Flame' bears chartreuse edged, red foliage on wiry stems. Inconspicuous flowers. Makes good groundcover. Self sows.

E. martinii 'Red Dwarf' or **'Red Martin'** has red flushed foliage.

E. 'Purple Preference' has leaves flushed purple with gingery flowers in spring. 75cm (2.5ft).

E. polychroma 'Candy' and **E. 'Redwing'** both have purple-tinted foliage.

FAGUS

Must surely be the most well-known and planted purple foliage tree in the northern hemisphere. Has always been my favourite tree, which perhaps in part explains my passion for dark plants. Deciduous beech make superb, noble specimen trees in an open site and are also found in woodland. Use fastigiate types in smaller gardens. Also make a superb purple hedge.

HOW TO GROW

Very tolerant of a wide range of soils including chalk, best in light to medium, well-drained soil. Best positioned in full sun, when their exquisite colour will dazzle. In late summer or early spring remove wayward or crossing shoots to maintain a good framework. Trim hedges in late summer. *F. sylvatica* does not need the usual long hot summers to do well. Hardy.

Sow seed in a seedbed in autumn or stratify and sow in spring. Cultivars are grafted in spring.

F. sylvatica 'Ansorgei' is a rare shrubby, willow-leaved form producing brownish purple, lanceolate, almost entire leaves. Slow growing with an open habit which allows underplanting.

F. sylvatica Atropurpurea Group, can be rather variable in purple hue, turning coppery in autumn. Striking and vigorous. Mentioned as early as 1680 around Zurich and planted at Knap Hill nurseries in 1826. 30m (100ft).

F. sylvatica Atropurpurea Group 'Swat Magret' was raised in Germany, having very dark purple leaves which retain their colour until late summer.

F. sylvatica 'Black Swan' bears dark purple foliage which holds its colour well, with a handsome weeping habit. Tall and slender, a graceful beauty and a distinguished vertical element in the garden.

F. sylvatica 'Brocklesbury' has deep purple leaves which are larger than the norm. There is a beautiful specimen at Kew.

F. sylvatica Cuprea Group is used to denote trees of a paler purple leaf colour, the copper form.

F. sylvatica 'Dawyck Purple' is narrowly upright with deep purple foliage. 20m (70ft) with a spread of just 5m (15ft), making it a candidate for smaller gardens.

F. sylvatica 'Frisio' bears purple foliage.

F. sylvatica 'Haaren' found in North Brabant, Holland, this weeping beech features handsome dark purple foliage.

F. sylvatica 'Purple Fountain' is a seedling of *F.s.* 'Purpurea Pendula' raised in Holland. It makes a narrowly upright tree with purple leaves and weeping branches.

F. sylvatica 'Purpurea Nana' is a slow-growing, dwarf form, eventually making a mushroom-shaped bush. 3m (10ft).

F. sylvatica 'Purpurea Pendula' the weeping purple beech has stiff, pendulous branches which bear deep purple-blackish leaves. Rarely exceeds 4.5m (15ft).

F. sylvatica 'Purpurea Tricolor' has purple leaves unusually marked at the edges with pink or pinkish white. Markings are inconsistent.

F. sylvatica 'Remillyensis' bears purple foliage.

F. sylvatica 'Riversii' has very dark purple leaves, perhaps the darkest, holding colour well into summer with rich autumn tints. A fine old cultivar making a large tree, listed since the 1870's.

F. sylvatica 'Rohan Obelisk' (Red Obelisk') is a narrow form of the copper beech with feathery purple foliage. By midsummer the secondary flush of growth is red giving a wonderful glowing appearance against older and darker leaves.

F. sylvatica 'Rohan Pyramidalis' is a columnar form with attractive purple leaves, incised on margins.

F. sylvatica 'Rohan Trompenburg' originated at the famous Arboretum in the Netherlands, a seedling of 'Rohanii' with lustrous deep purple leaves, delicately feathered with an elegant faint silver margin.

F. sylvatica 'Rohanii' differs in that its reddish brownish purple leaves are attractively and deeply cut, earning the name of the fern leaf beech. A beautiful, slow-growing tree, raised in 1888 from seed, it has been in commerce since 1908.

F. sylvatica 'Spaethiana' is a small version of the copper beech with

Fagus sylvatica 'Dawyck Purple' (above right), Fagus sylvatica Purpurea Group (above far right) Fagus sylvatica 'Haaren' (right)

dark glossy colour holding very well through the summer.

F. sylvatica 'Tortuosa Purpurea' is wide spreading with twisted branches. 3m (10').

FICUS

Figs are handsome plants. The Rubber Plant is often grown as a houseplant in cooler areas. Dark cultivars have an added extra on an already extremely handsome plant.

Ficus elastica 'Black Prince' is a superb dark leaved cultivar of the rubber plant. Tolerant of poor light and best kept on the dry side. Min -3°C overnight. Z10.

Ficus elastica 'Burgundy' is known as the purple-leaved Rubber Plant.

FRITILLARIA

Sumptuously dark, dusky bell-shaped flowers are to be found amongst the 100 or so species of this genus of bulbous perennials, beloved by specialist collectors. Nomenclature is very confused.

HOW TO GROW

Since Fritillarias come from many different habitats around the world, their cultural requirements differ. Handle fragile bulbs with care and never allow to dry out if lifted. Successful cultivation is more assured if well-drained, lime-free, low nutrient compost is provided. Excess nitrogen is one nutrient not appreciated. Fully to frost hardy depending on the species. Plant early to mid autumn, covering bulbs with soil 4 times the height of the bulb.

Seed sown ripe, exposed to winter cold, should germinate in the following spring when it can be transferred to a cold greenhouse. Grow small species in containers for two years before planting out. Divide offsets and sow basal bulbils in late summer.

The dark forms of **F. acmopetala** found in S.E. Turkey are worth seeking, they increase easily in the open garden in full sun or dappled shade. Dainty and perfect for the rock garden. 2.5-7.5cm (1-3"). Z7.

F. affinis v tristulis is found on cliff tops in California, a triploid with large flowers which is easily cultivated, provided dry summer and autumn and moist winter and spring conditions are available. There are also maroon and purple forms of the species itself, the chocolate lily, which is much taller. 20cm (8").

F. armena bears beautiful dark purple flowers on short stems 4-7cm (around 2") from May to June, dark on the inside too. Slow to increase. Same growing conditions as *F. pinardii*.

The purple-brown flowers of **F. assyriaca** shine in March to May. Semi-pendent and often faintly chequered green, they are held on very weak stems. In rich, moist leaf mould, kept rather dry, this Turkish and northern Iraq species increases readily. Provide frost protection in early spring. 20-25cm (8-10").

F. biflora is known as the black fritillary. It offers bell-shaped, brownish flowers tinged purple to black and flushed green. Easy to grow, best with protection. Along the coast of San Luis Obispo in California is to be found one of the finest dark forms. Keep cool in summer. 24-40cm (10-16").

F. biflora 'Martha Roderick' has deep red-purple flowers with two thirds of the outer tepals being white or creamish chocolate brown. 20cm (8").

Far darker, the "Black Queen" of this genus is **F. camschatcensis**, the enchanting black sarana whose roots can be dried and eaten and are known as Eskimo's potatoes. It can be variable and produce green or yellow flowers, of differing size. When you have a good form, the bells produced in late spring to early summer are unbelievably black, nectaries too are the colour of the midnight sky. Petals are smooth and silky on the outside and corrugated on the inside, exuding a pungent smell in mid-late summer, the last fritillary to flower. Needs rich leaf-mould and grows best in areas with cool, damp summers as its native habitat is moist open woods in subalpine meadows and grassy places near

Fritillaria aff tristulis

Fritillaria camschatcensis

F. camschatcensis flore pleno

the coast, but it has the widest distribution of any fritillary. Easy in moist, peaty soil in partial shade, never allowed to dry out. 45cm (18").

F. camschatcensis black is more consistent in its colouring. 20-40cm (8-16"). The double form is extremely intriguing and quite rare.

F. camschatcensis 'Amur' is brownish-black and **'Tomari'** is bluish black. These are best in full sun. Z. 3-8.

F. caucasica from Turkey will appreciate heavy, peaty soil in open areas and a cool summer to display its large, glaucous, purple-brown bells, dusted with a grape-like bloom, showing ruby highlights in sun. Easy.

F. crassifolia ssp kurdica bears dark, plump bells with faint green striping, but you must search for these rare dark clones. In flower early winter or late spring. Needs protection.10-12cm (6-8").

The dark chocolate, semi-pendulous bells produced in late spring or early summer of **F. davisii** are worth growing, not least because this is the speediest of fritillaries, flowering in 2-3 years from bulbs which are produced regularly around the parent. A native of southern Greece, it is happy in a pot, or outside in a trough or scree with plenty of grit. 8-16cm (3-6").

F. drenovskii is particular as to growing conditions but worth perservering with for its small near black flowers, tipped yellow, which appear in May to June above narrow, glaucous leaves. A slightly moist soil in summer and autumn, a cold but not too wet winter, and a warm spring are required to grow this well. Admirable and elegant. Almost extinct in its native Bulgaria and Greece. 20-25cm (8-10").

F. elwesii, a native of S. Turkey, bears dark flowers in March-May on thin, weak stems. It is close to, but usually taller than *F. assyriaca*. Increases well by bulbils. Has charm and grace. 25-40cm (10-16").

F. ehrhartii from Greece, appears early in the year, from February to April and will therefore appreciate some protection. The dark grape-black flowers have a yellow tip to each petal and glow in the evening sun. Stout stems produce up to 6 flowers. Easy under glass. An absolute charmer. 20-30cm (8-12"). E.K.Balls collected **F. epirotica** in Greece in 1937, from the same location comes a good dark purple-brown form, dimly tessellated green. Flowers sit just above the twisted and curled foliage almost at ground level in summer. The plant is then dormant in dryish soil. A very desirable, dwarf, alpine species, exquisite in an alpine-house pan. A plant to cherish. 7.5-10cm (3-4").

F. graeca has deep green flowers, almost wholly chequered with brownish purple. It is intolerant of wet, especially when dormant, but easy to grow. 10-20cm (4-8").

F. grandiflora is dark and checkered, found in rocky woods and scrub, flowering in May. An easy species producing bulbils.

The dark, slender flowers of **F. latakiensis** appear in April above narrow foliage. Easy in a bulb frame or outdoors in mild areas. Needs little water in summer. Increases rapidly. 20cm (8").

F. latifolia displays broadly bell-shaped, smallish, dark maroon to purplish flowers from May to June. Worth trying outdoors, but is intolerant of wet and in general not an easy species being temperamental and on the slow side to increase. 15cm (6").

F. lusitanica bears purple-brown bells though the species hybridises readily with *F. pyrenaica* above shining green leaves. Does well in half shade, with dryish soil in summer. 20-30cm (8-12").

F. meleagroides bears black-brown hanging bells on a 70cm (28") stem above narrow leaves. A Russian species, best in a moist spot.

The delightful and very well-known **F. meleagris**, the snake's head fritillary, bears dark purple broadly bell-shaped flowers with strong pinkish tessellation. Can be quite robust and is excellent for naturalising in damp grass. The natural sites of *F. melegris* are sadly diminishing in Great Britain and it is strictly protected. Flower colour is variable, the darker forms being **F. meleagris 'Charon'** and **F. meleagris 'Jupiter'**. An easy subject to grow, happily increasing in damp soil. Flowers in April. Up to 25cm (10"). Z4.

F. **michailovskyi** from Turkey is a gem for the bulb frame or alpine house needing to be kept dry when dormant in summer. Shining damson-coloured flowers, tipped with yellow or yellowish green are charming. Easy to grow, producing up to seven flowers per stem, but slow to increase. Is becoming widely available, but beware that many commercial stocks are poor and variable. 10-20cm (4-8"). Z7.

F. **micrantha** is attractive with small, brownish purple bells in April to June. Needs to be kept dry in summer, wet in winter and spring. 20-25cm (8-10").

F. **minuta** is a dainty, leafy species, not easy to get into flower, when they do appear they are purplish. Try in a deep pot with grit and loam. 10-15cm (4-6").

The chequered, purple bells of **F. montana**, usually tipped yellow, lighter on the inside, are very desirable and are reliably borne from late spring to early summer. Easy to grow and tolerant of wet British summers, though preferring dry summer soils found in its native habitat of southern France to northern Italy and Greece. Also found in Turkey is a fine, tall, elegant form with exceptional big, dark, brown-purple bells. Small shrubs provide adequate shade. 25cm (10"). In semi-shade, **F. montana ruthenica** appears even darker and is taller than the species. Soil must not dry out. 25-50cm (10-20").

F. **nigra** bears deep purple flowers netted gold on tall thin stems above narrow glaucous leaves.

F. **obliqua** is similar to the desirable *F. tuntasia*, but with larger flowers of bloomy black in March and April. A native of Greece, rapidly losing its natural habitat in the suburbs of Athens, rendering it very rare and sought after. 15-20cm (6-8").

F. **persica** bears up to 20 greenish brown to deep purple flowers from April to May. It is a robust, very striking species with sturdy, upright stems. Suitable for a very sunny border or rock garden in full sun by a south-facing wall in well-drained, rich, deep soil. Superbly dark, but often shy to flower in northern Europe. Grown in U.S. gardens since at least 1830.

Fritillaria persica

104

Sumptuous. 1m (3ft), though usually half that height. Z5b-7.

F. persica 'Adiyaman' is taller and more free-flowering than the species, bearing brown-purple flowers. 1.5m (5ft). 75.

F. persica 'Senkoy' is darker and even more free-flowering. Z5.

F. pinardii is variable but can be superbly dark, the flared bells are very enticing. A widespread Turkish species relatively easy to grow, flowering from late spring in a warm spot with protection. Grow in loam and grit, keep cool in winter and moist in spring, with shade and just a little moisture in summer. 20cm (8").

F. pyrenaica which has been known under the synonym of F.nigra h., has deep brownish-purple flowers, occasionally yellow, which are strongly tessellated, flaring to show off their yellow-green interiors. Quite adaptable to garden conditions, grow as for F. persica. 25-45cm (10-18").

F. reuteri is like a tall *F. michailovskyi*, flowers are shorter but the same colouring, appearing in mid-spring. Best in an alpine house with a cold, moist winter and cool, wet spring and summer. 18-25cm (7-10").

F. rhodocanakis has petals half maroonish purple, the lower half pale yellow. Each petal is recurved and flared. 10cm (5").

F. sewerzowii (Korolkowia) is a variable species which bears greenish-yellow to vivid purple flowers, each yellowish within. The flared bells of a good black form are irresistible and exciting. Intolerant of wet, easy in a bulb frame kept dry in summer. 25-40cm (10-16").

F. straussii flowers from May to June, its dark purple flowers can appear green at first. Demands very gritty soil and is best in a bulb frame. 8-13cm (3-5").

F. tubiformis will produce its lightish purple flowers from May to June in peaty soil with overhead protection and moist soil in summer. Colour can be variable. Its natural habitat is alpine meadows. 10-20cm (4-8").

F. tuntasia is a native of Greece. The dark, plummy to near-black flowers are borne from March to April and are very attractive. However, this is not an easy species, nevertheless exceptionally desirable for its depth of colour. 30-45cm (12-18").

F. uva-vulpis is choice, almost wholly greyish purple petals with bright gold tips. Found growing in cornfields in its native Turkey, Iran and Iraq, it increases easily in cultivation in damp soil. Good for naturalising. 30-45cm (12-18").

F. zagrica is a classic dwarf species which is challenging to grow and extraordinary with its distinctive black to dark plum-purple bells, tipped yellow which enchant from March to May. Grows on gravelly clay in its native Iran.

There are numerous spotted purple-black species, such as **F. cirrhosa** and the combination of green and deep purple occurs in many species.

FUCHSIA

The promise of near black tantalises in the bells of *Fuchsia*. Bronzed foliage is also tempting.

HOW TO GROW
Full sun or light shade in fertile, moist soil which is well-drained. Softwood cuttings in spring, semi-ripe cuttings in late summer.

F. 'Alice Hoffman' has purple-tinged, bronze-green foliage to compliment the small, semi-double flowers with rose-pink tubes and sepals and white corollas veined rose-pink. May not be frost hardy in some areas. 45-60cm (18-24").

The double-flowered **F. 'Black Beauty'** (Fairclough 1952) and **F. 'Black Prince'** (Banks 1861) are perfectly good flowers, but not that black. 30 years ago they were much darker, but have sadly declined in colour in cultivation. Z8.

F. 'Lady Boothby' (Raffil 1959) is hardy and very dark. Z6.

F. 'Lechlade Magician' (Wright 1985) and **F. 'Whiteknights Amethyst'** have aubergine (eggplant purple) skirts. Z8.

F. 'Zulu King' (de Graaf 1990) from Holland is also very dark, nearest to black I have seen. Z8.

F. triphylla has leaves purple on the underside and the two frost-tender cultivars **'Thalia'** and **'Gartenmeister Bonstedt'** have velvety bronze-red leaves with delightful, long-tubed flowers of orange-red. Z9.

GERANIUM

Hardy Geranium are long-season, herbaceous perennials which look good in the mixed border and can be used to effect with roses or as groundcover. Found in all but very wet habitats in temperate regions throughout the world. The combination of attractive leaves, sometimes dark or blotched and dark flowers is a sure winner, and a second flush is often possible on some varieties when cut back after flowering. Excellent companions for other dark-leaved plants such as *Heuchera*. Usually hardy and easy.

HOW TO GROW
Larger species and hybrids are grown in moderately fertile soil, in full sun or partial shade. Small species require sharply-drained soil with added grit in full sun.
Sow fresh seed outdoors when ripe or sow in spring. Divide in spring.

G. 'Bertie Crug' has dark bronze foliage and forms low mounds studded with deep pink flowers. A charming prostrate creeper. Z. 5-11. 15cm (6").
G. 'Black Beauty' is extremely dark and retains its colour well.
G. 'Black Ice' (A.B.) produces dark grey-brown leaves and white flowers. Prefers full sun and well-drained soil.
G. 'Bullfinch' has blood coloured leaves with pink flowers.
G. 'Crug's Delight' (Crug's Darkest) has dark silky leaves with pink flowers just above the foliage.

G. 'Crug Strain' is low growing with dark foliage and pink flowers.
G. 'Dusky Crug' produces low-growing, velvety brown leaves.
G. 'Foie Gras' is so called because it reminded the raiser of chopped liver! Has pink flowers.
G. 'Kate' has dark bronze foliage, with extending flower stems and pink flowers showing its Folkard parentage. 20cm.
G. 'Libretto' bears dark foliage and white flowers. 20cm (8").
G. 'New Dimension' is a smaller, compact sport of *G.* 'Victor Reiter'.
G. 'Orkney Pink' (A.B.) has dark bronze-grey foliage and purple-pink flowers from June to frost.
G. 'Persian Carpet' bears mats of near black, small leaves.
G. phaeum, the dusky cranesbill, is clump-forming with soft-green basal leaves, often with brown marks. In late spring to early summer, it bears pendent, white-centred, deep purple-maroon flowers, occasionally paler, rarely white on lax stems. An understated beauty which is best en masse. 80cm (32").
G. phaeum 'Chocolate Chip' is an American form with very dark flowers of chocolate-maroon. Z5.
G. phaeum 'Raven' is another darker blue-maroon form claiming to be the darkest, a seedling of 'Lily Lovell'. Z5.
G. phaeum 'Samobor' has outstanding large leaves, handsomely marked by an artist's hand with a chocolate blotch vying for attention with the silky, midnight-purple flowers. Good rich soil for best effect in shade, drought tolerant when established. 60cm (2ft). -23°C (-10°F) Z 5.

Geranium phaeum 'Samobor'

G. phaeum v phaeum ('Mourning Widow') is a strong grower in shade with dark purple-black, silk-textured blooms in early summer. 80cm (32"). Z5.

G. pratense Midnight Reiter Strain has purple tinged foliage. 'Night Reiter' has black-burgundy leaves. 'Victor Reiter' has deep red leaves which are black-red when young. Fertilise well. Z4-8.

G. pratense 'Purple Haze' is a dark leaved seed form selected from the Reiter clones. Z4.

G. pratense 'Purple Heron' is a clone of 'Midnight Reiter' which keeps its purple foliage colour right through the season. Z4.

G. 'Rosie Crug' has unusual pewter-grey foliage.

G. 'Sea Spray' (A.B.) has bronze foliage and a succession of small pink flowers until the first frosts.

G. sessiliflorum 'Rubrum' with darkest red mahogany foliage studded with contrasting white flowers all summer.

G. sessiliflorum ssp novae-zelandiae 'Nigricans' has tufts of olive-bronze basal divided leaves. Greyish-white flowers in summer.

G. sessiliflorum ssp novae-zelandiae 'Porter's Pass' has prostrate chestnut-brown leaves, contrasting with pink flowers on this tiny gem. Watch for slugs. 5cm (2"). -12°C (10°F). Z 8-10.

G. sinense has astonishing red beaks protruding from the darkest deepest maroon-purple, reflexed petals, 2cm (almost 1") across. Flowering from August-October, this is one of the darkest.

G. 'Strawberry Frost' forms a small clump of rich purple-brown leaves and pink flowers all summer in a sunny, well-drained position.

G. 'Welsh Guiness' (A.B.) is a prostrate creeper weaving a dark glossy mat studded with many small white flowers which give perfect contrast to the foliage.

G. x monacense 'Muldoon' is a clump-forming perennial with dark purple, reflexed flowers and dark-variegated leaves. Best in part to full shade in well-drained soil.

G. x oxonianum 'Buttercup', 'Fran's Star' and 'Walter's Gift' as well as G. reflexum have distinctive dark markings on the leaves. G. x monacense has leaves heavily spotted with chocolate. G. phaeum 'Calligrapher' has dark contour lines.

GLADIOLUS

Towering spikes of gloriously near black Gladiolus.

HOW TO GROW

Grow in fertile, well-drained soil in full sun. Corms should be planted at a depth of 10-16cm (4-6") deep in spring. A bed of sharp sand will aid drainage. Lift when the leaves turn yellowish and snap from the corm, store frost-free. Z9.

Sow seed of species in containers in spring. Separate cormlets when dormant.

G. 'Black Lash' available in the U.K. bears small-flowers of black-rose. An excellent dark, bred by Ed Frederick, introduced in 1976, still wins at Gladiolus shows today.

In the U.S., the dark red-black G. 'Black Beauty' is worth looking for, G. 'Black Jack' is a deep red with a black edge, G. 'Black Mystery' is a very dark red and G. 'Black Swan' is very dark maroon.

Most blackish Gladiolus are bred in the Czech Republic or U.S.A. Large-flowered Gladiolus to look out for include 'Black Dancer', 'Blackwood', 'Dark Victory'. Of the medium-flowered types try 'Burgundy Queen' and small-flowered types are 'Dark Mystery' and 'Dave's Memory'.

Bill Murray of Edinburgh has bred some dark-flowered primulinus type Gladiolus including 'Brush Strokes' which is a black-rose with grey dusting.

G. atroviolaceus, a native of E. Turkey to Armenia, is found in cornfields on dry hillsides from May to July. Dusky-purple flowers are a delight in spring. Extremely hardy. Well drained site in full sun. 60cm (24").

G. kotschyanus is available in a dark, deep crimson and grows in wet meadows, usually at high altitudes. Reaches 40cm (16") in cultivation, much smaller in its native Turkey.

The tender G. callianthus bears strongly-scented white flowers marked with purple in the throat. Very attractive. Z9.

G. papilio Purpureoauratus Group is another attractive species not quite as tender as the above. Alluring flowers can vary from cream to yellow, but all are heavily marked with dusky purple. Z8.

HEBE

Handsome in both foliage and flower are just two reasons for growing *Hebe* in the dark garden.

HOW TO GROW

Grow in poor or moderately fertile, moist but well-drained soil. Neutral to slightly alkaline soil in sun or partial shade. Small leaved types are the hardiest. Fully hardy to half hardy.

Seed is not normally recommended and *Hebe* hybridise freely. Semi-ripe cuttings are easy to root in late summer or autumn with bottom heat.

H. 'Amy' has elegant large, purple-bronze leaves when young and colours well in winter, with purple flowers. Needs some shelter in colder areas. 75-120cm (30-45").

H. 'Autumn Glory' has green leaves, purplish especially when young and dark chunky violet flowers in June to September. 45cm (18").

H. 'Caledonia' has narrow blue-green leaves and violet blue and white flowers. Turns deep maroon in winter. 75cm (30").

H. evansii has dark purple foliage.

H. 'Fairfieldii' is an upright shrub, with coarsely toothed, glossy mid-dark green, red-margined leaves, having lavender-violet flowers. Frost hardy.

H. 'Hinderwell' was bred in the north and has sumptuous, red-purple leaves and deep violet flowers. 60cm (24").

H. 'Midsummer Beauty' has bright green leaves, red-purple beneath when young.

H. 'Mrs Winder' has purplish-brown shoots and leaves of dark-red purple when young.

H. 'Pascal' has deep burgundy foliage and mauve flowers.

H. 'Purple Shamrock' has lime green leaves turning deep purple and pink during winter with blue flowers in summer.

H. 'Rojo' bears black-purple foliage with variegated edges with black stems, a sport of 'Autumn Glory'.

H. speciosa 'La Seduisante' has dark purple shoots and green leaves, purple on the underside. It bears medium-sized, dark purple-red flowers. 90cm (3ft).

HELLEBORUS

Some of my favourite flowers are found in this genus and *H. orientalis* hybrids are tops with most black flower lovers for their very dark, near black petals, with purple or blue undertones. Sultry queens of the dark garden.

HOW TO GROW

Moist, fertile, humus rich soils in sun or partial shade, in a warm and sheltered spot. Hardy below -15°C, but needs to be out of wind. The golden rule is not to move them around, they dislike disturbance. Allow them to self-seed.

Named varieties are slow to increase and will cross-pollinate in gardens. Hardy. Z. 5-10.

Sow fresh seed in a coldframe. Divide after flowering.

H. orientalis hybrids are available in colour selections ranging from deepest reds, darkest purples and blues to black. Tones are exquisite. Froebel's catalogue of 1890 is testimony to the breeding which had taken place by that time and already produced colours of indigo blue-black, dark violet, crimson, purple red, dark steel blue, often with dark stems and dark leaf colour. Sadly, none of these wonderful plants have survived to this day, but the colour ranges formed the basis of today's modern hybrids. E. B. Anderson of the Tooting nursery was responsible for many dark hellebores. To obtain the colour, the dark and bluish Balkan hellebores and *H. torquatus* were used. Helen Ballard was a lady I would have dearly loved to have met. She raised some of the best blacks of her time, having large rich dark purple flowers. Ballard's aim was to produce larger, rounded flowers with a more upfacing habit. By and large she succeeded beautifully. Most of her darks are complemented by cream stamens. There are many dark, blue-black seedlings, just like midnight, from this strain. Many years ago there was a German hybrid named **H. 'Black Knight'** but I believe it is no longer available. **H. 'Little Black'** and a nearly black are available at the time of writing. There is also a single black with petals so dark it will stop you in your tracks, the best colour I have found in the U.S. are at Heronswood, but many of these have downfacing petals. In the U.S. you might also look out for **H. 'Birkin's Black'** or **H. 'Smokey Blue'**. There is also a maroon foliaged and flowered form. Wow!

H. 'Dusk' (1985) is a beautiful Ballard hybrid, purple with a blue bloom.

H. 'Hades' is an incredible flower, slate-blue and very desirable, raised by Ballard in 1988.

H. 'Harvington Shades of Night' is a lovely slate purple, well-toned and long flowering, appearing early in the season and flowering one year for me until September. Floriferous and robust with maroon young foliage.

The deepest blue, **H. 'John Burbeck'** raised by Ballard in 1994 was sadly never listed.

H. 'Indigo' (Ballard 1983) is a deep blue-black with wonderful undertones.

Eric Smith's selected purples from what he named **H. 'Midnight Sky'** are a mouthwatering purple with an even dusting of darker speckles.

H. 'Mystery' (Ballard 1991) has a mauve spotted droopy flower.

The small flowered **H. 'Nocturne'** (Ballard 1988) is bluish black.

H. orientalis ex 'Pollux' gives small, cup-shaped flowers of rich, purple-black, with well-tinted red-purple cut foliage as it unfolds in spring.

H. orientalis 'Purpurascens' bears blooms of dusky purple, this is now widely available.

H. 'Philip Ballard' (Ballard 1986) bears large cup-shaped, deep, dark dusky blooms. A robust plant which is always early. The similar **H. 'Blue Rook'** was raised in 1992. **H. 'Pluto'** is an intriguing colour being purple on the outer petals, purple with a green tint within.

H. purpurascens has leathery, basal mid-green leaves to 27cm (11"). Pendent, cup-shaped flowers of purplish or slate-grey, often flushed pink or purple are borne before the leaves make their appearance. 5-30cm (2-12").

H. 'Queen of Night' (Elizabeth Strangman 1970's) is a dark purple with dark nectaries. Pleasant to grow, with handsome maroon foliage at first, turning green, but not as dark a flower as the black I have seen.

H. 'Rembrandt' (1988) with young dark foliage, complimenting the reddish brown flowers.

H. 'Saturn' is an upfacing smoky blue-purple raised by Ballard but never found on a nursery list.

H. 'Tom' and **H. 'Tom Wilson'** were both raised by Ballard in 1989, both a deep bluish black.

H. 'Violet' (Ballard 1993) is a deep violet shade.

H. 'Vulcan' raised in 1980 by Ballard is a red black.

H. 'William' is a blue-black with purple undertones.

Note: **H.niger** has black roots, green leaves and white flowers.

Helleborus 'Harvington Shades of Night'

HEMEROCALLIS

Flowers last but a day, but are usually borne in profusion, nevertheless bud count is important, particularly in cooler areas. Dark colours tend to be intolerant of full sun and rainfall, so need a little midday shade. Hybrids are tolerant of a wide variety of conditions and can do well on heavy clay. Grow with red-stemmed Cornus, grasses and feathery foliage such as Foeniculum and Nigella.

HOW TO GROW

Best in fertile, moist but well-drained soil in an open site. Mulch in late autumn or spring. From spring until buds appear, water freely and apply a balanced feed every 2 weeks. Very drought tolerant once established. Hardy Z4.

Divide every 2-3 years, evergreen hybrids in mid to late spring, deciduous in spring or autumn.

H. 'Africa' (Kropf-Tankesley-Clark 1987) is one of the darkest black-reds, a repeat bloomer with narrow petals and a bright orange throat. Colour is sun tolerant. 68cm (27").
H. 'African Diplomat' (Carr 1992) bears ruffled near black petals with a lemon-green throat. Fairly sunfast and good in harsh climates. 74cm (29").
H. 'American Revolution' (Wild 1972) is often sold as a black, but this was the first dark *Hemerocallis* I had and I would call it wine red.

Fades badly in sun. Hardy. 70cm (28").
H. 'Baby Jane Hudson' (Petit) is a tetraploid of very dark hue with a chartreuse throat and ruffled yellow edges. Fine form.
H. 'Baltimore Oriole' has smallish deep plum flowers.
H. 'Bela Lugosi' is a semi-evergreen tetraploid which is suitably dark. 80cm (33").
H. 'Black Ambrosia' (Salter 1991) has superb large, ruffled velvet black flowers with a yellow throat. In hot climates this is a reliable repeat bloomer. Quite hardy, but foliage is susceptible to damage in frost. Good branching and bud count. 75cm (30").
H. 'Black Briar Bay' bears dark flowers on a vigorous grower.
H. 'Black Cat' (Wild 1980) bears 10cm (5") blooms of black-red with a small yellow eye and green throat. 70cm (28").
H. 'Black Cherry' is a cherry-red purple. 90cm (36").
H. 'Black Emperor' is a good dark purple. 60cm (24").
H. 'Black Eye' is dark purple with a black eye and yellow throat.
H. 'Black Falcon' is a plum-purple.
H. 'Black Friar' has deep purple flowers with black shading and a brilliant yellow throat.
H. 'Black Knight' is purple from darker buds. Flowers appear June-August. 90cm (3ft).
H. 'Black Magic' has thin, reflexed petals, very dark plum-purple, 10cm (4") across from dark buds with a contrasting green throat. 60cm (2ft).

H. 'Black Plush' (Connell 1956) has velvety spider flowers of black-red, a self, holding its colour well even in Florida heat and sun. Upright and vigorous but slightly tender. 95cm (32").
H. 'Black Prince' is on the heritage list, bred by Russell in 1942. A striking combination of medium blackish flowers with an orange throat. Excellent with deep purple foliage, such as *Cotinus*.
H. 'Black Siren' has a blackish centre fading to the tips.
H. 'Blackjack Cherry' (Carr '95) is a tetraploid with red-black flowers and a burgundy watermark. Fragrant. Cold hardy. Mouthwatering. 45cm (20").
H. 'Caviar' (Moldovan 1984) bears blackish-red tetraploid flowers 12cm (5") across. Good rebloomer. Very cold hardy to -40°F.
H. 'Charcoal' is such a deep purple appearing almost black.
H. 'Chicago Blackout' (Marsh 1970) Intense dark black cherry blooms with red overtones to 7.5cm (6") across. A mid-season tetraploid. 75cm (30").
H. 'Dark Avenger' (E.Salter 1990) bears well formed, velvety black-red blooms with vivid yellow-green throats. Superbly branching, semi-evergreen, miniature plant. 40cm (18").
H. 'Dominic' (Williams 1984) is semi-evergreen. Blackish-red, velvet-textured blooms with a large, vibrant gold centre appear in mid-season and rebloom later making this an excellent garden variety. Tetraploid with large 12cm (5")

Hemerocallis from top to bottom left
H. 'American Revolution', H. 'Bela Lugosi', H. 'Dominic', H. 'Jay'
H. 'Dakar' (above) H. 'Midnight Magic' (below)

blooms. Superb. 75cm (30").

H. 'Double Firecracker' is very attractive, having black flowers with purple streaks.

H. 'Ed Murray' (Grovatt 1970) is a sunfast maroon-black with a green throat. An oustanding garden plant. 65cm (26").

H. 'Edge of Eden' (Petit 1996) is a sumptuous evergreen tetraploid with deep black-purple petals, ruffled and edged in gold to match the throat. Needs shade in heat and sun, but is an excellent plant in cooler climates. 55cm (22").

H. 'Jungle Beauty' (Apps 1991) is a midseason diploid with luscious dark near black flowers. Good branching and bud count makes this a good choice. Can be slow to establish. 75cm (30").

H. 'Little Christine' (Croker 1987) is an early to mid bloomer bearing prolific flowers of dark purple with a black eye which stay open until evening. Withstands temperatures to -40°F. 45cm (18").

H. 'Little Fred' (Maxwell 1977) is a deep black-red self, with a lemon-green throat. Has good heat tolerance. 60cm (24").

H. 'Midnight Magic' (Kinnebrew 1979) is a ruffled dark black-red,

extremely velvety 12cm (5") blooms holding fairly well in sun. A tetraploid, early to mid bloomer which increases well. May need protection. 70cm (28").

H. 'Midnight Raider' (Stamile 1996) is a midseason evergreen tetraploid with fine, rich burgundy purple blooms with crisp green throats. High bud count on tall, branched scapes. 80cm (30").

H. 'Minstrel Boy' has a dark 12cm (5") across flower blooming in midseason. 60cm (2ft). Z 4-9.

H. 'Nebuchandnezzar's Furnace' (Talbott 1988) bears almost ruffled maroon-red-black flowers. An evergreen in Z. 8-10, needs protection if temperatures fall below (50°C) 10°F. 55cm (22").

H. 'New Swirls' (Wild 1983) is a good burgundy-black with a green throat. Must have shade in hot areas. 75cm (30").

H. 'Night Beacon' (Hansen '88) is a velvety deep purple-brown, with a large yellow throat and tiny green eye and pale midribs. Early to mid flowering rebloomer. 45cm (18").

H. 'Night Raider' (Webster 1986) stands up to the weather producing dark red petals with

Hemerocallis 'Paradise Princess'

Hemerocallis 'Baby Jane Hudson'

near black veining and edges contrasting with the green throat. Well branched and blooms well. 70cm (28").

H. 'Night Wings' (Williams 1985) bears black-red flowers with a bluish sheen and a lemon-green throat. Good branching and bud count. 75cm (30").

H. 'Nigrette' has deep purple flowers with dark mahogany overtones. 65cm (26").

H. 'Paradise Princess' (Lewis 1977) is a semi-evergreen midseason diploid. Deep purple with black shading. 50cm (20").

H. 'Purple Rain' is a deepish burgundy purple. 40cm (16").

H. 'Rebel Boy' bears 6 superb black petals, star-shaped with black stamens. To -40°F.

H. 'Rue Madelaine' (Carr 1992) bears ruffled, rich red petals with black undertones and a green throat. A vigorous, fairly hardy well-branched choice. 68cm (27").

H. 'Siloam Stormy Night' bears wonderful deep purple flowers with lighter veins. Attractive form.

H. 'Sir Modred' (Webster 1992) bears sturdy, well-branched scapes with a good bud count opening to give a long display of near black blooms, holding the deep colour well. Vigorous growth on this hardy, dormant daylily. 60cm (24")

H. 'Soot Storm' (Kirby 1969) bears dark blackish purple 12cm (5") blossoms of a velvet texture and deep yellow throat.

H. 'Spanish Harlem' bears good dark blooms.

H. 'Starling' is a red-black daylily

with a bright gold reverse and medium-sized flowers. Colours better out of full sun. 1m (3ft).

H. 'Super Purple' has very dark maroon-purple flowers 14cm (5.5") across. Throats are lime-green and yellow. 65cm (26"). Not quite fully hardy, but does have the bonus of an extended flowering period.

H. 'Total Eclipse' (Durio 1984) bears rounded petals, near black-red with a green throat. A good choice in Europe. 60cm (24").

H. 'Tuxedo' (K. Carpenter 1987) bears ruffled black-purple petals with a vivid green throat. This is a stoloniferous, dormant variety which retains its dark colouring in sun. 53cm (21").

H. 'Vintage Bordeaux' (Kirchoff 1987) is an evergreen tetraploid with 10cm (5") blooms of purple-black with cherry red edges and a yellow throat. A little heat encourages the blooms to open. A sunfast, early bloomer and fairly hardy, doing well in 7. 5 9.

H. 'Voodoo Dancer' (John P Peat) is a fabulous double with near black-purple colouring having a lighter edge and a yellow throat. Totally bewitching.

Hemerocallis 'Voodoo Dancer'

HERMODACTYLIS

This handsome plant is not the easiest to grow well, but worth the effort. Found on dry, rocky slopes in S.Europe to N.Africa and Israel and Turkey, it needs long hot, dry summers to bake the tubers.

HOW TO GROW
Plant tubers at a depth of 10cm (4") in autumn. Choose moderately fertile, sharply drained, alkaline soil in full sun. Dislikes excessive summer rain. Needs a hot spot, and is best positioned at the base of a warm, sunny wall. In frost-prone areas, although hardy, the early flowers may be damaged, grow in a bulb frame if in doubt. In warmer areas it can be naturalised in grass. Hardy.
Divide as soon as leaves die back.

H. tuberosus, the widow iris is a perennial which slowly forms clumps The delightful flowers have a most unusual, irresistible, subtle colouring. Some describe the green as glass-green (Beth Chatto) others as jade-green (Avon Bulbs). The greenish yellow flowers are 5cm (2") across with wondrous velvety blackish-brown falls borne in spring. In addition, these extraordinary flowers exude a sweet perfume. Linear bluish or greyish-green leaves die back in early summer. 20-40cm (8-16").
An intriguing flower but not the easiest to grow.

HEUCHERA

This is one genus, with recent developments, mostly from Dan Heims of Terranova nurseries in the USA, now offers an outstanding number of purple-leaved hybrids. Excellent ground cover and superb container plants mixing well with *Ajuga* and *Geranium*. Offering good contrast with reds and pinks or underplanted with gold foliage. Once grown for their coral bell flowers to which bees are attracted, but now one of the foremost plants in the foliage stakes for those fabulous dark scalloped leaves.

HOW TO GROW
Grow in fertile, moist but well-drained soil in sun or partial shade. The woody rootstock can have a tendency to push upwards . Mulch well. Hardy to -29°C(-20°F) Z 5 or 6-9.
Sow seed in a cold frame in spring and select the best purple foliage. Divide in autumn.

H. 'Amethyst Myst' (TN) is beatifully marked with cream flowers. 40-50cm (16-20").
H. 'Beauty Colour' bears brownish leaves netted with green and silver.
H. 'Black Beauty' (TN) has deep, near black leaves which retain their colour well. A perfect foil for the pink flowers. 40cm (16").
H. 'Black Velvet' has blackish red leaves.
H. 'Blackbird' (W) bears pink flowers over brownish-black

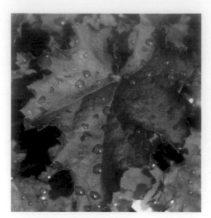

Heuchera 'Blackbird'

foliage. 50cm (20").

H. **'Burgundy Frost'** (TN) has cream flowers above purple foliage. 70cm (28").

H. **'Can-can'** (TN) has cream flowers over well-ruffled, dark foliage flushed in purple tones, excellent in winter. 40cm (16").

H. **'Cascade Dawn'** produces a mound of huge reddish-purple leaves marbled with pewter grey.

H. **'Cathedral Windows'** (TN) sprays of cream flowers rise over excellent dark foliage veined in black. 40cm (16").

H. **'Chocolate Ruffles'** (TN) has luxuriant deep chocolate-purple foliage with nicely scalloped, ruffled edges and maroon undersides. Excellent winter foliage. 50cm (20").

H. **'Chocolate Veil'** bears very dark near black leaves highlighted with light silver. 30cm (12").

H. **'Crimson Curls'** has well-ruffled edges and is a good purple.

H. **'David'** bears large beige-pink bells in May to June over deep burgundy foliage. 50cm (20").

H. **'Diana Clare'** bears rose flowers over brownish red leaves. 40cm (16").

H. **'Ebony and Ivory'** (TN) has dark leaves to contrast with the white flowers. 35cm (14").

H. **'Eden's Mystery'** (W) pushes forth dark, shiny purple leaves becoming glossy silver with age. Good young colouring. Has creamy-white flowers. 25cm (10").

H. **'Eden's Shine'** (W) is similar but not as hardy.

H. **'Emperor's Cloak'** has wondrous puckered, folded and pleated foliage in shades of beetroot to deep purple, appearing almost transparent in sun. Thin stems of fluffy white flowers.

H. **'Fireworks'** (TN) bears large red flowers over dark reddish bronze foliage. 40cm (16").

H. **'Frosted Violet'** has the vigour and habit of *H. villosa* with the new pink-violet foliage darkening in winter. 30cm (12").

H. **'High Society'** bears pewter leaves with charcoal veining and large ivory flowers in April to June. 45cm (18").

H. **micrantha v diversifolia 'Bressingham Bronze'** has bronze green leaves with a plum reverse, overall too greenish. 70cm (28").

H. **micrantha v diversifolia 'Palace Purple'** bears overlapping leaves of dark bronze-red on the surface, lighter on the underside. Faint puckering between the veins accentuates the sheen. Can look brown. Dark wiry stems carry tiny white flowers held well above the foliage. This and a selected form are seed strains. 46cm (18"). Z4.

H. **'Midnight Claret'** has darkest purple leaves and creamy-greenish flowers. 46cm (18").

H. **'Montrose Ruby'** has burgundy leaves, glowing red in cool weather against white flowers.

H. **'Oakington Jewel'** bred by Alan Bloom in the 1930's is a good dark and according to Barry Glick of Sunshine Farms, USA, is "as good as modern day cultivars".

H. **'Obsidion'** (TN) is hard to beat for near black foliage. Tremendous.

H. **'Palace Passion'** (TN) bears small pink flowers and purple-brown foliage. 40cm (16").

H. **'Persian Carpet'** (TN) displays purplish leaves marbled pink-grey with cream flowers. 80cm (32").

H. **'Petite Ruby Frills'** bears dwarf mounds of purple, scalloped leaves. Heat tolerant. 30cm (12").

H. **'Pewter Moon'** (Oudolf) bears palish pewter-marbled, red-purple scalloped leaves with pale flowers in May to August. 20cm (8").

H. **'Pewter Veil'** (TN) has scalloped purple and silver foliage and cream flowers. 60cm (2ft).

H. **'Pink Ruffles'** (TN) bears cream flowers over purplish foliage. 50cm (22").

H. **'Plum Pudding'** bears evergreen, large foliage of a deep, shiny plum-burgundy with silver markings and clouds of tiny maroon flowers in May to August. Good winter foliage, retains its colour well. 60cm (24").

H. **'Prince'** (W) has purple foliage which turns green, losing its good looks by midsummer, with white flowers. 35cm (14").

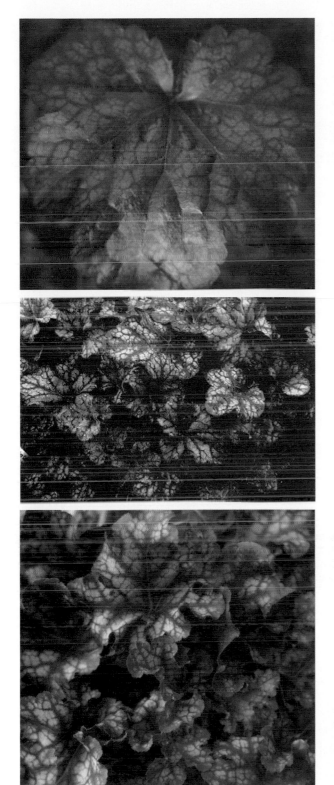

Left top to bottom
Heuchera 'Plum Pudding', H. 'Cathedral Windows', H. 'Amethyst Myst'.

Heuchera 'Can-can' (above), H. 'Obsidion' (below)

115

H. 'Purple Petticoats' (TN) has heavily ruffled leaves of deep, darkest maroon with cream flowers. The colour deepens with colder weather. Outstanding. 30cm (12").

H. 'Purple Sails' (TN) bears dark bronze-purple leaves with a silver overlay. Best in shade. 50cm (20").

H. 'Rachel' is a real dark beauty with purple-brown leaves and pink flowers, but turning green later in the season. Easy. 40cm (16").

H. 'Regina' (PP) bears pink flowers over dark purple-brown leaves with silver markings. 60cm (24").

H. 'Ruby Veil' (TN) is a very sun tolerant reddish-purple leaved form with cream flowers. 100cm (36").

H. 'Stormy Seas' (TN) has attractive, crinkled purplish foliage netted with silver. 40cm (16").

H. 'Swirling Fantasy' combines purple foliage with red flowers.

H. 'Tinian Bronze' bears white flowers over bronze foliage.

H. 'Van Gogh' (W) bears cream

flowers over foliage veined near black. 50cm (20").

H. 'Veil of Passion' (TN) has red flowers over bronze foliage. 40cm (16").

H. 'Velvet Night' (TN) bears dark maroon to black leaves with metallic purple and silver overlays. When established the leaves are of enormous proportions. 40cm (16").

H. 'Vesuvius' bears hot pink flowers from red buds over compact burgundy foliage.

H. villosa 'Biddulph Brown' bears large white flowers with brownish-red glossy leaves. 50cm (20").

X HEUCHERELLA

A cross between Heuchera and Tiarella. Prefers slightly acid soil. Hardy.

x H. 'Burnished Bronze' is a superbly dark bronze form with large and glossy cut leaves. Excellent.

x H. 'Chocolate Lace' has large, dark glossy leaves and star like flowers. Reblooms. 45cm (18").

x H. 'Heart of Darkness' bears white flowers and dark maroon foliage marked with silver and grey-green.

x H. 'Quicksilver' has metallic purple foliage with bronze veining and bears pink and white flowers from May to July. 30cm (12").

x H. 'Silver Streak' has paler purple foliage overlaid with silver white and bears white and lavender pink flowers in April to July. 30cm (12").

Heuchera 'Van Gogh' (above left)
x Heucherella 'Burnished Bronze' (above)
Heuchera 'Stormy Seas' (left)

HIBISCUS

Known for such exotic flowers, it is a delight to see the combination of coppery purple foliage too.

HOW TO GROW

Under glass, grow in loamless or loam-based compost in bright, filtered light. Requires moderate humidity and good ventilation. When in growth, water freely and apply a balanced feed monthly. Water sparingly in winter.

Where there is no danger of frost, grow outdoors in humus-rich, moist but well-drained, neutral to slightly alkaline soil in full sun. Frost tender. Z10.

Sow seed under glass in spring. Divide perennials in spring. Root greenwood cuttings of shrubs, or semi-ripe cuttings in summer. Layer in spring or summer.

H. acetosella 'Coppertone' ('Red Shield') is a short-lived perennial often grown as an annual. The leaves of the species are often flushed red, but 'Coppertone' has broadly ovate, usually deeply lobed leaves of a brilliant maroon-purple. Together with its 5cm (2") across flowers of old rose this is one plant which will delight whether you grow it inside or out. Flowers indoors, but reluctantly so outdoors unless in tropical areas.

H. 'Kopper King' bears copper-red leaves with orange-red undersides.

HUERNIA

Huernia are frost-tender perennial succulents from hilly, semi-desert areas with a faintly unpleasant scent. Flowers are interesting.

HOW TO GROW

Under glass, grow in cactus compost with added leaf mould in bright, filtered or indirect light with low humidity. Water moderately in growth, applying a half-strength, high nitrogen feed monthly. Keep virtually dry in winter. Outdoors, grow in poor, sandy, well drained soil with leaf mould. Grow in dappled shade or in full sun with midday shade. Dislike excessive winter wet.

Sow seed under glass in spring. Root cuttings of stem sections in spring or summer.

H. macrocarpa v arabica bears deep maroon purple flowers with white hairs borne in early autumn. 10cm (4"). 11°C (52°F).

H. oculata bears blackish-red flowers with a pure white centre.

H. schneiderana has bell-shaped flowers, brownish on the outer surface and velvety, deep purple inside, the margins pinkish and edged with maroon.

H. striata bears greenish or maroon flowers on the outside, yellow on the inside, all marked with brownish-maroon bands.

H. zebrina has greenish yellow flowers to 3.5cm (1.5") across, marked with maroon and a very deep maroon centre. 8cm (3").

HYDRANGEA

Superb large shrubs, usually grown for their flowers, but with some interesting dark foliage.

HOW TO GROW

Moist but well-drained moderately fertile, humus-rich soil in full sun or partial shade with shelter from cold winds. Cut *H.* 'Preziosa' down to the base in early spring. Hardy. Sow seed in a cold frame in spring. Root softwood cuttings in early summer, or hardwood in winter.

H. quercifolia with its bold, oak-leaves is the best to my eye, turning a good bronze-purple with the onset of colder weather as its sterile white flowers become pink-tinged with age. Flowers appear from midsummer to autumn. 2m(6ft).

H. quercifolia 'Sikes Dwarf' bears very closely spaced foliage, dusky black when nights are cool with lacy white flowers fading to pink, then beige.

H. 'Preziosa' bears reddish-brown foliage and deep rose-red flowers.

Hibiscus acetosella 'Coppertone'

Ipomoea batatas '*Blackie*'

Ipomoea batatas '*Black Heart*'

HYPERICUM

A sensational shrub, flushed in dark tones.

HOW TO GROW

Grow in moderately fertile moist but sharply drained soil. Position in full sun or partial shade. Hardy. Greenwood or semi-ripe cuttings in summer.

H. androsaemum 'Albury Purple' is a deciduous shrub with erect branches and broadly ovate to oblong leaves which are flushed purple. The cupped yellow flowers to 2cm (1") across are borne in midsummer. The red, spherical berry like fruit which follows ripens to black. 75cm (30").

H. x odorum 'Golden Beacon' has sensational gold-coloured foliage which turns black when growing strongly. Clusters of yellow flowers appear in June to August and ornamental red fruits turn black. Bushy. 40cm (16").

IPOMOEA

Superb dark foliage on sweet-potato types and darkish flowers on a morning glory are welcome additions to container gardens. Contrast with lime leaved plants for great effect.

I. batatas 'Blackie' has irresistible dark foliage with 5-fingered leaves. Extremely heat tolerant, the foliage is darker in warmth. A superb trailing plant, suitable for hanging baskets or containers. Z8-10.

I. batatas 'Black Heart' is equally delightfully dark, featuring exquisite heart-shaped foliage.

I. batatas 'Lady Fingers' 7-lobed dark leaves with purple raised veins on the reverse. Revels in acquatic conditions, but equally at home in containers.

I. batatas 'Vardaman' bears purple-toned heart-shaped leaves which mature to a dark green. A vigorous, maroon-stemmed heirloom.

I. purpurea 'Kniola's Purple-Black' bears dark flowers though not as dark as its name suggests. Foliage on this morning glory darkens as the season progresses. **Convolvulus 'Star of Yelta'** is similar.

Ipomoea purpurea 'Kniola's Purple-Black'

IRESINE

Superb tropical dark foliage not to miss, providing excellent contrast with flowering plants.

HOW TO GROW

Under glass, in loam based compost in full light with shade from hot sun. In growth, water freely. Apply a liquid feed once a month. Outdoors, moist but well-drained soil in full sun for best leaf colour. Revel in heat and good light. Pinch back when young in spring to encourage bushiness. Frost tender. 10°C (50°F). Z 10-11. Stem tip cuttings at any time. Softwood in late winter or spring.

I. herbstii (beefsteak plant) and its cultivars are grown for their fabulous foliage alone. These short-lived perennials are dwarf, shrubby natives of Brazil, often used as annuals. Excellent pot plants.

I. herbstii 'Acuminata' has sharply pointed black-red leaves with carmine and lilac veins.

Iresine herbstii 'Brilliantissima'

I. herbstii 'Brilliantissima' bears near black foliage with iridescent red-pink veins. Positively volcanic.
I. herbstii 'Wallisii' offers black-purple leaves.
I. lindenii (blood leaf) this erect, bushy and compact perennial is fabulously dark with very attractive, smooth, glossy leaves. From Ecuador, in ideal conditions this can reach 1m (3ft). Quickly became a favourite and permanent member of my garden.
I. 'Purple Lady' from seed, makes annual trailing cover of cranberry and burgundy tones in leaf and stem.

Iresine lindenii

IRIS

This genus of over 300 species is split into groups. Their individual cultivation requirements differ. Mostly hardy, but some thrive only in specific conditions. Dark *Iris* are one of the great delights of the plant world, mainly falling into the bearded category, available in shimmeringly dark colours.

GENERAL CULTIVATION
Plant in late summer and early autumn. Grow in well-drained, moderately fertile neutral or slightly acid or alkaline soil in full sun to light, dappled shade.
Plant bearded irises with the rhizome level with the soil, and partially exposed (thinly covered in very hot sites). Do not let other plants overshadow them. They also dislike nitrogen.
Sow seed in a cold frame in autumn or spring. Divide rhizomes, it is usual to cut the leaves down to one third and the rhizome can also be cut.

SPECIES
I. chrysographes is a rhizomatous beardless Siberian *Iris* with linear grey-green leaves to 50cm (20") long. In early summer, each unbranched stem bears 2 fragrant, dark red-violet flowers, up to 7cm (3") across, having gold streaks on the falls. Easy in peaty, moist soil. Hardy. 40-50cm (16-20"). Z5.
I. chrysographes 'Black Beauty' is a purple-black, darker from afar, purple tones showing close-up.

I. chrysographes 'Black Knight' has very dark black flowers. Z5.
I. Black and 'Kew Black' are also reliable. Z5. All these are wow!
I. ewbankiana bears black and white mottled flowers.
I. iberica is a rare beauty, a rhizomatous, bearded Onocyclus with narrow grey-green leaves, strongly curved. Each stem produces a solitary brown-veined, white flower 7cm (3") across in mid to late spring, the falls are near black, giving the appearance of a black and white flower from afar.
I. iberica ssp elegantissima is very similar. Hardy. 15-20cm (6-8").
The small, furry falls of I. paradoxa are near black, standards are purple.
I. sibirica 'Tropic Night' has gorgeous flowers of dark purple.
I. spuria 'Stars at Night' has velvety brown-black flowers with clear yellow signals.
I. 'Arabian Midnight' (L.Rich 1989) is a very dark purple-black, darker on the falls with a black beard. Aril bred.

BEARDED IRIS
Superb, large flowers, often ruffled are an excellent choice. Many of these are award winners, the elite are multi-award winners. A whole spectrum of dark hues are associated with this flower , mainly amongst tall bearded iris. Allow them to revel in a spot where the rhizomes can bake. Long, hot summers ensure good performance. Z 3-10.
Season, E early, M mid L, late.

Iris 'Around Midnight'

Iris 'Old Black Magic'

Iris 'Paint it Black'

TALL BEARDED

70cm (28" or more) usually with multiple large flowers per stem. Dark flowers appear to be cut from black silk, taffeta and velvet. Z6.

I. 'About Last Night' (Black 1999) standards have a purplish-black midline, falls are black with cream veining having a bright yellow beard, well-branched and fragrant.
I. 'After Dark' (Schreiner 1963) is a dark violet blue black, with deep red beard.
I. 'After Eight' (H.Stahly 1995) is a deep blackish-violet self with near black beard.
I. 'Anvil of Darkness' (Innerst 1998) is a pure black self with a round, wide flaring form.
I. 'Around Midnight' (Schreiner 1995) has dark violet standards and black falls with a ruffled yellow tipped violet beard. 8-10 buds per stem. Sumptuous. 1m (3ft).
I. 'Back in Black' (Schreiner 1986) is a velvety rich black self with red undertones.
I. 'Baltic Star' (Stahly 1994) has unusual colouring of blackish purple washed white over the falls. Wonderful.
I. 'Bar de Nuit' (P. Anfosso 1987) has violet highlights shining through black petals with a dark blue beard.
I. 'Basic Black' (B.Hager 1971) the standards and beard are dark purple, the falls shading to black.
I. 'Batman' (Byers 1986) is a deep blackish purple, lightly ruffled variety with a musk fragrance.
I. 'Before The Storm' (Innerst 1989) is heralded as one of the darkest, moderately sized flowers of elegant shape, all black with well-flared falls, good growth and slight fragrance. 90cm (36").
I. 'Bill Bailey' (B.Hager 1989) is black-maroon with a bronze beard.
I. 'Black Accent' (C.Tompkins 1985) is a black-red self with violet tinting on the beard.
I. 'Black As Night' (D.Meek 1992) is a red-black bitone, darker on the falls with wide, ruffled flowers and a yellow beard. A fragrant rebloomer. ML. 92cm (37").
I. 'Black Bart' is black, with well-pronounced red overtones and velvety falls.
I. 'Black Belle' (Stevens 1951) is a black self with a rich blue, velvet sheen having a ruby overcast. ML. 80cm (32").
I. 'Black Butte' (Schreiner 1999) is a dark purple-black self with an attractive form.
I. 'Black Dragon' (Schreiner 1982) has purple-black flowers, velvety and intensely dark with matching beards. ML. 95cm (38").
I. 'Black Falls' (Nebeker 1996) bears black-violet standards and falls with a violet-yellow beard.
I. 'Black Fantasy' (Meek 1988) has dark wine standards and maroon-black falls with a yellow beard. Nicely ruffled petals.
I. 'Black Flag' (1984) has deep violet standards and deeper falls.
I. 'Black Grapes' (Hamner 1993) is a black-purple self.
I. 'Black Hills' (Fay 1951) is a blue-black self, one of the first of a string of ever darker varieties.
I. 'Black Hope' (Austin 1963) is deep mulberry-black, Austin does not specialise in blacks.
I. 'Black Ink' has very dark blue-black flowers and a good scent.
I. 'Black Madonna' (H.Stahly 1985) is a very deep violet, blacker on the falls.
I. 'Black Market' (G.Plough 1974) is a deep purple-black self.
I. 'Black Nitie' (Z.Benson 1962) bears plummish purple standards and near black falls with a green overlay, having a bronze-gold beard. M.74cm (29").
I. 'Black Pansy' (C.de Forest 1969) is a black self with a brown beard.
I. 'Black Pearl' (D.Meek 1984) is a deep reddish black with velvety black falls.
I. 'Black River' (D.Morrison 1987) has black petals with a brownish-black band on the falls, the black beard fades to brownish gold.
I. 'Black Sergeant' (F.Gadd 1983) bears deep ruffled black blooms with brown beards. 81cm (32").
I. 'Black Sultan' (Austin 1966) is a red-purple bitone with velvety falls and a striking black centre.
I. 'Black Suited' (Innerst 2000) is a black-self.
I. 'Black Swan' (Fay 1960) is a translucent, silky purple-black contrasting with the broad, black velvet falls. One of the first I grew, and still one I admire. 75cm (30").
I. 'Black Taffeta' (Songer 1954) glistens with black-purple standards and broad velvety black, slightly ruffled falls. 75cm (30").
I. 'Black Tie Affair' (Schreiner 1993) is a shimmering, velvety,

inky black with black beards. Large, ruffled flowers. 90cm (36").

I. 'Black Tornado' (G.Plough 1983) is a purple black with a contrasting mustard beard and a sweet fragrance.

I. 'Black Ware' (L.Powell 1980) is a rebloomer with tailored blue-black petals and a pale yellow beard exquisitely tipped in blue.

I. 'Blackout' (Luihn 1986) is a good dark, silky red-black with darker falls. Fragrant mid-spring bloomer which reblooms. 95cm (38").

I. 'Blacky' (M.Beer 1992) has black-blue standards and velvety falls with a dark blue beard.

I. 'Boogie Man' (D.Meck 1986) is a dark violet with black-violet falls bordered in the colour of the standards and with lighter veining around the bronze beard.

I. 'Bordello' is a rich black infused with purple-red. Rebloomer.

I. 'Bye Bye Blackbird' (G. Sutton 2000) is one that everyone will love, ruffled shiny black with a deep, dark violet purple edge on the falls. Rebloomer.

I. 'By Night' (Schreiner 1976) is a sumptuous uniform ebony blue-black self.

I. 'Can't Wait' (Black 2000) is a superb black with old gold beards and very vigorous growth.

I. 'Charcoal' (G.Plough 1969) bears deep violet standards with a black cast, and black-violet falls.

I. 'Cherry Smoke' (D.Meek 1978) is a stunning velvety red-black, heavily ruffled with a bronze beard tipped violet. 85cm (34").

I. 'Christina Diane' (C.Hahn 1995) is a black self with a hint of purple and a hint of fragrance too.

I. 'Coalignition' (T.Burseen 1993) this spicily fragrant variety has dark red-maroon standards, and velvety, sooty black-maroon falls, with a bright gold beard.

I. 'Congo Song' (Christensen 1963) has dark violet standards, with darker purple falls lighter at the edge and a purple beard.

I. 'Count Dracula' (J.Hedgecock 2000) bears dark violet standards with near black falls, with a wonderful sheen and a burnt gold beard. Fragrant.

I. 'Cracken' (Schreiner 1974) is deep blue-black with a white centre on the standards.

I. 'Dark Boatman' (P.Cook 1954) bears violet standards with darker near black-purple falls.

I. 'Dark Freeze' (T.Burseen 1998) has red violet standards redeemed by much darker purple-black falls with a reddish violet rim and an unusual cream beard with orange hairs. A fragrant variety.

I. 'Dark Passage' (Pinegar 1997) has blackish-maroon falls, near black-

Iris 'Dark Passion'

maroon standards with gold hafts, and a white beard. Rebloomer. 80cm (32").

I. 'Dark Passion' (Schreiner 1998) A dark, licorice almost ebony hue with a hint of blue on compact flowers which are gently ruffled and exude a pronounced sweet fragrance. 6-9 buds. 90cm (36").

I. 'Dark Past' (J.Hedgecock 1999) is a red-black with darker falls. Fragrant.

I. 'Dark Ritual' (B.Hager 1972) is a dark red with much darker falls and a bronze-yellow beard.

I. 'Dark Side' (Schreiner 1985) is a vivid rich purple-black with superb ruffling and ebony beard. A floriforous rebloomer. 85cm (34").

I. 'David Keith' (Stadler 1991) is a maroon-black with a slight sweet fragrance.

I. 'Dirty Dancing' (J.Saia 1990) is a black self with a sooty sheen on the falls, a dark purple beard and a slight sweet fragrance.

I. 'Draco' (P.Anfosso 1988) is a ruffled deep violet-black.

I. 'Dracula's Shadow' (J.Hedgecock 1989) is a deep red-black self with gentle ruffling and a blue-black beard. Simply sparkles. 85cm (34").

I. 'Dusky Challenger' (Schreiner 1986) is a rich, silky dark purple with large ruffled flowers, well branched with up to four flowers open at the same time. Deservedly the top iris three years running with the A.I. S. 97cm (39").

I. 'Dusky Dancer' has very dark violet-black self ruffled flowers. 90cm (3ft).

I. 'Dusky Flare' (Powell 1984) is a

Iris 'Dracula's Shadow'

spicily fragrant sooty black with a bronze beard.

I. 'Ebony Angel' (L.Johnson 2000) bears royal purple-black standards with slightly lighter falls at the edge, ruffled. Spicy fragrance.

I. 'Ebony Dream' (Stahly 1993) deep violet-black with darker falls.

I. 'Ecstatic Night' (P.Cook 1963) is a black with a good tinge of violet.

I. 'Edenite' (Plough 1959) An excellent sooty red-black. Early-mid season rebloomer. 74cm (29").

I. 'Evening Gown' (Ghio) comes dressed for dinner with deep, suave blue-black flowers.

I. 'Elizabeth Carol' (J.Burch 1986) is a reddish black with a rust beard.

I. 'En Garde' (Maryott 1994) is a heavily ruffled, velvet purple-black.

I. 'Evening Silk' (Aitken 1990) is a sumptuous deep purple-black.

I. 'Fantasm' (L.Meininger 1997) bears velvety, blackish purple petals streaked and splashed in white.

I. 'Fine Precedent' (P.Blyth 1977) is a good red-black self.

I. 'Fright Night' (J.Hedgecock 1995) has blue-black standards and laced falls of the same colour.

I. 'Ghost Train' (Schreiner 2000) is a violet-black self with, luxuriously smooth, well ruffled flowers. Each stem averages 7 to 11 buds.

I. 'Halogram' (T.Burseen 1998) bears ruffled petals of dark red-violet with a black-burgundy overlay and a bronze beard.

I. 'Harlem Hussy' (D.Meek 1982) is a heavily ruffled red black.

I. 'Hello Darkness' (Schreiner 1992) has a rich colour, an unsurpassable degree of velvet black and extra large, ruffled flowers. Strong stems yield 6-7 buds. E-M.92cm (37").

I. 'Hell's Fire' (Roberts 1976) is superb with its reddish-pink standards combining with near black falls. Rebloomer.

I. 'Hollywood Nights' (R.Duncan 2001) Deep purple black standards are coupled with even darker falls with a black sheen and a white spray near the blue-violet beard with an orange throat.

I. 'Holy Cow' (T.Burseen 1998) has black burgundy falls with redder standards. A frgrant variety.

I. 'Houdini' (B.Maryott 1985) is a ruffled, velvety deep red-black with violet undertones.

I. 'Huntsman' (Sass 1955) is a very dark blackish-brown self.

I. 'Interpol' (G.Plough 1973) is a fluted black-purple variety.

I. 'Jazz Jubilee' (R.Dunn 1985) has red-black standards and deeper falls with a velvet blue-black beard.

I. 'Jet Black' (R.Brizendine 1962) is a rebloomer with delightful deep blue-black standards and jet black falls with a black beard.

I. 'Kentucky Coal' (G.Slade 1985) is a blue-black with a sooty overlay.

I. 'Licorice Stick' (Schreiner 1961) bears deep blue-black velvet standards and darker falls, excelling in lustre. Midseason rebloomer. 97cm (39").

I. 'Men in Black' (L.Lauer 1998) has dark purplish black falls and standards with a deeper flush on the falls. Well ruffled and fragrant. 85cm (34").

I. 'Midnight Caller' (Byers 1989) has silky deep purple standards and velvet black-purple falls with a lighter edge. A reliable repeat bloomer in Z4b.

I. 'Midnight Dancer' (Schreiner 1991) has ruffled and flaring purple-black petals.

I. 'Midnight Express' (Schreiner 1988) bears ruffled purple-black-blue petals and deeper blue-black beard. M-ML. 98cm (35cm).

I. 'Midnight Fragrance' is heavily ruffled, a violet black self with a pronounced sweet fragrance.

I. 'Midnight Madonna' (R.Dunn 1996) is a very dark purple-black with a velvety texture in evidence on the falls, dark purple beard.

I. 'Midnight Masterpiece' (R.Annand 2001) is a velvety maroon black enhanced by a bronze beard.

I. 'Midnight Oil' (K.Keppel 1998) is sooty with a matt finish and grape beard. Emits a slight, sweet fragrance. 90cm (36"). Excellent.

I. 'Midnight Special' (N.Sexton 1973) bears deep violet standards and black falls with a dark blue beard.

I. 'Muriel Neville' (H. Fothergill 1963) of complicated parentage,

Iris 'Black Dragon'

Iris 'Before The Storm'

Iris 'Dusky Challenger'

Iris 'Hello Darkness'
Iris 'Black Butte'

Iris 'Black Tie Affair'
Iris 'Tuxedo'

Iris 'Ghost Train'
Iris 'Night Ruler'

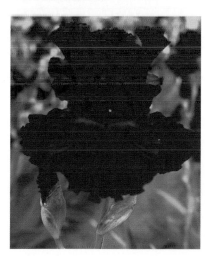

Iris 'Midnight Express'

produces a good dark brown-purple flower in mid-season.

I. 'Mystic Magic' (B.Blyth 1987) bears standards of a deep rich blue-violet and velvety smooth black falls with a blue-violet edge and an unusual tangerine beard.

I. 'Neon Cowboy' (H. Bradshaw 1998) bears ruffled red-black petals with a faint mauve rim and a daring white sunburst surrounding the yellow beard on the falls. 107cm (42").

I. 'Night Club' (McWhirter) is a rich velvet black.

I. 'Night Flame' (J.T.Aitken 1992) bears glossy red-black standards and black falls with a black beard tipped mustard.

I. 'Night Game' (K.Keppel 1996) is aubergine (eggplant) purple-black having a velvet sheen, with a slate violet rim on the velvety falls and smouldering brick-red beard. Fragrant. 107cm (42").

I. 'Night Lady' (Stahly 1986) has red-black standards and slightly deeper falls.

I. 'Night Owl' (Schreiner 1970) has rich dark violet, blue-black petals and a velvety sheen on the falls.

I. 'Night Raider' (C.Burrell 1976) is a velvet blue-black self. 84cm (34").

I. 'Night Ranger' (W.Simon 1982) is a ruffled black purple with black falls and a navy beard.

I. 'Night Ruler' (Schreiner 1990) has well-ruffled, dark deepest purple standards with darker black falls, with a blue-black inky sheen. 7 double-socketed buds. 97cm (39"). Excellent.

I. 'Night Song' (Luihn 1965) is a dark violet-black self with black beard. M-L. 92cm (37").

I. 'Night Stalker' (J.Hedgecock 1994) bears velvet purple-black fluted petals. Fragrant.

I. 'Night to Remember' (R.Ernst 1997) has ruffled, dark blue-black petals with black-purple beard.

I. 'Night Vision' (D. Meek 1993) bears light red-black standards and black falls, the beard being black tipped bronze.

I. 'Nights of Gladness' (R.Ernst 1990) has velvet black-purple petals.

I. 'Nightfall' (D.Hall 1942) is a purple-black self. M. 90cm (3ft).

I. 'Nightside' (Schreiner 1967) is a black-blue self with a deep blue-black beard and a uniform darkness having a deep, silky sheen. L. 90cm (3ft).

I. 'Oklahoma Crude' (P.Black 1989) has dark, satiny purple standards and velvety black falls with a white ray pattern around white beards, tipped mustard. Reblooms.

I. 'Old Black Magic' (Schreiner 1996) is coal black with yellow beards. Smallish flowers but an amazing 8-12 buds per stem. Pleasantly scented. 90cm (36"). Evokes the magic of planting black.

I. 'Paint it Black' (Schreiner 1994) bears dark black-purple falls with a black beard and lighter standards on this dusky small flowered, reblooming variety with excellent form and ruffling. 90cm (36").

I. 'Patent Leather' (Schreiner 1971) is a dark, blue-black violet self.

I. 'Phantom Masquerade' (Spoon 1997) bears dark purple flowers, the beard is surrounded by white.

I. 'Quiet Night' (P.Cook 1968) is a blackish violet to black self.

I. 'Raven Hill' (Carr) is a deep blue-black.

I. 'Raven's Return' (J.Weiler 1997) has ruffled dark violet standards with darkest near black-violet falls. A sweet, fragrant rebloomer.

I. 'Raven's Roost' (G.Plough 1981) is a deep purple black self with a mustard tipped beard.

I. 'Raven Wing' (Oliver 1955) has deep purple-black falls with much lighter standards. M. 87cm (35").

I. 'Ravenwood' (Lowry 1971) is a blue-black rebloomer, the dark beard is tipped yellow.

I. 'Royal Salute' (Milliken 1934) This early variety is a dark bitone.

I. 'Sable Night' (P.Cook 1952) bears rich black-violet petals with a claret undertone and a silky, bronze beard. Attractive, vigorouss form. E-M. 87cm (35").

I. 'Sable Robe' (P.Cook 1966) is a blackish violet self.

I. 'Satan's Mistress' (G.Spellman 1983) is red black.

I. 'Satin Satan' (J. Weiler 1986) has deep violet-black standards and uniform shiny, near black falls with 9-11 buds. Slight sweet fragrance. 90cm (36").

I. 'Set the Tone' (Burch 1994) is a maroon-black self with a contrasting yellow-orange beard.

I. 'Silk Silhouette' (Gartman 1992) is a ruffled almost black violet with a deep blue beard.

I. 'Sir Knight' (Ashley 1934) is an early variety, a dark black bitone.

I. 'Spectacular Bid' (D.Denney 1981) bears ruffled, smooth red-black petals.

I. 'Spirit Raiser' (Schreiner 1979) has wonderfully ruffled petals of deep blue-black.

I. 'Storm Flurry' (Schreiner 1975) is a velvety blue-black self with a purple-black beard.

I. 'Study in Black' (G.Plough 1968) bears purple-black flowers with a dark violet beard tipped antique gold. Vigorous and a reliable rebloomer. 90cm (36")

I. 'Stygian Night' (G.Slade 1982) is a blue-black.

I. 'Style Master' (C.Tompkins 1965) bears violet blue-black flowers and beard.

I. 'Sunday Punch' (F.Crandall 1977) is a ruffled black with red undertones and a bronze beard.

I. 'Superstition' (Schreiner 1977) is a dark black-purple, with a blue-black beard. Sleek and vibrant. A classic rebloomer. 90cm (3ft).

I. 'Swahili' (G.Plough 1965) has red-black petals and a brown beard.

I. 'Swazi Princess' (Schreiner 1978) is a tailored, intensely dark indigo blue with a luxuriant velvety sheen. 91cm (36").

I. 'Tabu' (Schreiner 1954) is a deep blackish-violet with a velvet lustre on the falls.

I. 'Tar Barrel' (L.Powell 1976) has blue-black standards with velvety black falls and a blue-black beard.

I. 'The Black Douglas' (J.Sass 1934) is a dark blue-black self. M. 90cm (36").

I. 'Thunder Spirit' (Schreiner 1996) bears big, bold dark purple-indigo flowers. Fragrant.

I. 'Tinder Box' (E.Hill 1998) is a red-black self with a bronze beard.

I. 'Totentanz' (Dyer 2001) "Death Dances" is named after a Franz Liszt piano piece. A pulsating bicolor, similar to Strozzapreti with a different texture and form. Rich wine standards and near black falls edged in wine and gold

Iris 'Superstition'

beards tipped bronze. Moderate ruffling and waving evocative of a dancer in full swing.

I. 'Tuxedo' (Schreiner 1965) is a superb midnight blue-black self. M. 92cm (37").

I. 'Vintner' (M.Smith 1996) has glowing blackish garnet petals, blacker at the edges. Fragrant.

I. 'Walkora' is a red-black self with a maroon beard, well ruffled, laced and fragrant.

I. 'Wild Echo' (Kelway) is a dark blue-black with bronze beard. 96cm.

I. 'Wild Wings' (K.Keppel 1999) bears dark violet standards with jet black falls and orange beards.

I. 'Winesap' (Byers 1989) is a fragrant rebloomer with deep wine, near black flowers.

I. 'Wintry Night' (Pond 1966) bears black petals with white centres.

I. 'Witch's Sabbath' (W.Maryott 1986) has heavily ruffled, purple black, velvety falls and dark purple beards. Excellent. M. 92cm (37").

I. 'Witch of Endor' bears ruffled, black-crimson flowers with a gold beard and a small white circle at the haft. Reliable rebloomer.

I. 'Witch's Wand' has ruffled black-crimson flowers and a

Iris 'Thunder Spirit'

tangerine beard.

I. 'Zaton' (Dyer 1999) is a dark black-violet bitone. 90cm (36").

I. 'Zebra Night' (Kasperek 1998) is a dark violet with orange beard, not that dark, but included here as it is the only dark iris to have variegated green and white leaves.

I. 'Zombie' (T.Craig 1957) bears intensely rich red-black flowers.

INTERMEDIATE

Ranging from 40-70cm tall (16-28").

I. 'Black Teddy Bear' (D.Spoon 1997) is a purple-black rebloomer.

I. 'Black Watch' (Rosengels 1973) is very dark with the deepest purple flowers and bluish beards with a satin texture. Attractive form. 58cm (23").

I. 'Darkness' (Hager 1993) bears near black-purple petals with bronze beards. Late season rebloomer. 53cm (21").

I. 'Deep Black' (P. Cook 1955) has very dark purple, almost black flowers. Best in poor soil in full sun. 60cm (2ft).

I. 'Devil May Care' (Black 2000) has black-purple velvet petals and red-orange beards.

I. 'Heaven's Bounty' (Miller 1982) bears ruffled purple flowers with black highlights and a bronze beard. Reblooms.

I. 'Helen Proctor' is a ruffled, darkest purple-black . 55cm (22").

I. 'Langport Midnight' (Kelway) is a deep purple-black self. A free flowering and vigorous intermediate. 45cm (18").

I. 'Langport Wren' (Kelway 1995) is a deep magenta self with black veining on the petals and unusual brown beards. Early intermediate. 66cm (26"). Z. 7-10.

I. 'Michael Paul' is a good dark dwarf bearded iris, ruffled black-purple. 27cm (11").

I. 'Midnight Moonlight' is the perfect iris for the black and white garden, bearing white standards and near black-purple falls.

I. 'Midsummer Night's Dream' (Baumink 1999) is a silky, smooth very dark purple self. A good rebloomer. 47cm (19").

I. 'Tommyknocker' (R.Lyons 1994) is a red-black self with a dark bronze beard.

I. 'Walt Luihn' (L.Barnard 1995) bears satiny black-red petals with darker midribs and velvety falls and a bushy, blue beard.

STANDARD DWARF

20-40cm (8-16") tall with smaller flowers.

I. 'Black Bandit' (D.Meek 1998) bears red-black flowers, deeper on the falls with a brown beard tipped purple.

I. 'Darkover' (N. K. Stopes 1983) is an early flowering, deep maroon self dwarf with blue beard. 25cm (10").

I. 'Dark Vader' (R&L.Miller 1987) produces ruffled flowers with dark blue-violet standards and black falls with bushy blue-violet beards. 28cm (11").

I. 'Demon' (Hager 1971) has dramatic flowers of the deepest velvety purple, appearing almost black. Purple beards are tipped with gold. A scented, floriferous dwarf variety. 30cm (12").

I. 'Little Black Belt' (O.D.Niswonger 1980) has the darkest blue-black petals with a pale blue beard. Reblooms. 30cm (12").

I. 'Little Blackfoot' (M.Reinhardt 1967) is a velvety dark red-black rebloomer.

I. 'Pumpin Iron' (P.Black 1990) bears dark, sooty red black flowers with a purple beard.

I. 'Well Suited' (P.Black 1990) is a dark purple-black bitone of good form. 30cm (12").

MINIATURE DWARF

I. 'Black Stallion' (Hite 1982) bears near black flowers with a yellow beard. 20cm (8") tall.

LOUISIANA HYBRID

I. 'Black Gamecock' (Chowning 1978) is an intense dark purple-black. Not fully hardy. Does well near pond margins. 60cm (24").

Iris 'Black Gamecock'

Jovibarba 'Be Mine'

JOVIBARBA

To all intents and purposes, these look like and can be treated like *Sempervivum*. They like a hot, sunny dry spot.

J. hueffelii 'Be Mine' raised by Howard Wills is a superb dark cultivar, in sun it approaches black, so dark, so enticing.

J. hueffelii 'Bora' is extemely dark too forming handsome rosettes.

J. hueffelii 'Chocoleto' has beautiful form and shape and is very dark.

J. hueffelii 'Gold Rand' has dark rosettes exquisitely tipped with gold. A favourite.

J. hueffelii 'Mystique' is an excellent dark cultivar, one of my favourites.

Jovibarba 'Cholcoleto'

JUGLANS

A rare purple leaved form of the common walnut.

J. regia 'Purpurea' bears superbly dark leaves up to 90cm (3ft) long when established. Leaves are wonderfully aromatic. In England this retains its colour well. Superb.

LATHYRUS

Perfect climbers for summer screening. Scented flowers are excellent for cutting. Black ones are a little disappointing, especially on opening, but they do darken. Combined with whites for effect.

HOW TO GROW
Prefer a well-manured and prepared site in the previous autumn to planting. Best in full sun in humus-rich soil. Apply a balanced feed every two weeks when in growth. Dead head.
Easy from seed. Best sown in a cold frame in autumn. Can be sown direct into the flowering position in spring.

L. 'Black Diamond' bears darkish purple-maroon flowers.
L. 'Black Knight' has flowers of a dark purple-maroon. Good scent.
L. 'Black Prince' bears dark purple flowers.
L. 'Bridget' is a dark velvety violet-blue with real depth of colour.
L. 'Charlie' is one of the darkest, deepest maroons with slight scent.

Lathyrus 'Midnight'

L. 'Midnight' is a different colouring, finest dark maroon. Large, frilly flowers on long stout stems. A very vigorous grower, lightly scented.
L. 'Windsor' bears rich, chocolate-maroon flowers with a good scent.

LEPTINELLA

Small near black button flowers are suitable for paving crevices and gravel gardens. These members of the daisy family are a common feature of New Zealand alpine flora.

HOW TO GROW
Grow in moderately fertile, sharply drained soil in full sun. Hardy.
Sow fresh seed in containers in an open frame. Divide in spring.

L. atrata (Cotula) is a creeping, tufted perennial with fern-like foliage of a grey-green which can be purple-tinged. In late spring and early summer, it bears purplish-black flowers to 1.5cm (3") across, with yellow anthers becoming prominent as the flower matures. Suitable for an alpine house or scree bed. 15cm (6").

L. atrata ssp luteola differs in having dark red-brown centres and creamy white stigmas. Leaves are less deeply divided.

L. squalida 'Platt's Black' is the best of the bunch, carrying its black button flowers with pride over dark, creeping foliage.

LEPTOSPERMUM

Attractive Australian plants in leaf and flower. Sun brings out the best dark tones in the foliage.

HOW TO GROW
Under glass, grow in loam-based potting compost in full light, or filtered light. Water freely. In growth, apply a balanced feed every month. Needs little water in winter. May need restrictive pruning. Outdoors, grow in moderately fertile, well-drained soil in full sun or partial shade. Intolerant of chalk soils. Borderline hardy to frost tender.
Sow seed under glass in autumn or spring. Root semi-ripe cuttings with bottom heat in summer.

L. macrocarpum 'Copper Sheen' has deep bronze purplish-green glossy leaves and single reddish flowers. Unusual flowers have a central, greenish-yellow receptacle 18mm (7") across, glistening with nectar. The petals are white, marked purple.

The new foliage of **L. petersonii** is bronze-red, narrow leaves have a lemon-scent when crushed.
L. rupestre turns bronze-purple in very cold weather.
L. scoparium 'Black Robin' is a compact shrub of conical habit, spectacular for its combination of dark reddish-purple foliage and numerous flowers of 1cm across, pink with a deep purple almost black centre. Tender. To 2m (6ft).
L. scoparium 'Burgundy Queen' has bronzed foliage with double red flowers. Tender.
L. scoparium 'Chapmanii' bears bronze-coloured foliage, whilst **L. scoparium 'Nanum'** has dark bronze-green leaves. Tender.
L. 'Crimson Glory' bears double flowers of the darkest red with burgundy foliage. 150-180cm (5ft).
L. 'Dark Shadows' is a fast, broad, spreading shrub with the darkest, largish leaves of the bunch, flushed dark burgundy-maroon in sun with creamy white single flowers.
The small leaves of **L. scoparium 'Nichollsii'** and of **'Nichollsii Nanum'** are deep bronze-purple when grown in open ground. **L. scoparium 'Ruby Glow'** is a double-flowered form with bronze foliage and red stems.

LILIUM

Lilies named black are not that dark however a succession of flowers is possible if you grow all three from early to late summer.

HOW TO GROW
Prefer well-drained soil enriched with leaf mould, or any well-rotted organic matter. Full sun without shade. Plant bulbs in autumn at a depth of 2-3 times their height. Hardy to frost tender.
Remove scales, offsets or bulblets from dormant bulbs as foliage dies down, stem bulbils in late summer.

HYBRIDS
L. 'Black Beauty' raised in 1957, is the darkest of the three. A vigorous, long-living oriental hybrid. In midsummer racemes of scented, medium-sized turkscaps of a dark-blackish red are produced with green centres and white tepal margins.1.5m (5ft).
L. 'Black Dragon' has been available since 1950. Bears stout racemes of large, scented, outward-facing trumpet-shaped flowers of a dark purplish-red on the outside and white within in early to mid summer. 1.5m (5ft). Z 5-8.
L. 'Black Magic Group' is a vigorous trumpet-shaped lily flowering in mid-late summer. From maroon buds opening to reddish black on the outside to white within, as the trumpet opens the white predominates, fragrant. 1.5m (5ft).

Lilium nepalense

L. nepalense has a large reddish purple blotch inside the yellow to greenish flared petals. A stunning rhizomatous lily requiring acid soil and partial shade. Frost tender. Unscented or unpleasant smelling.

L. souliei is found in wet alpine meadows and scrub in China. Scented 3cm (1") dark purple flowers appear in June and July. Grow in cool, well-drained soil which is moist in summer.

LOBELIA

Hardy perennial Lobelia offer dark foliage and vibrant red flowers.

HOW TO GROW

Grow in deep, fertile, reliably moist soil in full sun or partial shade. Hardy to -12°C (10°F) Z 8. Sow fresh seed of perennials as soon as ripe, or sow in spring.

L. 'Bees' Flame' is slightly hairy with reddish-purple stems and linear lance-shaped leaves. In mid to late summer racemes of brilliant crimson flowers to 15cm (6") long are borne, slightly larger flowers than *L.* 'Queen Victoria'. 75cm (30").

L. 'Dark Crusader' bears maroon stems and velvety deep ruby-red flowers. 60-90cm (24-36").

L. 'Fan Zinnoberrosa' bears bronze leaves and spires of pink flowers.

L. fulgens 'Elmfeuer' bears bronze foliage with dark red flowers in August to October. A winter mulch will see it through the colder months. 30cm (12").

L. 'Queen Victoria' is a short-lived perennial with deep red-purple stems and lance-shaped leaves of the same glorious colour. From late summer to mid-autumn, the striking, scarlet flowers are borne on racemes to 45cm (18") long. Benefits from a mulch and overwinters better in moist soil, better still in a shallow pool margin. A favourite with me. 90cm (3ft).

L. 'Russian Princess' in cultivation often has purplish flushed leaves and red-purple flowers. The plant that should be sold under this name has green leaves and pink flowers.

L. 'Tania' bears dark leaves, rose underneath with brilliant magenta flowers. Happiest in semi-bog conditions in full sun. Z6.

L. 'Will Scarlet' has bright blood-red flowers over green foliage flushed maroon. 90cm (36").

L. splendens and **L. x speciosa** cultivars bear reddish foliage.

Lobelia 'Queen Victoria' (below)
Loropetalum chinense f rubrum 'Burgundy' (right)

LOROPETALUM

Evergreen shrubs or small trees with purplish foliage, best grown in woodland.

HOW TO GROW

Grow in fertile, humus-rich, moist but well-drained neutral to acid soil in partial shade. Undemanding but will respond to regular watering and fertiliser. 5°C (41°F) to flower well. Borderline frost hardy.

Sow fresh seed in an open frame. Root semi-ripe cuttings with bottom heat.

L. chinense f rubrum bears very dark, shiny foliage, even better is the cultivar **'Burgundy'** with handsome dark leaves.

L. chinense f rubrum 'Fire Dance' is a neat, compact evergreen shrub with tiered branches and fuchsia pink flowers in early spring. Purplish red foliage all season. Grown in pots. To 2m (6ft).

L. chinense f rubrum 'Zhuzhu' bears purple foliage.

L. chinense 'Pizzazz' bears burgundy foliage maturing to bronze-green on a spreading evergreen shrub. Z.8-9.

LOTUS

Unusual species with silvery foliage and claw like flowers. 0°C (32°F).
L. jacobaeus is a lax evergreen perennial with brownish or black flowers, a native of the Cape Verde Islands, flowering mainly in summer. Dry, sunny position.
The flowers of **L. berthelottii** are orange-red to scarlet with a blackish centre, contrasting with the grey-silver foliage.

LYCHNIS

Dark bronze foliage and red hot orange flowers which simply glow are two reasons for including this unfussy Lychnis in your garden.

Worthy of the dark border is **L. x arkwrightii 'Vesuvius'**. A short-lived perennial with very dark, brownish to dark purple foliage and knock-out orange-scarlet flowers in early to midsummer. Another hot combination for the dark garden. Hardy. 45cm (18").

Lychnis x arkwrightii 'Vesuvius'

LYSIMACHIA

Offering two forms one with dark foliage and the other with dark flowers which are excellent for the border, enjoying good leafy moist soil in partial shade.

L. atropurpurea available from seed has dark spikes of very dark burgundy flowers from spring through to summer set off by fleshy glaucous green leaves. Makes a good accent amongst paler flowers. 'Beaujolais' is a selected seed form.
L. ciliata 'Firecracker' is a real cracker with its handsome purple - brown foliage and yellow flowers in midsummer. Propagate by division in autumn or winter. Enhanced by pale contrast. Hardy to -40°C (-40°F). Z 3-10.

Lysimachia ciliata 'Firecracker'

MALUS

Malus are valued for their foliage, blossom and fruit. Dark foliage is highly prized.

HOW TO GROW

Moderately fertile, moist but well-drained soil in full sun for purple-leaved forms. Hardy.
Sow seed in autumn. Bud in late summer or graft in midwinter.

M. x purpurea is an erect, open tree with usually broadly ovate, dark green leaves. The young wood and spring foliage are both purplish red. In mid-spring purplish-red flowers open from ruby red buds and are followed by dark red fruit.
Many cultivars, offer similar colour such as M. **'Aldenhamensis'**, M. **'Eleyi'** and M. **'Lemoinei'**. 4-7m (12-22ft).
M. x moerlandsii 'Profusion' has bronze-purple leaves, purple-red when young, dark reddish flowers and dark purple fruits.
M. 'Red Barron' is a broadly upright tree with ovate bronze-green leaves, purple when young. A good contrast to the dark pink flowers opening from dark buds in late spring, followed by glossy, dark red fruit. 6m (20ft).
M. 'Royalty' is a spreading tree with ovate dark red-purple foliage which retains its colour well, finally turning red in autumn. Crimson-purple flowers are borne in mid to late spring, followed by dark red fruit. 8m (25ft).

MARANTA

Cultivated for their mesmerisingly handsome leaves with black markings, Maranta are from rainforests in tropical America. Grow indoors in frost-prone areas.

HOW TO GROW

Under glass, grow in loam-based or loamless compost in bright filtered or bright indirect light. Their shallow root systems make them ideal subjects for half pots. Require high humidity. When in growth, water moderately and apply a balanced feed monthly. Water sparingly in winter. Outdoors, grow in humus-rich, moist but well drained soil in deep or partial shade. Tender.

Sow seed when fresh. Divide in spring. Take basal cuttings 7-10cm (3-4") long and root with bottom heat in spring.

M. leuconeura v erythroneura known as the Herringbone plant bears velvety olive and black-green leaves with interesting red midribs and veins. To add to the effect there are jagged light yellow-green markings around the midribs and the undersides are deep red. 30cm (12"). 15°C (59°F).

M. leuconeura v kerchoveana is more common having black or dark brown squarish markings on the leaves which have led to the common name of rabbits' tracks. Very effective.

M. leuconeura v massangeana has blackish-green foliage with silver-grey feathering along the midribs and veins and purple undersides.

Maranta leuconeura v massangeana

MUSA

Superb exotic tropicals with large paddle shaped leaves.

M. samatrana (zebrina) has 120cm (4ft) long leaves with a wide black stain on the upper and solid wine underneath, complimented by dark red trunks.

M. 'Royal Ruby' is a stunning ornamental banana with a dark ruby red inflorescence and green foliage 240cm (8ft) long. Cut flowers are very long lasting.

MUSCARI

Discard the usual blue, invasive Muscari, for the darker, choice varieties which are less aggressive.

M. commutatum is distinguished by its small, blackish flowers with black teeth in March to May. Easy in well-drained soil in sun.

M. grandifolium comes from Morocco and needs protection to prevent flowers from spoiling. Flowers are large and blue-back from china-blue buds. Hardy.

M. latifolium from Turkey is an easy plant in the U.K. with racemes of deepest violet-black flowers from pale-blue buds. Single leaf. Z4.

M. neglectum has blackish flowers with white teeth. Variable in size. Easy in well drained soil and increases well.

NEMOPHILA

An easy to grow annual with delightful near black flowers.

HOW TO GROW

Fertile, moist but well-drained soil in full sun or partial shade. Water well to maintain flowering in hot weather. Hardy.

Sow seed outdoors in early spring or autumn where they are to flower. Self-seeds freely. Sold under various names in seed catalogues.

N. 'Pennie Black' is a little gem and useful for filling in gaps. The trick with this is to keep it moist or it will stop flowering. Flowers are small but prolific, of a very dark purple, near black with a white edge. A little gem, performing well in containers or as a front of border plant, most welcome to fill any gaps. Bears pinnate green leaves and produces saucer-shaped flowers of a very dark purple, near black. A superb choice for the black and white garden and an ideal and easy filler. 15-30cm (6-12").

Nemophila 'Pennie Black'

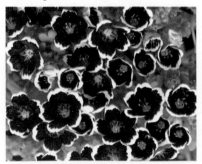

NYMPHAEA

Water lilies are a decorative addition to any pool. Shade from their leaves reduces algae. Flowers are unbelievably elegant and beautiful floating on water. A sea of floating dark lily pads or dark flowered lilies enhance any pond.

HOW TO GROW

Grow in undisturbed water in full sun. Plant in firm, loamy soil inserting the rhizomes just under the surface and covering with washed pea gravel. Submerge. Hardy or frost tender.

Surface sow fresh seed and cover with 2.5cm (1") of water, hardy species need a germinating temperature of 10-13°C. The seed heads of water lilies sink as the seed ripens. Divide rhizomes or separate offsets.

N. 'Almost Black' is excellent, outer petals are very dark turning black toward the centre. Flower size is 15cm (6") across. Excellent bloomer for medium to large pools. Leaves are reddish. Hardy.

N. 'Atropurpurea' has semi-double, flat dark red flowers, the young foliage is purple turning to dark green.

N. 'Black Princess' is a deep red, blackish towards the centre on large flowers, 12cm (5") across. Hardy.

N. 'Burgundy Princess' bears smallish deep burgundy flowers which are good for a container water garden.

N. 'Perry's Black Opal' is an intensely deep red, overlaid with a sheen of black on spidery blooms which darken with age. An exotic hardy which will thrive in any size pond.

N. 'Perry's Darkest Red' is a very similar colouring to 'Black Princess'.

N. 'William Falconer' the darkest red before the arrival of the new lilies bred in America. Large deep green leaves splashed with brown.

A number of *Nymphaea* also bear foliage which is red, bronzed or purple, often only when young, or marked or flecked red, these include **N. 'Caroliniana'**, the deep dark leaves of **N. 'James Brydon'** which bears lovely pink flowers, **N. 'Laydeckeri Fulgens'**, **N. 'Laydeckeri Liliacea'**, **N. 'Laydeckeri Purpurata'**, **N. 'Madame Maurice Laydecker'**, **N. 'Perry's Red Star'**, **N. 'Pygmaea Rubis'**, **N. 'Sirius'**, **N. 'Pearl of the Pool'** whose leaves are bronze when young and **N. 'Lucida'** is one of the best having leaves heavily marked with purple. There is also an unnamed black flower.

Nymphaea 'James Brydon'

OPHIOPOGON

This plant, the so-called Black Grass, or mondo grass, even though it is not a grass, is the one that started off my interest in black plants many years ago. Resist the dark temptation if you can.

HOW TO GROW

Grow in moist but well-drained slightly acid, fertile, humus-rich soil in full sun. Give a dressing of leaf mould every autumn. Hardy, -12°C (10°F) Z 6-10. Survives winters in Ohio given protection from winter sun and overwinters through freezing temperatures in my Sheffield garden in the U.K. without protection.

Can be sown from seed, but only expect a percentage to come true and watch for green at the bases which really spoils the effect. Sow fresh seed in a cold frame. Divide in spring as growth resumes.

O. planiscapus 'Nigrescens' goes under many synonyms, you may find it listed as 'Arabicus', 'Black Knight' or 'Black Dragon' or 'Ebony Knight'. The blackest leaves of any plant are alluring with a clump-forming habit, slowly spreading by rhizomes. Its arching, strap-shaped, spidery leaves make a year round feature. In summer, it bears short sprays of tiny mauvish bells, and the shiny black berries last well into winter. 20cm (8").

So versatile and suitable for so many garden situations. The Japanese use variegated forms as a grass substitute. Excellent as an edging plant or could be used to good effect in a rock garden as well as being superb in containers. Associates well with pink flowers or silvery foliage and looks magnificent with a paler contrast scattered around and through its leaves, like the Sedum shown here. Truly remarkable for its colour which is the nearest to black you will see, often silvery in full sun. Truly versatile and yes, those leaves are black! My number one black plant. If you are only growing one black foliage plant, then this is the one to choose. Keeping its good looks all year round, with attractive foliage, tiny lilac bells, interesting leaf shape and persistent berries, Ophiopogon is not only trouble free but easy.

OXALIS

Some dark-leaved *Oxalis* are very well-worth growing.

HOW TO GROW

Plant the tiny rhizomes just below the surface of the soil. Requires well-drained, fertile, humus-rich soil. Water moderately in growth and apply a balanced feed every month. Keep barely moist in winter when dormant. Fully hardy to frost tender.

Divide in spring. Small sections of rhizome root readily.

O. **hedysaroides** '**Rubra**' is a seldom seen native of S. America which requires humid conditions and bright light to display its spectacular deep maroon red leaves and brilliant yellow tiny blossoms. Can reach 60cm (2ft) but is far better pruned and bushy.

Oxalis vulcanicola 'Copper Tones'

O. **oregana** has mid green foliage, tinged purple underneath, particularly in cool weather, with pink flowers. Seed pods suggest that this may be promiscuous.

O. **triangularis 'Cupido'** has very dark purple leaves and soft pink flowers. O. **triangularis 'Myka'** is a hardy perennial with lilac flowers above rich, bronzy-purple foliage.

O. **triangualris ssp papilionacea 'Atropurpurea'** has dark purple leaves with an attractive lighter purple-maroon splash and flowers of rose-pink. Rather muddled in commerce over time. The plant I grow under this name has a soft lilac flower with fascinating leaves, deep purple, like butterflies when folded (papilionacea). In a pot outdoors, this looks truly magnificent all summer. As the weather turns cooler, I put it into the cold frame, keeping it on the dry side and it comes back year after year. Prone to rust. *O. rubra* is similar.

O. **vulcanicola** (siliquosa), the Red Velvet Oxalis, has red succulent stems, with copper maroon leaves and almost continual yellow flowers. Z9-11. 15-25cm (6-10").

O. **vulcanicola 'Copper Tones'** (siliquosa) was a great success for me producing fabulous small purple leaves all summer, turning coppery in autumn to contrast with the butter yellow flowers. Survived some frost in my garden and still looking good in November. Z9-11. 15-25cm (6-10"). Note: *O. triangularis* is known as *O. regnelii* in the U.S.

PAEONIA

Large, showy flowers of an impeccable beauty and rich foliage tints in spring are features of these fabulous plants. Like most extraordinarily beautiful flowers, blooms are fairly fleeting.

HOW TO GROW

Grow in deep, fertile, moist but well-drained, humus-rich soil in full sun or partial shade. Shelter from wind. Fully to frost hardy.

Sow species seed in containers outdoors in autumn or early winter. Divide herbaceous peonies in autumn or early spring. Take root cuttings in winter. Take semi-ripe cuttings of *Paeonia* in summer or graft in winter.

P. **'Beauty of Livermere'** is a large single blood-red flower with a black centre.

P. **'Belle Center'** (Mains 1956) bears shallow cup-shaped semi-double flowers of a mahogany-red

Paeonia 'Black Pirate'

with yellow stamens. 75cm (30").

P. **'Bifuku-mon'** is a Japanese tree peony with beetroot red flowers and black flares.

P. **'Black Monarch'** (Glasscock 1939) is a double hybrid with dark red flowers, appearing bright in sun. 78cm (31").

P. **'Black Panther'** (Saunders 1948) bears deep mahogany-red, semi-double flowers against yellow stamens. 1m (3ft).

P. **'Black Pirate'** (Saunders 1935) is a hybrid tree-peony, having dramatic deep mahogany-red flowers, very dark towards the centre, with black flares. Semi-double flowers open at an angle resembling small trumpets. Finely cut foliage is admirable on this vigorous, compact plant. 1m (3ft).

P. **'Buckeye Belle'** (Mains 1956) bears darkest red, crinkled semi-double flowers. Early and free flowering. 85cm (34").

P. **'Chinese Dragon'** (Saunders 1950) semi-double, purplish red flowers with black flares. The iridescent petals appear blue as they reflect the light. 1m (3ft).

P. **'Chocolate Soldier'** (Auten 1939) is an herbaceous perennial with deep green leaves, flushed bronze when young. Bears large, satiny, deeply cupped, deep purple-red to chocolate flowers. Registered as a Japanese hybrid, it can produce single or double flowers. Very early. 1m (3ft).

P. **'Dauntless'** (Glasscock 1944) is a good substitute for the above, slighter redder, but does produce many flowers. 90cm (36").

The species, **P. delavayi** is also quite dark, often raised from seed, the flowers are small 8cm (3") across and vary in colour from blood red to deep maroon and almost chocolate brown. Deeply dissected leaves are red-tinted. A large shrub up to 150cm (5ft). Z6.

P. 'Guan Shi Mo Yu' is a black-purple with a sheen, bearing large upright flowers with large leaves tinged purple. Described to me by Shuo Wang as the best 'black' one.

P. 'He Hai Jin Long' bears single dark flowers.

P. 'Hei Sa Jin' is mulberry with a sheen, lotus shape flowers.

P. 'Hui Hua Kui' (Black Flower Chief) bears deep red blooms, darkening to almost black in the centre against yellow stamens with purplish leaves and stalks. Slow growing but free flowering.

P. 'Hei Xiu Qiu' bears near black flowers.

P. 'Illini Warrior' (Glasscock-Falk 1955) is a superb dark red having a slight fragrance and good vigour. 1m (3ft).

P. 'Iphigenia' has large single flowers shaded black. Outer petals have a white line on the reverse. 93cm (37").

Paeonia 'Guan Shi Mo Yu'

P. 'Kenrei-mon' is a tree peony with semi-double, purple-red flowers and black flares, let down by the foliage.

P. 'Kokko Tsukasa' bears cupped flowers, an inviting combination of deep red, shaded black against prominent yellow stamens.

P. 'Kronos' bears single or semi-double burgundy flowers with near black flares. 96cm (3ft).

P. 'Mai Fleri' has dark, bronzy foliage.

P. 'Mo Yu Shuang Hui' is a very deep purple-black, anemone double-flowered with fragrant blooms to 10cm (4") across.

P. 'Mo Zi Rong Zing' bears black-purple flowers.

P. 'Qing Long Wo Mo Chi' (Hyacinthine Dragon Lying in Ink Pool) bears long pointed greenish-yellow buds opening to black-purple flowers up to 25cm (10") across with conspicuous green pistils. Leaves are yellowish green. Occasionally produces greenish petals in the centre. 3m (10ft).

P. 'Santorb' (Kelway 1925) is a

Paeonia 'Kokko Tsukasa'

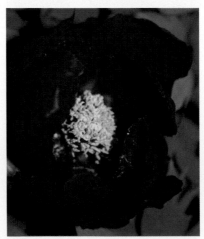

jewel among reds, an intensely rich, dark crimson maroon. It has good stiff stems and is sweetly scented. Late flowering, into July. 66cm (26").

P. suffruticosa 'Hana-daijin' is a double-flowered peony of the darkest red with black undertones.

P. suffruticosa 'Kokuryu-nishiki' ('Black Dragon Brocade') has very dark red, crinkled double flowers with blackish undertones.

P. suffruticosa 'Rimpo' ('Bird of Rimpo') has maroon-red semi-double flowers and is fragrant.

P. 'Thunderbolt' (1948) bears crimson-red flowers often streaked black with yellow stamens. Finely dissected foliage. 1m (3ft).

P. 'Wilbur Wright' (Kelway 1909) is a very dark single with crimson-maroon flowers. 1m (3ft).

P. 'Wu Jin Yao Hui' is a virtually black semi-double with glossy flowers.

P. 'Yan Long Zi Zhu Pan' bears black-purple flowers. Erect and free-flowering.

P. 'Zhong Sheng He' is a traditional black flower.

Try the bronze foliage of **P. 'Yachiyo-tsubaki' or 'Hei Hai Bo Tao'**.

Paeonia 'Hei Hua Kui'

PAPAVER

Sumptuous silky petals on large cupped flowers dressed in black. Superb decorative seedheads. Easy.

HOW TO GROW

Grow in deep, fertile, well-drained soil in full sun. Hardy.

Sow seed *in situ*. Divide perennials in spring or take root cuttings in late autumn or winter.

P. orientale 'Black and White' is a perennial with mid-green leaves to 30cm (12") long with lance-shaped toothed segments. Produces white flowers with a large crimson-black mark at the base of each petal. Z3.

P. orientale 'Choir Boy' and **P. orientale 'Snow Goose'** look very similar. 1m (3ft).

P. somniferum 'Black Beauty' is a double peony-flowered poppy of a silken dark maroon-purple. Stunning and delightful.

P. 'Nubian Prince' is an enchanting fringed variety.

Papaver somniferum 'Black Beauty'

PELARGONIUM

Wonderful plants with most dark flowers found in the Regal Pelargonium types and dark foliage from zonals.

HOW TO GROW

Under glass, grow in loam-based or loamless compost in full light with shade from hot sun and good ventilation. Water moderately during growth, applying a balanced feed every 10-14 days in spring and early summer, followed by a high-potash fertiliser when in flower. Water sparingly in winter. Plants kept at a temperature above 7°C (45°F) will most likely continue to flower through winter. Can be cut back up to two thirds and kept almost dry and frost free.

Outdoors, grow in fertile, neutral to alkaline, well-drained soil. Regal cultivars prefer partial shade and zonals prefer sun, though they are tolerant of a little shade. Re-pot overwintered plants in late winter as new growth resumes. Dead-head regularly. Z10.

Sow seed under glass in late winter and early spring. Take softwood cuttings in spring or late summer and early autumn.

REGAL PELARGONIUM

Wonderful houseplants bloom in late March for around a month in a cool room, and can then be deadheaded and put outside to bloom again throughout summer. Will last for several years if kept frost free. Z 10.

P. 'Aldwyck' bears good dark markings on red flowers.

P. 'Ann Hoystead' (D. Saddington) is vigorous with dark red flowers, and upper petals almost black.

P. 'Australian Bute' is nowhere near as attractive as 'Lord Bute', petals of burgundy-purple tone, of a not too attractive form.

P. 'Babylon' (J. Ritchie) bears black-red petals with a white throat and an orange ring. Unusual.

P. 'Black Gold' (G. Morf) has large flowers, almost jet black.

P. 'Black Knight' a decorative pelargonium with small purple-black petals, edged in lavender.

P. 'Black Magic' has the darkest mahogany-black flowers.

P. 'Black Prince' has purple-black blooms which shade into the throat, with white edging, a miniature regal.

P. 'Black Top' has upper black petals with a red sheen.

P. 'Black Velvet' is an old variety, with very dark velvet black, glossy flowers, having a light purple edge around the petals. A strong grower. 45cm (18") height and spread, flowers 6cm (2"+) across in summer. 0°C (32°F).

P. 'Black Wings' (J. Ritchie) is a black flowered butterfly type.

P. 'Bronze Velvet' with bronze flowers and darker blotches.

P. 'Brown's Butterfly' ('Black Butterfly') (Brown 1953) bears black, ruffled flowers flecked with mahogany. A favourite, very dark.

P. 'Burgundy' is a good dark red with a black throat.

P. 'Carrum Purple' (J. Ritchie) is a deep purple-black.

P. 'Dandy' (J. Ritchie) this small flowered variety is perfect for the black and white theme.

P. 'Dark Mabel' ('Dark Presidio') has rose-pink flowers with purple-black on the upper petals, a lovely bi-tone with a splash of dark.

P. 'Dark Secret' has flowers a deep mahogany feathered burgundy.

P. 'Dark Shadow' is a dark red-black with a large black blotch on petals. A compact plant.

P. 'Dark Venus' is dark mahogany, almost black. Free flowering.

P. 'Dee Jay Picotee' (J. Ritchie) bears purple-black flowers with pale edges.

P. 'Dollar Bute' is extremely dark, with flared petals tipped rose.

P. 'Ebony' (J. Ritchie) is a black flowered variety.

P. 'Eureka' bears dark purple,

Pelargonium 'Australian Bute

Pelargonium 'Dollar Bute'

140

Pelargonium 'Tomcat'

Pelargonium 'Lord Bute'

Pelargonium 'Brown's Butterfly'

Pelargonium 'Springfield Black'

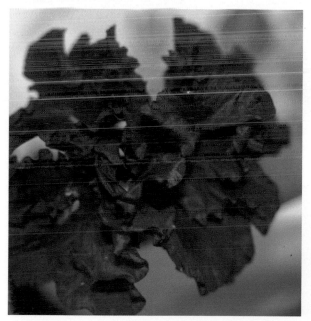

almost black flowers.

P. **'Fifth Avenue'** bears dark flowers.

P. **'Gordano Midnight'** is intriguing with its dark, mahogany, almost black flowers on a short, bushy plant.

P. **'Harewood Slam'** makes a bushy plant with darkest red flowers blushed black. Good specimen.

P. **'Imperial'** for the black and white garden, sumptuous dark purple blooms are edged in white.

P. **'Jedda'** has very dark purple, amost black flowers.

P. **'Jungle Night'** is a wine purple, with much black marking.

P. **'Lady Madonna'** (E. M. Middleton) has flat red-black flowers, a seedling of 'Morwenna'.

P. **'Lara Rajah'** (C. Blackman) bears deep red pansy-shaped flowers with black-red upper petals.

P. **'Lord Bute'** is a purple-black, edged wine and long considered one of the darkest. An excellent plant for bedding, capable of good dimensions and wonderful as a specimen. Excellent colour, flower form and growth keeps this one in the top ten.

Pelargonium 'Rimfire'

P. **'Marchioness of Bute'** is almost black, edged purple. Petals are well-crimped, looks like a double.

P. **'Minstrel Boy'** is a good dark, floriferous form.

P. **'Morwenna'** is a dark purple-maroon, shading to black.

P. **'Pompeii'** is nearly black, narrowly edged pink-white. A distinctive, short, bushy plant.

P. **'Princess Josephine'** bears flowers of pinkish-purple with a black blaze and feathering.

P. **'Regalia Chocolate'** is a dark mahogany with darker blotches on good-sized blooms.

P. **'Rimfire'** is a very dark near black, with a rim of fire-red, ready to burst into flame. Attractive.

P. **'Rogue'** with huge mahogany-crimson flowers shaded black.

P. **'Rosalie'** is dark with good shading, an excellent performer which is easy to bloom.

P. **'Royal Guernsey'** is a new cultivar with deepest red blooms shading to black with just the hint of a white throat.

P. **'Springfield Black'** is a very deep darkest red-black with large blooms, the darkest regal I have grown. Robust and floriferous.

P. **'Thundercloud'** is a very deep purple-black.

P. **'Zorro'** (G. Morf) is a bushy plant with maroon-black flowers.

Pelargonium 'Royal Guernsey'

SCENTED PELARGONIUM

Useful in the dark garden for the markings on the leaves, these smell good as well as look good.

P. **'Chocolate Peppermint'** is a large plant with softly hairy leaves having a dark patch in the centre and veins, up to 15cm across. Peppermint and spice scent. Small pink flowers.

P. **'Royal Oak'** has central brown zones on its spicily fragrant bold oak shaped leaves. Small pink flowers have dark blotches.

P. **quercifolium** bears a similar dark patch on oak-shaped leaves.

UNIQUE PELARGONIUM

P. **'Voodoo'** has light wine-red flowers, blazed purple-black on each petal. Tall and striking with triangular-shaped leaves.

ZONAL PELARGONIUM

Several zonal-leaved pelargonium display a black zone on their leaves, enhanced by the other leaf colours.

P. **'Abba'** (B. Monahan) bears black-dark maroon flowers on a compact, low-growing plant.

P. 'Chocolate Peppermint'

P. 'Alcyone' is an easy miniature with a very deep red flower and blackish green leaves.

P. 'Aldehan' (1953) is a dwarf with small black leaves and single bright salmon-pink flowers.

P. 'Bewerley Park' is a black zoned leaf with biscuit-pink flowers.

P. 'Bird Dancer' is a dwarf, salmon-pink single flowered zonal with dark green maple-shaped leaves dramatically zoned black.

P. 'Black Knight' is a single-flowered miniature zonal pelargonium with salmon flowers.

P. 'Black Pearl' bears flowers with a black blaze overlaid with cerise-red.

P. 'Caligula' is a miniature, double scarlet flowered form with very dark green, almost black leaves. Best indoors.

P. 'Currant Red' (L. R. Bodey) bears currant red flowers aglow over a near black leaf.

P. 'Etna' is a miniature zonal with scarlet flowers and perfectly contrasting black leaves.

P. 'Friesdorf' is a dwarf, fancy-leaved with rounded, almost black leaves and narrow-petalled, single crimson flowers.

P. 'Goblin' is a double red flowered miniature with blackish green leaves.

P. 'Grandad Mac' bears brown foliage and orange flowers.

P. 'Grenadier' is a dwarf with dark green, almost black foliage and single, bright crimson flowers.

P. 'Imp' is a slow-growing variety with almost black flowers and single salmon flowers.

P. 'Madame Fournier' is a delightful miniature, bearing scarlet single-flowers with purple-black leaves and stems.

P. 'Marmalade' bears double soft orange flowers, with black-green foliage. Free-flowering.

P. 'Meadowside Midnight' has dark leaves which contrast well with the bright flowers.

P. 'Mephistopheles' is almost identical to 'Red Black Vesuvius'.

P. 'Osna' bears very dark leaves and scarlet flowers.

P. 'Peace' is a miniature with almost black foliage accompanied by large single salmon-pink flowers.

P. 'Pink Black Beauty' (M. Bird) bears a dark green leaf with black markings, topped by pink flowers.

P. 'Red Black Vesuvius' ('Black Vesuvius') is a scarlet flowered miniature zonal with black leaves. Superb. 'Crimson Black Vesuvius', 'Pink Black Vesuvius' and 'Salmon Black Vesuvius' are also worthy.

P. 'Red Brooks Barnes' is a U.S version of 'Red Black Vesuvius' but faster growing and more vigorous.

P. 'Royal Norfolk' is a double reddish-purple flowered miniature with blackish green leaves.

P. 'Salmon Splendour' is a miniature with almost black foliage and single flowers of azalea pink.

P. 'Stellar Ragtime' has a large blackish blotch on the dark green leaf and double stellar flowers.

P. 'Timothy Clifford' is a zonal miniature with dark green leaves appearing black. Lovely double, salmon-pink flowers.

P. 'Turkish Delight' has a deep bronze and green leaf.

P. 'Vancouver Centennial' (Ian Gillam 1986) is leafy with a good brown patch covering all but the golden green edge. This fades out in poor light. Small, single scarlet-orange flowers.

The seed-raised 'Black Magic' series would be wonderful if it came true from seed. The plants I saw at the breeders were superbly dark, but what I grew from seed is a very poor imitation.

IVY-LEAVED PELARGONIUM

P. 'April Hamilton' (G. Baker) is very dark with its near black velvet flowers with red overtones.

P. 'Barbe Bleu' bears deep blackish purple double flowers with bluish-green leaves and short, bushy growth.

Pelargonium 'Meadowside Midnight' (left)
P. 'Black Magic' (below)

P. 'Rigoletto' is black in bud opening to beetroot red with white centres.

P. 'Rio Grande' has almost black flowers with a white reverse.

P. 'Tomcat' is the darkest of the ivy-leaved with its near black, maroon overlay on rosebud type petals. Wonderful.

SPECIES PELARGONIUM

P. ardens has a head of small, richly coloured scarlet flowers with black markings and much divided leaves. Spoiled by overlong stems.

P. x glaucifolium has bi-coloured flowers of near black edged in bright yellow. Sweetly scented and superb. **P. lobatum** and **P. bicolor** are very similar.

P. x lawrencianum has lobed leaves and velvet dark maroon and paler margined petals.

P. sidoides has fantastic black but very tiny flowers with silvery-leaves. A South African native with tuberous roots, easy to grow if kept on the dry side. 10°C (50°F).

P. tricolor is a native of South Africa with striking flowers, it is a variable species but can occur with

Pelargonium ardens

the upper petals blackish maroon and the lower superbly contrasting in white. Flowers open in the sun from September to December. Greyish-green leaves are long stalked and toothed. Easy in sandy, peaty soil on the dry side. There is a hybrid **'Splendide'** which is sometimes sold as this species, but the colouring is much lighter. Hardy to -3°C.

P. triste has small, dark brownish-purple and greenish white flowers in umbels of 6-20. Leaves are mostly basal and carrot-like, tuberous roots spread to form new plants. Exudes a wonderful evening scent. This native of South Africa is easy in sandy soil, kept dry in summer and moist in winter and spring. John Tradescant grew this in England in 1632.

PENSTEMON

Offering some dark-leaved forms and flowers, *Penstemon* should find a place in the border.

HOW TO GROW

Border perennials need to be grown in fertile, well-drained soil in full sun or partial shade. In areas prone to frosts, protect with a good dry mulch, plants detest cold, wet feet. Dead-head to maintain vigour. Hardiness varies.

Sow seed in late winter or spring. Take softwood cuttings in early summer or semi-ripe in midsummer. Divide in spring.

P. digitalis 'Husker Red' has beetroot-coloured stems and foliage in spring, fading to green, tinged purple forming the perfect background to the swaying clusters of green buds which open to palest pastel pink or white tubular flowers in early to midsummer. Does not flower well in some areas. 90cm (3ft). Z3.

P. hirsutus normally has green leaves but there is a bronze form to look out for. Fully hardy spreading subshrub.

P. 'Merlin' (Beeches Nursery 1995) is similar to 'The Raven' in flower, slightly lighter, low growing, with glossier leaves. 55cm (22"). Z7.

P. 'Midnight' is possibly the same as 'Russian River', there seems to be no difference, although this is the earlier name. Z7.

P. 'Russian River' is one of the darkest European hybrids. Graceful, dusky purple bells with a white throat are closely set on upright stems with dark green foliage. 70cm (24"). Z7.

P. 'The Raven' (Sidwell 1970) Duskiest purple, beautifully marked large flowers with a blackish purple tube, lips slightly lighter and a white throat. Z7.

P. whippleanus has deep mauve-purple, almost black flowers.

PERILLA

Cultivated in Japan as a salad crop and herb and used for its decorative purple-leaved foliage.

HOW TO GROW

Grow in fertile, moist but well-drained soil in full sun or partial shade. Remove insignificant flowers to prevent self-seeding. Can be planted out early in the season, withstanding light frosts. Sow seed in spring.

P. frutescens v purpurascens is an attractive foliage plant bearing dark purple-bronze leaves. Deserving of wider and more imaginative planting than the usual council bedding plot. 45cm (18").

PERSICARIA

P. microcephala 'Red Dragon' makes a good container plant. Three greys might sound like a dull combination of colours, not so with this plant. It bears a bright, red vein on metallic, pewter foliage, impeccably coloured and marked. Shear over in late summer. 60cm (2ft).

PHILODENDRON

Members of the aroid family grown for their handsome leaves. Found in tropical forests with little direct light. Juvenile and mature foliage often differ. Spathes are seldom seen in cultivation.

HOW TO GROW

65°C day temperature and 60°C night temperature, plenty of humidity and indirect light. Z10.

P. 'Black Cardinal' bears large 20-25cm (8-10") long leaves, emerging bright burgundy to red-black.

P. 'Burgundy' has dark green-red new growth and deep red undersides to the 20cm (8-12") long leaves.

P. erubescens has a red edge to the leaf which bears a purple sheen and purple stalks.

P. 'King of Spades' bears heart-shaped dark leaves with black stems.

P. melanochryson bears sensational large, velvety, heart-shaped leaves with a touch of black shading, growing to 90cm (3ft) long when mature. Incredibly handsome. Go for it.

P. melanochrysum 'Black Gold' is a climbing epiphytic vine with velvety heart-shaped leaves of deep purple, with light green veins. Easy to grow, yet stunning.

P. 'Royal Queen' bears wide, rich maroon leaves on a vining plant which maintains its colour well in low light.

P. scandens has bronzed leaves at first, turning green.

From left to right
Perilla, Persicaria, Philodendron

PHORMIUM

Ideal for coastal gardens. The upright accent of the leaves is irresistible anywhere. Superb foliage plants with stems of wondrous seed heads like beaks, making excellent focal points.

HOW TO GROW

Grow in fertile, moist, but well-drained soil in full sun. Protect in frost-prone areas with a deep dry mulch before the first frosts and by wrapping plants. Frost to half hardy, may tolerate temperatures as low as -12°C (10°F). Older plants are hardier, *P. tenax* being the hardiest species. Z 8-10.

Sow species seed in spring. Expect variable purple seedlings from *P. tenax Purpureum Group*. Divide cultivars in spring.

P. 'Amazing Red' bears deep reddish-bronze leaves.

P. tenax 'Bronze Baby' produces tufts of bold, stiff bronze-red leaves, pendent at the tips. 45-60cm (18-24").

P. 'Chocolate' has red undertones on chocolate brown leaves. Quite vigorous, grows to 1.2m.

P. 'Dark Delight' (M. Jones) bears bold, graceful foliage the colour of plain dark chocolate. One of the darkest. Slow to divide. Very hardy. 1-1.2m (3-4ft).

P. 'Dark Moon' has dark reddish-purple upright foliage. 90-120cm (3-4ft).

P. 'Dazzler' has arching bronze-red leaves, striped mahogany, orange and pink. The overall effect on this smallish plant is reddish. 1m (3ft).

P. 'Dusky Challenger' has dark brownish leaves, similar to 'Dark Delight'.

P. 'Dusky Chief' has narrow, dark purplish brown foliage with dark red margins.

P. 'Evening Glow' is an admirable dark with stiffish foliage.

P. 'Firebird' is a new variety from Margaret Jones of New Zealand producing gorgeous deep red leaves with bright red edges. Upright habit and as hardy as they come.

P. 'Fountains' has pewter-grey evergreen foliage, bearing black and gold flowers in June-July. Sounds wonderful. 1m (3ft).

P. 'Jack Spratt' is a dwarf species making a dense, compact clump of relatively grass-like, very dark, bronze-brown foliage. Fast growing. 45cm (18").

P. 'Platt's Black' (G. Platt) the real thing is one of the darkest with near black, narrow foliage of compact habit, slow growing. In a class of its own. Raised by G. Platt from seed collected from P. 'Black Knight' in Auckland.

P. 'Purple Giant' reaches vast proportions in its native New Zealand, less in the U.K.

P. tenax 'Coffee' is an interesting colour quite aptly named, the foliage less upright than many.

P. tenax 'Nanum Purpureum' this dwarf form has brownish-purple leaves. 40cm. (14").

P. tenax Purpureum Group has rich mahogany-purple to dark copper leaves and prefers an open site. 1m (3ft), but is capable of reaching a gigantic 2.5m (8ft).

P. tenax 'Stormy Dawn' has dark maroon-black leaves. 1m (3ft).

P. 'Shirazz' has deep maroon foliage on the reddish side. 60-90cm (2-3ft).

P. 'Thumbelina' (R. Burton) has bronze red leaves and a dwarf habit. Prefers good soil. 60x60cm (2ft). Hardy.

P. 'Wildwood' has long, dark purple, luxurious foliage. 120-180cm (4-6ft).

From left to right: Phormium 'Evening Glow', 'Platt's Black' and 'Amazing Red '

PHYLLOSTACHYS

Dramatic black canes on this slow-growing bamboo which makes a good container subject.

HOW TO GROW
Grow in fertile, humus-rich, moist soil, well-drained in full sun. In frost prone areas, protect from strong, cold winds. Protect emerging shoots from slugs. Divide in spring.

P. nigra, black bamboo is a clump-forming species with arching, slender canes which turn from green to a spectacular, lustrous black in their second or third year. Abundant lance-shaped, mid-green leaves 4-13cm (1.5-5") long. Reaches a height of 3-5m (10-15ft).
P. violascens is a spreading bamboo with swollen green canes, at first finely striped purple, becoming violet. Bears narrowly, lance-shaped, glossy green foliage to 12cm (5") long, glaucous on the undersides. 5m (16ft).

PHYSOCARPUS

An unusual recent introduction with dark attractive foliage on this deciduous shrub.

HOW TO GROW
Prefers acid soil. Moist but well-drained in full sun or partial shade. May become chloritic if grown in shallow chalk soil.
Take greenwood cuttings in summer. Remove rooted suckers in spring or autumn.

P. opulifolius 'Diablo' has spiny purple to very dark red-black leaves which are useful for flower arranging. White flowers are produced in summer followed by bladder-like fruit. I rate this very highly as a superb shrub, best planted in an open, sunny position. Good specimen in its own right, or equally good with gold or silver foliage. 1-2m (3-6ft).

PILEA

Native of Costa Rica, attractive for its green leaves with incredible texture, puckered with black-brown veins, the whole blushed this colour. Min 0°C.
P. repens bears tiny, coppery black leaves on a creeping plant.
P. spruceana has pointed, serrated chocolate leaves with pewter bands, a self-branching, compact plant suitable for a terrarium.

Phyllostachys 'Nigra' (far left)
Physocarpus opulifolius 'Diablo' (below)

PITTOSPORUM

Glossy, leathery leaves in very good colour tones. Many bear red-brown flowers with a wonderful honey scent. Excellent specimen plants in warmer areas and coastal regions.

HOW TO GROW
Under glass, grow in loam-based potting compost in full light. In growth, water moderately, applying a balanced fertiliser monthly. Water sparingly in winter. Outdoors, grow in fertile, moist but well-drained soil in full sun. Shelter from wind. Trim hedges in spring. Frost hardy to frost tender. May survive temperatures below 0°C (32°F) for short spells, provided wood has been well ripened in summer. Z 9-10.

Seed is best sown fresh or in spring in a cold frame. Take semi-ripe cuttings in summer, layer or air layer in spring.

P. tenuifolium 'Atropurpureum' bears glossy purple foliage and small honey-scented flowers.
P. tenuifolium 'James Stirling' has blackish-purple branchlets.
P. tenuifolium 'Nigricans' produces black twigs and deep bronze-purple mature leaves. Excellent for cut foliage.
P. tenuifolium 'Nutty's Leprechaun' is about half the size of 'Tom Thumb'. A superb compact plant for a small space. 30cm (1ft).
P. tenuifolium 'Purpureum' has purple mature foliage, being similar to *P. tenuifolium* 'Nigricans', but more open in habit. 3m (10ft).

P. tenuifolium 'Tom Thumb' forms a low bush with wonderful bronze-purple glossy foliage as it matures, new growth is light green, quickly turning burnished dark purple-black. Foliage is shimmer-glossy, combined with the honey scented flowers this has to be a winner. Good in containers. Hardy in mild areas. 60cm (24").

PLANTAGO

Decorative plantains are available which are not at all invasive.

HOW TO GROW
Prefer moist but well-drained soil, do not allow them to dry out. Unfussy.
Sow seed of species in autumn in a cold frame. 'Rubrifolia' will come true. Divide in spring.

P. lanceolata 'Streaker' bears variegated foliage and tubby dark brown flowers. Does not self-seed. Suitable for a pot. This will not tolerate acid soil.
P. major 'Rubrifolia' is easy to grow and although it seeds itself freely, it does not become a nuisance. Bears very large, wide, beetroot coloured foliage which is deeply veined. Spiky brown seedheads are useful for drying. Can easily look weedy. 30cm (12").

Pittosporum tenuifolium 'Tom Thumb'

148

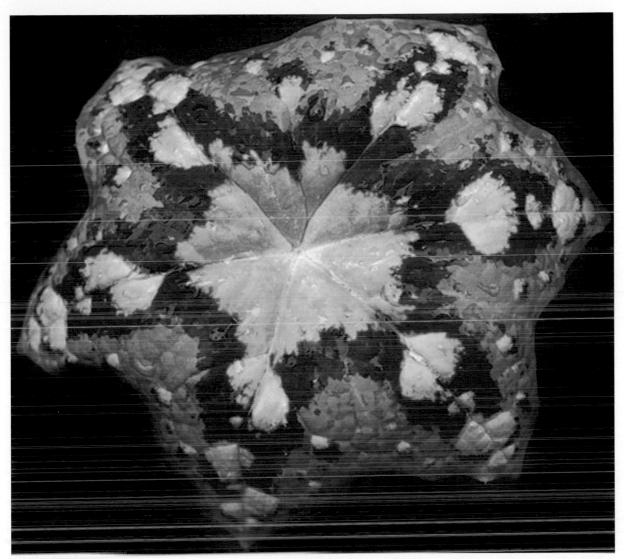

The fascinating leaf forms of Podophyllum make them an excellent choice for the woodland garden.

PODOPHYLLUM

Shade-loving plants with attractively marked foliage. Taxonomy for species is under discussion, I have retained the name Podophyllum.

HOW TO GROW
Grow in humus-rich, moist soil in full, partial or dappled shade. Ideally suited to woodland or a moist, shady border. Hardiness is not certain in cold areas.
Sow fresh seed in an open frame.

P. delavayi (P. veitchii) has some of the best foliage of all, beautifully marked in dark patches, tones of black-purple at first becoming rich plum-purple with a green centre. Deep red flowers. First described by Helms and Wilson in 1906.
P. difforme has attractively marked leaves, variable in its seedlings, but worthy. Salmon-pink flowers are borne beneath the leaves, followed by clusters of yellowish-green fruits.
P. hexandrum bears handsome, marbled bronze foliage which emerges and unfolds like an umbrella. Pure white, sometimes pink, cupped flowers, hidden by the foliage, are followed by large, brilliant red fruits. 45cm (18").
P. hexandrum v chinese has dark markings on pale olive leaves maturing to deep green.
P. mairei is a Chinese species having branching stems with tooth-edged leaves. Clusters of pear-shaped, pendent deep purple flowers. Z6.

P. peltatum is a north American species, lacking the ornamental value of the Asian species.
P. pleianthum is endemic to China, usually bearing a large single, plain umbrella leaf to 20cm (8"), deeply lobed. In March-April, 2-6 hanging flowers are produced in very deep purple to garnet red with a paler interior. Flaring as they age, they reveal yellow anthers. Clusters of 3-7 blooms are long-lasting with a meaty scent, only discernible at close quarters in an enclosed space. Followed by incredible silvery fruits. Easy in leafy soil, well drained in humid shade. Mulch well in cold areas. Possibly only hardy to -5°C. 25°F.
P. versipelle has highly ornamental deeply lobed and cut leaves splotched with maroon. The deep purple flowers appear in May in clusters of up to 15 on a short, bristly stem. Best in a sheltered spot, but has proved hardy at Kew and other parts of the U.K.
TOXIC: all parts if ingested.

Podophyllum demonstrating variation in leaf colouring and markings.

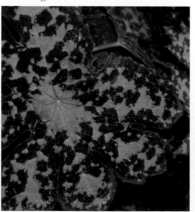

POLEMONIUM

Bronzed-foliage on a Jacob's ladder provides interest on these well-known plants.

HOW TO GROW
Grow in any fertile, moist, well-drained soil in full sun or partial shade. Dead-head regularly. Hardy.
Sow seed in a cold frame in autumn or spring. Divide in spring.

P. 'Bressingham Purple' is the latest addition to the bronze-leaved group.
P. 'Sonia's Bluebell' has dark bronzed foliage with pale blue flowers having white centres.
P. yezoense 'Purple Rain' produces a fine basal rosette of bronzed-purple foliage from which arise stems of purple ladders. Attractive rich lilac flowers are 2.5cm (1") across. Comes relatively true from seed, discard any seedlings not dark enough. 45cm (18").

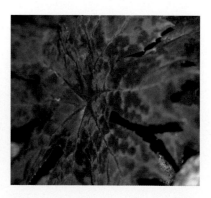

PRIMULA

Most of the dark-flowered *Primula* fall into the auricula group. Astonishing and amazingly beautiful flowers, little wonder they attracted very high prices in the past. Irresistible plants with sumptuous flowers in colours including brown, black, deepest reds and purples.

HOW TO GROW
Generally, *P. auricula* will grow in full sun with midday shade, or in partial shade. A moist, but gritty, sharply drained soil is required. Prefers humus-rich, slightly alkaline soil. Auriculas are hardy to Z3. Some alpine species require the protection of an alpine house. Border varieties are less fussy.
Surface sow seed in spring. Root offsets in autumn or early spring.

P. '**Barbarella**' is a nearly black show self whose dark colouring contrasts dramatically with the attractive foliage. Strong-growing.
P. '**Blackfield**' is a self which bears red flowers.
P. '**Blackhill**' is a show self which is a dark red with a lovely mealy centre.
P. '**Black Ice**' bears purple-brown self flowers.
P. '**Black Jack**' is a very deep burgundy with a white centre and glaucous leaves. Up to 20 heads on one plant, and scented too.
P. '**Butterwick**' is a sturdy-growing alpine auricula with rich velvety-brown flowers.

Primula auricula 'Neat and Tidy'

P. '**Consett**' is a dark red self.
P. '**Corrie Files**' bears double flowers with near black petals.
P. '**Cortina**' is a dark red self acclaimed for the velvety texture of its flowers and its thickly mealed foliage.
P. '**C.W.Needham**' is an alpine auricula that can always be relied upon to produce a wealth of dark purple flowers with almost white centres of an incredible velvety texture. Raised in 1939.
P. '**Dark Eyes**' is a superb double.
P. '**Doublure**' is a dark velvety red double with rose type flowers. Exquisite.
P. '**Douglas Black**' is a dark red self, with wonderful mealy foliage.
P. '**Dusky Maiden**' is an alpine auricula in dark purple-brown.
P. '**Eden Simon**' is a fairly dark border auricula of a shade of deep purple with a light centre.
P. '**Freda**' is a stunning, unrivalled black self. Worth seeking.
P. '**Guizabroon**' (Derek Telford) is a dark red self with handsome mealed leaves, almost white under protection. Telford has produced some superb darks.
P. '**Hinton Admiral**' is a show type with dark centres ringed white.
P. '**Matthew Yates**' is a purple-black double-flowered auricula with a wonderful incense-like scent. Smooth grey-green leaves. Superb.

P. auricula 'Guizabroon'

151

P. 'Merlin' bears black and white striped flowers.

P. 'Mikado' listed since 1906 has a fine truss of black pips contrasting well with the long green serrated leaves. One of the best show selfs

P. 'Neat and Tidy' is just that, a superb dark red, near black show self with silvery green farinose foliage. Approaches perfection.

P. 'Night and Day' is a good dark red show self.

P. 'Night Dancer' bears similar colouring on a show self.

P. 'Nocturne' is a very dark, almost black flower on a show self.

P. 'Remus' is a dark red show self with the white centre flaring a little into the darker colour.

P. 'The Raven' very dark red-black flowers on this self.

P. 'The Snods' is a dark show self, appears almost black, raised in the 1960's and its name is taken from a small village in the north of England.

P. 'Trouble' is one to add to your chocolate selection, double flower in a shade of light chocolate.

P. 'Typhoon' is an alpine auricula bearing brownish-purple flowers with a contrasting gold centre.

P. 'Wincha' is a very dark red-black self, a real delight.

The hardy Barnhaven strain also offer some dark flowers and foliage. Do not allow these to dry out. Divide regularly. All hardy.

P. 'Bergfruhlung Julianas Group' (PO) includes deep blue shades with a yellow eye and dark green leaves tinged bronze.

P. 'Cowichan Garnet Group' is a favourite with me for its dusky, velvet red flowers. Reddish brown tinted foliage. Easy to flower.

P. 'Gold-Laced Group' (PO) is a beautiful old-fashioned flower which if you only grow one Polyanthus, it would be well to make it this one. Gold or silver lacing on a red, mahogany or black ground. An absolute gem.

P. 'Guinevere' (PO) sometimes listed as 'Garryard Guinevere' bears soft pink flowers over rich bronze-purple foliage.

P. 'Midnight' (PO) is a deep blue-black and magenta-purple strain with dark foliage.

Try **Wanda** hybrids for their dark foliage amongst them is a violet-purple shade with a velvet sheen and little or no eye, rather like a Cowichan. Exceptionally beautiful flowers with gorgeous deeply bronzed foliage.

Good dark double primroses are *P. vulgaris* **'Crimson Beauty'**, **'Lady Bird'** and **'Sparkling Wine'**, all wine red.

P. x pubescens 'Hurstwood Midnight' is a hybrid with deep velvety purple-blue flowers suitable for an alpine house.

Primula 'Guinevere'

PRUNUS

Excellent specimen trees with good purple foliage, *Prunus* are not to be disregarded in the dark-leaf garden.

HOW TO GROW

Moist but well-drained soil is required in full sun. Hardy.

Sow seed of species outdoors in autumn. Root greenwood cuttings of deciduous species in early summer and semi-ripe cuttings of evergreens in midsummer, both with bottom heat. Bud cultivars in summer or graft in early spring.

P. cerasifera 'Nigra' has the most wonderful dark blackish purple foliage which is redder when young and bears pink flowers. A magnificent, deciduous specimen tree. Can also be used to good effect as a hedge, which needs to be trimmed after flowering. 10m (30ft).

P. cerasifera 'Pissardii' has dark purple leaves and pale pink flowers that fade to white. Superb and capable of making a dense hedge.

P. cerasifera 'Thundercloud' bears pink flowers and dark purple foliage.

P. x cistena is a small, erect shrub with glossy red leaves maturing to deep reddish-purple. Small bluish-white flowers in spring. 1.5m (5ft).

P. 'Fragrant Cloud' = 'Shizuka' bears scented, semi-double flowers and bronze foliage.

P. persica 'Terrace Garnet' bears superbly glossy dark leaves of a good deep bronze colour.

P. 'Royal Burgundy' has impressive

Prunus persica 'Terrace Garnet'

deep purple foliage throughout the summer, turning bronze in autumn. A good choice for the small garden, being a sport of 'Kanzan' but less vigorous.

P. spinosa 'Purpurea' is a dense, spiny deciduous shrub or tree which bears red foliage, later turning dark red-purple. The pale pink flowers in spring contrast admirably with the foliage. 5m (15ft).

The foliage of **P. 'Kiku-shidare-zakura'** (Cheal's Weeping') is bronze when young, so too **P. jamasakura**, and other *Prunus*. **P. padus** 'Colorata' bears leaves whose new growth is coppery purple. **P. sargentii** has bronze-red young foliage.

Pseudopanax lessonii 'Purpureus'

PSEUDERANTHEMUM

Often listed under Erantherum. Frost tender species grown for their colourful foliage.

HOW TO GROW
Under glass, grow in loam-based potting compost in bright filtered light with high humidity. In growth, water moderately, applying a balanced feed every month.

Outdoors, grow in humus-rich soil in partial shade in moist soil. Pinch out regularly when young. Cut back hard in spring if straggly. Protect from winds. Minimum temperature 13°C (55°F). Z 10-11.

Root semi-ripe cuttings in midsummer with bottom heat.

P. atropurpureum is an erect, open shrub with deep purple leaves spotted with various colours. Bears tubular white flowers, spotted rose or purple at the bases, during summer. 1-1.5m (3-5ft).

P. atropurpureum 'Caruthersii' bears wide, solid metallic purple leaves to 15cm (6") long, slightly haired. Purplish-red and white flowers. Bushy shrub to 2m (7ft).

P. atropurpureum 'Pygmy' is a compact form with slim leaves, lacquered purple, pink and grey on emerald.

P. atropurpureum 'Rubrum' has very wide, lacquered maroon oval leaves. Rare, dramatic and showy.

P. atropurpureum 'Variegatum' ('Tricolour') has bronze-purple leaves splashed with creamy yellow and pink. Bears pink flowers.

P. reticulatum has showy foliage varying in colour from green to purplish-black with oval leaves to 15cm (6") netted with golden veins and having wavy margins. Bears white flowers with cerise markings in summer.

PSEUDOPANAX

Purple leaves on superb foliage plants. Architectural and specimen plants with purple to black fruits.

HOW TO GROW
In frost-prone areas grow under glass in loam-based potting compost with added sharp sand, in full light, shaded from hot sun or in bright filtered light. When in growth water moderately, applying a balanced feed every month. Reduce watering in winter. Frost tender.

Sow seed in autumn or spring under glass. Take semi-ripe cuttings or air-layer in summer.

P. crassifolius, commonly known as lancewood, is an evergreen tree remaining unbranched for many years. Mature trees develop a rounded head and palmate foliage making an unusual dark accent. Huge, spiky leaves of purplish-red almost appear black from a distance. Hardy in Cornwall.

P. lessonii 'Purpureus' is an erect to spreading large evergreen shrub. Mature foliage is palmate and deep purple. Suitable for a large pot. 3-6m (10-20ft).

RANUNCULUS

A wonderful array of dark foliage is provided early in the year, mainly with contrasting yellow flowers.

HOW TO GROW
Best in partial or full shade in moist, humus-rich soil. Plant tubers at a depth of 5cm (2"). Summer dormant. Hardy. Z5. Divide tuberous species in spring or autumn.

R. ficaria 'Aglow in the Dark' was discovered by M.Cragg-Barber. The foliage opens almost black with a few small pale spots towards the edge. Ages to dark green.

R. ficaria 'Bitter Chocolate' has leaves of dark green surrounding the central brown bronze zone.

R. ficaria 'Brambling' is a distinct variant in dull bronze, overlaid with a filigree of silvery green.

R. ficaria 'Brazen Child' is a seedling from 'Brazen Hussy' by R.Hoskins. The dark chocolate leaf is splashed burgundy red.

R. ficaria 'Brazen Hussy' is a little gem of a plant producing glossy, chocolate-brown to purple leaves and the usual shining golden yellow flower with a bronze reverse. Seedlings often have bronzed leaves. Found by Christopher Lloyd. The shiny leaf distinguishes the plant from others of similar colouring. **R. ficaria 'Binsted Woods'** is not considered distinct enough to warrant a name of its own, but is said to be a more compact form from Mike Tristram.

R. ficaria 'Burnivale' found by M.Cragg-Barber bears dark, red-purple foliage and red-purple petioles. Its large and fat tubers are oddly pale white.

R. ficaria 'Coppernob' is a hybrid between *R. ficaria* 'Brazen Hussy' and *R. ficaria v aurantiacus*, bearing the foliage of the former with the glowing dark orange flowers of the latter. The clone **R. ficaria 'Brandymount Orange'** is a spontaneous cross of the two.

R. ficaria 'Crawshaw Cream' has dark foliage enhanced by a cream-coloured flower, with an unusual green reverse.

R. ficaria 'Deborah Jope' has bronze leaves admirably set off by single white flowers.

R. ficaria 'Holly Bronze' bears indented bronze leaves.

R. ficaria 'Holly Patchy' has holly-shaped leaves irregularly marked bronze.

R. ficaria 'Inky' is a rare form with deep, black-purple veining across the green leaf.

R. ficaria 'Jane's Dress' found by M.Cragg-Barber bears leaves of deep purple flecked with silver.

R. ficaria 'Mobled Jade' bears purple-bronze colouring which does not cover the whole of the leaf, the edges bearing green spots and splashes which extend into the darker zone. Distinctive.

R. ficaria 'Molten Lava' is a procumbent form with dark grey bronze leaves with a blue-black sheen and a ring of silvery spots at the periphery. It bears bright yellow flowers marked bright

chestnut on the reverse. The plant is smaller than many of the other variants.

R. ficaria 'Newton Abbot' is a wild collected variant found in Devon by C. Rogers which bears leaves of an olive khaki.

R. ficaria 'Suffusion' is similar to 'Mobled Jade', having the same spots and splashes but not entering the dark zone to the same extent. Both found by M.Cragg-Barber.

R. ficaria 'Sweet Chocolate' has a chocolate blob surrounded by green.

R. ficaria 'Tortoiseshell' has bold, large foliage with a bronze background wonderfully mottled with shades of green and red. The patterning is variable.

Rhodochiton atrosanguineus

RHODOCHITON

A delightful frost tender perennial not to be missed. A useful climber, making an attractive display in one season.

HOW TO GROW

Under glass, grow in loam-based potting compost in full light with shade from hot sun. During growth, water freely, applying a balanced liquid fertiliser monthly. In winter, keep just moist. Pot on in spring. Outdoors grow in fertile, humus-rich, moist but well drained soil in full sun.

Sow seed under glass in spring.

R. atrosanguineus (R. volubilis) is a slender-stemmed twining climber producing rich green heart-shaped leaves 4-8cm long. From summer to autumn, long, pendent stalks bear tubular black to reddish-purple flowers 4.5cm (2") long protruding from cup-shaped, rose-pink to magenta calyces. Deserves to be grown more. Easy from seed and attractive as an annual climber outdoors in Great Britain. I have seen a suggestion that it can also be used as ground cover, but the effect of the hanging bells would surely be completely lost. In a single season in a conservatory, it can reach 2.6m (8ft). A useful climber with interesting flowers which will make a good, quick display when fed and watered well. This is one I would choose to always grow in my garden. 3-5°C (37-41°F).

RICINUS

Architectural, palmate dark leaves make excellent specimen plants. Given the right treatment, they are capable of reaching large proportions in one season.

HOW TO GROW

Under glass, grow in loam-based potting compost in full light. Water freely when in growth, applying a balanced feed monthly. Reduce watering in winter. May need restrictive pruning. Outdoors, grow in fertile, humus-rich, well-drained soil in full sun. Feed, feed, feed. Plants in poor soil make less vegetative growth and smaller leaves. Half hardy.

Soak seed for 24 hours before sowing singly in pots under glass in spring. Dislike root disturbance. Plant out when all danger of frost has passed. Easy from seed. Please note seed is poisonous.

R. communis 'Carmencita' is well-branched with dark, bronze-red foliage and bright red female flowers. Annual growth of 2-3m (6-10ft).

R. communis 'Gibsonii' also bears dark leaves, flushed with red veins.

R. communis 'Impala' is compact with reddish-bronze foliage, young shoots and stems being carmine-red. 1.2m (4ft).

R. communis 'Red Spire' is tall with red stems and bronze leaves.

R. communis 'Sanguineus' is tall with deep bronze-flushed leaves. A stunning sight in a sunny position.

Ricinus communis 'Sanguineus'

ROSA

Red roses are the classic symbol of love, make mine the darkest rose. The elusive black beautifully shades some of the darker reds, most of which have gallica parentage, darkening as they age, hence the 'black rose'.

HOW TO GROW
Tolerant of a wide range of conditions, but preferring an open site in full sun. Thriving in moderately fertile, humus-rich soil, moist but well-drained.
Root hardwood cuttings in autumn. Bud in summer. Plant as bare root plants in winter.

R. 'Barkarole' (Evers 1993) is a hybrid tea, black in bud opening to deep velvet red, good for cutting. Very fragrant and heat tolerant. 1m (39"). Z5.

R. 'Black Baccara' is a beautiful near black rose, long-stemmed and perfect for cutting. Quite a robust grower. 60-80cm (24-32").

R. 'Black Beauty' (Delbard 1974). Rich, crimson scarlet with reflexes of darkest, velvety black. Excellent cutting rose.

R. 'Black Ice' is a nearly black rose of R. 'Iceberg' parentage. Near black buds open to scarlet. Compact. 60cm (2ft).

R. 'Black Jack' is a miniature deep red.

R. 'Black Jade' is a miniature with shimmering blooms of dark rich red velvet and good new red foliage. Spellbinding in its beauty, especially in bud when it appears black. Excellent in pots or in the garden. Open double flowers reveal yellow stamens. Emits a slight fragrance and blooms repeatedly. Burns easily in sun. Needs winter protection in Z5 and under. 45cm (18").

R. 'Black Magic' bears quite large dark red, shaded black flowers all summer long. 80-100cm (32-39").

R. 'Black Pearl' (Delbard-Chanert 1986) is a very dark red double, fragant flower. Z5.

R. 'Black Prince' bears fragrant, large-cupped flowers of rich carmine shaded almost black. 1866. 1.8m (5ft).

R. 'Chateau de Clos Vougeot' its deep claret-red blooms have blackish highlights, but this hybrid tea is a weak grower.

R. 'Conditorum' is thought to be of ancient origin with loose double dark flowers.

Rosa 'Deep Secret'

R. 'Dark Lady' (Austin 1991). Dark red flowers with hints of purple. Not very vigorous.

R. 'Deep Secret' (Tantau 1979) is a hybrid tea with a strong, rich fragrance. Perfect near black buds open far too pale. 1.5m (5ft).

R. 'Duc de Guiche' has splendid flowers of intense magenta-crimson, flushing purple in hot weather. Good foliage and sweetly scented. Gallica. 1.8m (5ft).

Rosa 'Black Baccara'

156

Rosa 'Hocus Pocus'

R. 'Eclair' 1833, is a very dark red variety, almost black. Fairly vigorous, free flowering, scented hybrid perpetual. Well-formed.

R. 'Hocus Pocus' is a magical combination of deepest red with creamy white specks and stripes. Available as a cut flower, these long stemmed varieties are not always suitable as garden plants.

R. 'Josephine Bruce' (Bees 1952) is the first rose I ever knew the name of at the tender age of ten, it has remained a favourite ever since, it is not merely sentiment which makes this rose special. Shapely, fully double flowers of a deep velvety red. Not the darkest, but lovely nevertheless. A strong, vigorous climber, also available as a modern hybrid tea. Scented. Sometimes, one of the parents is sold under this name, having a weak neck and little scent. (HT).

R. 'Louis XIV' (Guillot fils 1859) bears fully double flowers of very dark red almost black and quite flat, with a good fragrance which is unusual in the old China roses. Needs kingly care, hates wet conditions, but worth the effort.

60cm (2ft). A favourite with many, grown by Graham Fraser at Stoneacre and by Helen Dillon amongst others. 1.2-1.5m (5ft). Z 5-10. Min -15°C.

R. 'Midnight Magic' (1995) has exquisite, deep velvety red blooms with an ivory reverse on large exhibition quality flowers. A fragrant, repeat blooming hybrid tea. Z5.

R. 'Nuits de Young' (1845) is the darkest of the old moss roses. Bears small, double, scented flowers of a deep purple-maroon, very velvety with yellow stamens. Erect, compact bush with small, dark leaves, purplish when young, flowering in early summer. Thornless stems are mossy.

R. 'Papa Meilland' (Meilland 1963). Crimson-red, shading to black, strong fragrance. (HT).

R. 'Prince Camille de Rohan' bears very deep, blackish-red blooms of almost colossal size on a vigorous plant that unfortunately has a rather weak neck. Hybrid Perpetual. 120cm. (4ft).

R. 'Raven' bears largish, velvet blooms, attractive when open with rounded petals and dark stamens.

R. rubrifolia is a species wild rose bearing probably the best wine-coloured foliage, particularly on the undersides. The flowers are red at first, then greenish-white. Profuse number of hips in autumn. Makes a good hedge. Naturalises readily from seed.

R. 'Ruby Celebration' (Pearce 1995). A red so dark that you can almost see black shading. Flowers

are smallish and plentiful. Performs well throughout the season. Celibrate its darkness by placing this small rose where it is visible. 90cm (3ft).

R. 'Schwarze Madonna' (Black Madonna) (Kordes 1992) is a deep velvet red, large flowered cutting rose with shiny foliage. A slightly fragrant upright spreader. 60-80cm (24-32"). Z4.

R. 'Souvenir du Docteur Jamain' is a dark climbing rose with an intoxicating scent. Hybrid Perpetual.

R. 'Taboo' is a popular dark red rose in the U.S. with buds appearing black.

R. 'Tuscany' Pre 1800. Semi-double flowers open flat and display the yellow stamens which contrast superbly with the dark maroon purple petals. Slight fragrance. Gallica. 120cm (4ft).

R. 'Tuscany Superb' is larger, bearing semi-double blooms of the deepest velvety crimson, emphasised by prominent gold stamens. Good scent, erect and well foliated. Pre 1848. Gallica. 120cm (4ft).

R. 'Souvenir du Docteur Jamain'

R. 'Violacea' 18th century or earlier. Single, dark crimson flowers rapidly turn purplish with yellow stamens. Almost thornless. Small, rounded leaves. Sweet scent. 180cm (6ft).

Confronted with so many dark red beauties, and given the subjectiveness of colour, it is difficult to maintain the perfect vision, other dark roses you might like to consider are R. 'Charles Mallerin', R. 'Crimson Glory', the delightful floribunda R. 'Dusky Maiden', R. 'Zigeuderknabe' ('Gipsy Boy') a lovely Bourbon, the dark buds and flowers of R. 'Roundelay' or the rich velvety burgundy-purple flowers of the gallicas R. 'Cardinal de Richelieu', 'Charles de Mills', the deep beetroot purple of hybrid tea R. 'Big Purple', or red turning to purple of the shrub rose R. 'The Prince'. Of the climbers R. 'Guinee' is a very dark blackish-red hybrid tea with fully-cupped double flowers and R. 'That's Jazz' is also dark red. Noteworthy too is the rambler 'Violette' (1921) not to be confused with the similarly named 'Violetta'.

Rosa pimpinellifolia is used in the dark garden for a different reason. It bears creamy-white flowers which are followed by blackish hips. R. 'Single Cherry' has the same coloured hips.

Roses of other flower colour, often bear foliage of bronze or red.

The new growth of the hybrid tea R. 'Bride' is a distinctive shiny red, and that of R. 'Eternally Yours' is bronze-red, so too the shrubby climber R. 'Too Hot to Handle'. The hybrid tea R. 'Kathryn McGredy' bears glorious plum-red new growth as does R. 'Paddy Stephens'. The new growth of the floribunda shrub R. 'Oranges and Lemons' is a glossy red turning dark green as it ages.

The striking young foliage of the floribunda R. 'The Painter' is a glossy reddish bronze which ages to dark green, and shading to the same colour but beginning bronze-reddish is the patio rose R. 'Panache', whilst that of the floribunda R. 'Piccolo' is a glossy reddish colour.

The hybrid tea R. 'Ice Cream' is clothed in bronze-green foliage, likewise the floribundas R. 'Arcadian', R. 'Edith Holden', and R. 'Hannah Gordon' which is quite glossy. The hybrid tea R. 'Lovers Meeting' bears deep bronze foliage as do R. 'Solitaire' and the miniature R. 'Firefly' as well as the patio roses R. 'Regensburg' and R. 'Thank You'.

The new foliage of the patio rose R. 'Fiesta' is shaded red.

The floribunda R. 'English Miss' bears purplish to dark green foliage and R. 'Gordon's College' bears purplish tinted young foliage. R. 'Brown Velvet' bred by Sam McGredy in 1983 is a lovely hue of russet brown with reddish shadings and bronze foliage.

SALPIGLOSSIS

An annual or short-lived perennial from the southern Andes to add to your chocolate collection with long lasting richly dark flowers.

HOW TO GROW

Under glass grow in loamless or loam-based compost in full light with shade from hot sun. Requires low to high humidity when in growth. Apply a balanced liquid fertiliser every 2 weeks. Keep just moist in winter at a temperature of 17°C (62°F).

Sow seed under glass in mid-spring or in autumn or late winter for early flowering pot plants.

S. 'Chocolate Royale' ('Chocolate Pot') is compact with an elegant branching habit. Produces masses of rich, chocolate-brown trumpet flowers with a velvet sheen. Each one is veined in a darker tone and is enhanced by yellow stamens. Looks good in a drift. 30cm (12").

Salpiglossis 'Chocolate Royale'

SALVIA

This varied genus includes fabulously dark flowers and foliage.

HOW TO GROW

Outdoors, grow in light, moderately fertile, humus-rich, moist but well-drained soil in full sun or light dappled shade. Tender varieties need protection from winter wet as well as frost and can be raised under glass.

Species can be raised from seed, hardy varieties in a cold frame in spring, annuals in mid-spring under glass.

S. 'Black Knight' flowers unfurl slowly, darkening in late season to the deepest black-purple. Needs protection. Very desirable. Can reach 180cm (6ft).

S. castanea is a Himalayan native found growing on open turf on limestone. Dark brownish-maroon flowers are produced from July-August. Softly hairy, ovate, glutinous leaves. Well-drained soil, plenty of moisture in the growing season, fairly dry in winter. -20°C.

S. discolor is a tender perennial from Peru, with densely white-woolly branched stems, leaves paler and more attractive underneath, but less hairy on the surface. Bears racemes of deep indigo-black flowers to 2.5cm (1") protruding from finely white-hairy, silvery-green calyces in summer to early autumn. Rather floppy, but scintillating nevertheless. Unlikely to survive outdoors in the U.K. Flowers well into winter in a slightly heated glasshouse. 45cm (18"). Z 10.

S. guaranitica 'Black and Blue' (S.caerulea h) is a subshrubby tender perennial bearing rich blue flowers, more vigorous, larger and deeper coloured than the type with very dark purple-black calyces. Tender, top growth will be destroyed in winter in mild areas of the U.K. 2.5m (8ft). 0°C.

S. mexicana 'Black Sepals' is a fast growing, very erect salvia bearing dark green heart-shaped leaves blushed black in sun when mature, with terminal spikes of dark blue flowers. Best in sun to part shade. 180cm (6ft).

S. officinalis Purpurascens Group has red-purple young leaves. A subshrubby, evergreen hardy perennial with aromatic leaves to 8cm (3") long. Cultivated since the early 17th century. Looks fabulous with dark foliage and *Foeniculum*. 1m (3ft). Z5.

S. semiatrata bears blue-violet lipped violet flowers from purple calyces in short spikes in autumn. 60cm (24").

S. sinaloensis is a low growing Mexican native, fairly hardy but intolerant of prolonged cold and wet. Beetroot-red young leaves turn green as they mature unless kept very cool and dry. Intense deep blue flowers are held well above the foliage. Cool greenhouse in winter. Thrives in acid, peaty soil. The burgundy-leaved **S. lyrata 'Burgundy Bliss'** or **'Purple Knockout'** are worthy too.

S. officinalis Purpurascens Group

SAMBUCUS

Increasingly darker cultivars of *S. nigra* are making their way on to the market. A purple leaved clone was grown at Kew in 1957 from a plant found growing in the roadside in Yorkshire in 1954, propagated by Robert Howat, the leaves were bronze-purple, with or without streaks of green. In the 1970's, Hilliers cultivated a clone called 'Foliis Purpureis' from a garden in N. Ireland.

HOW TO GROW
Moderately fertile, humus-rich, moist but well-drained soil in full sun or dappled shade. Can be pruned hard to restrict size. Hardy. Take hardwood cuttings in winter. Take greenwood cuttings in early summer.

S. nigra 'Black Beauty' is now considered to be the darkest elder available. The dark, almost black foliage is combined with lemon-scented pink flowers in June, followed by berries in autumn. Will reach a height of up to 3m (10ft) in eight years if left unpruned, when it should make a good free-standing specimen, or can be cut back hard like other elders at the end of each season and used for its excellent dark foliage. Part of a breeding programme which promises to introduce more new varieties in the near future.

S. nigra 'Black Lace' is a very handsome dissected leaf form from the same breeding programme. Bears bright pink flowers. Stunning.

S. nigra 'Guincho Purple' was long considered the darkest black elder. Bearing dark green leaves which turn a blackish-purple then red in autumn, purple-stalks and pink-tipped flowers are heavenly against the dark backdrop. Prune hard, good in the herbaceous border. 4m (12ft).

S. nigra 'Thundercloud' is a darker mutation from S. nigra 'Guincho' whose dark red-black leaves colour best in full sun. The red-pink flowers are startling in May-June.

Sambucus nigra 'Guincho Purple'

Sambucus nigra 'Black Beauty'

SANGUISORBA

Dark reddish-purple or maroon small bottlebrush flowers can be found on some burnets.

HOW TO GROW

Grow in moderately fertile retentive soil which does not dry out in full sun or partial shade. Taller species may require staking. Sometimes invasive. Fully hardy. Sow seed in cold in spring or autumn. Divide established clumps at the same time.

S. menziesii has deep maroon bottlebrush flowers from May to July over pinnate green foliage. 60cm (2ft). Z5.

S. officinalis bears pinnate basal leaves with red-brown to maroon flowers borne on red stems from early summer to mid-autumn. 1.2m (4ft). Z4.

S. officinalis 'Shiro Fururin' produces broad serrated leaves with a sparkling white variegated edge, and burgundy flowers from June to July. 60cm (2ft). Z4.

S. officinalis 'Tanna' is a well-behaved dwarf version of the Great Burnet which has deep burgundy-maroon flowers arising on spikes to 30cm (12") from June - September. A neat, compact plant of 25cm (14") Perfect front-of-the-border plant. Z4.

S. tenuifolia 'Purpurea' bears tall maroon-purple spikes from August to October. 1.2m (4ft). Z4.

Saxifraga 'Black Ruby' (right)
S. 'Maroon Beauty' (far right)

SAXIFRAGA

A large genus varying in habit and leaf form with different cultural requirements, offering interest for the dark garden.

HOW TO GROW

Sow seed in autumn in an open frame. Divide herbaceous perennials in spring. Detach rosettes in late spring or summer. Hardy.

S. 'Blackberry and Apple Pie' (fortunei) has green foliage spotted dark and the undersides being bright red. 15cm (6").

S. 'Black Beauty' bears tiny maroon flowers over mossy green foliage. Useful in the rock garden.

S. 'Black Ruby' (fortunei) ('Black Leaf') from Japan is a most valuable addition with almost black stems and leaves. Bearing red-pink flowers from October to December. A glossy plant requiring moist shade and good soil, colours best in deep shade. 15cm (6").

S. cortusifolia is valuable not only for its dark leaves suffused with metallic purple, but also for its deep maroon undersides.

S. 'Maroon Beauty' (stolonifera) bears large, glossy, dark green, maroon marked leaves for dry shade under trees. 30cm (12").

S. 'Miss Chambers' (x urbium) bears crimson flowers in April-June with maroon-green leaves. 30cm (12").

S. 'Rokujo' (fortunei) has red and brown leaves with contrasting white flowers from September to November. 25cm (8").

S. 'Rubrifolia' (fortunei) is a compact plant for cool soil in a sheltered position. Bears round leaves, suffused deep red on the surface, carmine on the underside. In October white flowers are borne on the red stems. 30cm.

S. 'Velvet' (fortunei) is another dark-leaved form.

S. 'Wada' (fortunei) bears very large glossy, coppery leaves, red on the underside, with clouds of white flowers. 50cm (20").

S. 'Wisley' (frederici-augusti ssp grisebachii) has a pleasing, tiny dark maroon flower over spoon-shaped silver-grey leaves. Arching pink stems are clothed in green-tipped purplish bracts. 10cm (4").

SCABIOSA

One of my favourite flowers for their almost black buds, opening to velvety maroon.

HOW TO GROW
Moderately fertile, well-drained, neutral to slightly alkaline soil in full sun. Protect from excessive winter wet. Hardy.
Sow seed in early spring under glass or *in situ* mid-spring.

S. atropurpurea is an annual or biennial dark purple to lilac-pink, more often reddish pink flower, just 2-3cm (around 1") across. Flowers May-August. Many dark selections have been made from this, which have become very confused in horticulture.
S. 'Ace of Spades' is a dark annual with largish flowers. 3ft (1m).
S. 'Chile Black' ('Black Prince') bears small flowers, near black in bud, remaining dark in flower, around 2-3cm across, much shorter than 'Satchmo'.
S. 'Midnight' has fine foliage, and dark flowers.
S. 'Satchmo' the first I had was so named, superbly black, especially in bud. From a basal rosette of toothed leaves, arises a long stem in the second year, bearing solitary blackish buds, opening to astounding deep dark velvety maroon black-red flowers with pinkish stamens all summer. 5cm (2") across. Definitely a biennial in my garden. Stunning and easy from seed. 90cm (3ft).

Scabiosa 'Ace of Spades'

SCOPOLIA

Dark pendent bells on a clump-forming perennial, woodland plant. Dies back after flowering.

HOW TO GROW
Humus-rich, leafy, moist but very well-drained, neutral to slightly alkaline soil in partial shade. Hardy. Z5.
Sow seed in a cold frame or *in situ* in autumn. Divide in spring.

S. carniolica 'Zwanenburg'

S. carniolica is a creeping, rhizomatous perennial with pointed, veined and wrinkled leaves to 15cm (6") long, bearing solitary purple to red bells 2.5cm (1") long, yellow-green inside are borne from the leaf axils in mid and late spring. 60cm (2ft).
S. carniolica 'Zwanenburg' carries fascinating, drooping deep purple, much deeper than the species, bells from March to May. 30cm (1ft). All parts are toxic if ingested.

Sedum spathulifolium 'Purpureum'

162

SEDUM

Red or purple tinted foliage can be found on quite a number of succulent *Sedum* and there have been more than a few new introductions. Attractive fleshy leaves on tough plants which are easy to grow and useful in the mixed border.

HOW TO GROW

Grow in moderately fertile, well-drained, neutral to slightly alkaline soil in full sun. Excessive moisture, overfeeding and too much shade affect the colouring and habit of *Sedum* from *S. telephium ssp maximum* 'Atropurpureum' parentage. Hardy to -18°C (0°F) Z 7-10.

Sow seed in containers in autumn. Divide in spring. Take softwood cuttings of non-flowering shoots in early summer. Hardy.

Sedum album 'Murale' bears mats of small succulent stems with smallish purple leaves, flowers fading to pink.

S. 'Bertram Anderson', long a favourite of mine. Bears stunning black leaves on lax stems and deep pink flowers from August to October. 15cm (6").

S. 'El Cid' bears very dark foliage, similar to 'Lynda et Rodney'.

S. 'Joyce Henderson' is similar to 'Matrona' but looser and lax in habit, with mottling on the foliage. 55cm (22").

S. 'Lynda Windsor' (PBR) bears almost black, bitter chocolate foliage with glowing dark claret flowers, looks rather forlorn early season.

S. 'Purple Emperor' has matt purple foliage which is very deep at the time of flowering. Purplish pink flowers from July to September. Best kept on the dry side for an intensely-coloured, compact, upright plant. A favourite with me. 45cm (18").

S. 'Ringmore Ruby' is a seedling from S. 'Arthur Branch' with bright glossy red stems and dark red leaves and flowers in July to August. 45cm (18").

S. 'Ruby Glow' has soft grey-purple leaves with ruby red flowers in August to October. 50cm (20").

S. 'Strawberries and Cream' has dark foliage, pale flowers and a rather lax habit.

S. 'Sunset Cloud' has dark glaucous foliage and rich, wine-purple flowers.

S. telephium 'Arthur Branch' a well-established favourite with dark chocolate foliage and blood-red stems with pink flowers. 25cm (10").

S. telephium 'Jennifer' bears broad pink flowers in July to September with reddish purple leaves. 40cm (16").

S. telephium 'Leonore Zuuntz' bears very dark blue-black foliage which is narrower than usual. Open sprays of pale pinky flowers in August to September. 50cm (20").

S. telephium 'Matrona' (Ewald Hugin) is a German seedling of large and luxuriant proportions. Thick, succulent stems rise to 60cm (24"), kept in sun and in moderate soil they will remain strong and erect, overfed, they have a tendency to become weak and lax. The leaves are greyish-green in spring becoming suffused with purple as summer progresses. Pale pink flowerheads are borne in August and September. Z 3-9.

S. telephium 'Mohrchen' bears dark, glossy foliage and flowers from red stems in August to September. 40cm (16").

S. telephium 'Munstead Red' has purple-tinted dark green leaves and dark purplish red flowers, becoming darker with age. Makes a continuous attractive show into autumn, with flowers from raspberry red through to deep bronze. 35cm (14").

S. telephium 'Veluwe se Wakel' is similar to 'Lynda et Rodney'.

S. telephium spp maximum 'Atropurpureum' has dark purple, thick fleshy leaves and stems, superseded by some of the cultivars, even though it makes a good dark accent plant. Chocolate-brown seedheads add interest later in the year. 45cm (18"). Z4.

S. telephium ssp maximum 'Honey Song' is a plum foliage cultivar grown in the U.S. with dusky mauve flowerheads. Excellent with *Euphorbia dulcis* 'Chameleon'.

S. telephium ssp. telephium 'Lynda et Rodney' found in the wild by Jean-Pierre Jolivot and named after the proprietors of RD Plants in Devon, bears narrow brownish purple foliage, red stems

Sempervivum 'Poldark'
One of the darkest Sempervivum
(below)

Sempervivum marmoreum

Sempervivum 'Jungle Fires'

Sempervivum 'Quintessence'

Sempervivum 'Dark Beauty'

Sempervivum 'Damask'

Sempervivum 'Painted Lady'

Sempervivum 'Red Devil'

Sempervivum 'Graupurpur'

and tight, domed heads of flowers with pale pinkish-purple petals and strawberry-red ovaries. 80cm (32").

S. 'Vera Jameson' bears dusky pink flowers in late summer to early fall, on arching grey-pink branches. 25cm (10"). Z4-9.

The following are pleasing purple-flushed additions to the garden.

S. spathulifolium 'Harvest Moon' is a good purple. 10cm (4").

S. spathulifolium 'Purpureum' is a vigorous, evergreen perennial, producing succulent rosettes, richly suffused with delightfully contrasting tones giving a soft hued effect. 10cm (4").

S. spurium 'Purpurteppich' ('Purple Carpet') is compact with deep plum-purple leaves and dark purplish red flowers. 10cm (4").

S. spurium 'Schorbluser Blut' ('Dragon's Blood') has green leaves which are purple-tinted when mature. Bears deep pink flowers. 10cm (4").

Sedum telephium ssp maximum 'Atropurpureum'

SEMPERVIVUM

Evergreen succulents with thick, fleshy, pointed leaves which are often very dark with erupting stalks of starry flowers.

HOW TO GROW

Grow in poor to moderately fertile, sharply drained soil with added grit in full sun which is essential for dark colouring. Hardy.

Sow seed in a cold frame in spring. Rosettes die after flowering, so root offsets in spring or early summer.

S. 'Atropurpureum' is purplish black all summer with bold coloured but smallish rosettes.

S. 'Black Knight' is mahogany purple with red tips and forms tight rosettes.

S. 'Black Mini' has small rosettes of a very dark red tipped green.

S. 'Black Mountain' is attractive and vigorous with dark, black-red tipped leaves, rather similar to the above.

S. 'Black Prince' is a slow grower with beautiful purplish black leaves with leaf margins having silver hairs.

S. 'Bronco' is a handsome green and black dark form.

S. 'Cavo Doro' is a good dark cultivar.

S. 'Damask' (Ed Skrocki) has very large, shapely rosettes of purplish black leaves. Very distinctive.

S. 'Dark Cloud' is a good dark.

S. 'Dark Beauty' (Tom Lewis 1977) has very dark, almost black-red rosettes in summer. A good,

attractive grower.

S. 'Edge of Night' is green tipped black in summer, charcoal grey in winter.

S. 'Graupurpur' bears reddish-bronze leaves.

S. 'Jungle Fires' is similar to 'Quintessence' but the leaves are more pointed and the green edging extends further into the darker purple main colour.

S. 'Night Raven' has large dark blackish-purple leaves in summer.

S. 'Noir' is one of the darkest.

S. 'Othello' is an attractive variety I grew some years ago, a dark, dusky purple.

S. 'Painted Lady' is a good deep purple, a delightful form, soft with dusky colouring.

S. 'Poldark' is beautifully dark.

S. 'Quintessence' has deep reddish-purple leaves with green tips. Very attractive.

S. 'Red Devil' has very dark, near black tightly packed rosettes.

S. 'Red Shadows' has long, narrow very dark red leaves with black shading to red tips.

S. 'Rotkopf' produces large rosettes of a dusky dark purple.

S. 'Shawnee' is medium sized, bearing dark purple leaves which shade to almost black.

S. 'Zepherin' bears dark rosettes.

The species **S. marmoreum (schlehanii)** bears near black rosettes. This is superb.

SOLENOSTEMON

Still known as *Coleus*, this genus produces dramatic foliage plants for summer bedding or as houseplants, once beloved by Victorians but now regaining a spot in the garden as superb bedders in shade. Newer varieties are sun and heat tolerant.

HOW TO GROW

Under glass, grow in loam-based potting compost in bright filtered or moderate light. In growth, water freely, applying a high-nitrogen fertiliser every two weeks. Keep just moist in winter. Pot on annually in spring. Outdoors, grow in humus-rich, moist but well-drained soil, enriched with well-rotted organic matter. A sheltered position is preferred in full sun or partial shade. Water freely in dry weather. Pinch out young shoots to prevent straggly growth. For best foliage, remove flowers. Frost tender.

Surface sow seed under glass in early spring for summer bedding or anytime for use as houseplants. Seed varieties have a short life-span and are intolerant of hot sun. A decent plant can be had in 3 months from seed, much less from a cutting. Root softwood cuttings with bottom heat in spring or summer. Roots easily in water.

S. 'Apocalypse' (Frieling) makes a dark tower of wide, thick leaves of deep chocolate velour, closely packed, flared with violet veins and a green margin.

S. 'Atlas' bears very large, cupped leaves with a purple-black border and a green centre.

S. 'Black Dragon' produces a riot of frilled and crested leaves of deep purple to maroon-black around a raised medallion flecked fuchsia pink or violet. Colour holds well in winter. Seed raised.

S. 'Black Hitch' bears purple-black leaves.

S. 'Black Lace' is a frilly sport of S. 'Cantigny Royale' with tumbling mounds of purple foliage.

S. 'Black Magic' is a modestly statured plant of upright habit, full and well-branched, with mahogany purple dragon leaves outlined in avocado scallops with a lime-encircled central raised medallion. Darker in winter. Superb.

S. 'Black Night' has widely fingered pine green leaves with purplish maroon designs veined violet. Certainly not the darkest.

S. 'Black Prince' is a self-coloured almost black foliage plant, with just a hint of green edge to the leaf with a slightly serrated edge. Pinch well. Stunning.

S. 'Black Ruffles' bears attractively ruffled near black leaves.

Solenostemon 'Black Prince'

S. 'Black Trailer' bears almost black foliage edged in green with a superb cascading habit.

S. 'Blackheart' is red-black with a green margin on tiny leaves. Cute.

S. 'Brocade' is a deep magenta purple.

S. 'Bronze Pagoda' bears bronze chartreuse wide leaves with a central blood-red spattering and soft violet veins.

S. 'Burgundy Columns' ('Green Eyes') has reddish purple foliage, making a 120cm (4') mound.

S. 'Cantigny Royale' bears elaborately lobed mahogany-maroon leaves on much branched stems. 15-20cm (6-8").

S. 'Chocolate Bingo' is a dusky olive and pistachio green, modulating into chocolate purple crenated margins.

S. 'CJ' has the most exquisite smooth jet black leaves on a bushy plant. 30cm (12").

S. 'Coal Mine' is more coal dust than coal black. A strong stemmed, large-leaved type with bright green densely speckled burgundy.

S. 'Dark Frills' is a sport of S. 'Indian Frills' with a very dark, dramatic centre.

S. 'Dark Star' bears black-purple scalloped leaves, closely spaced on branching dark stems. Has very heat resistant foliage. A real star!

S. 'Dark Storm' has darkest purple, almost black, thick-textured foliage on a compact plant.

S. 'Dipt in Wine' bears smooth, shiny rounded leaves with a crimson-black centre and bright lime edge. 30cm (12").

Solenostemon 'Dark Star'
Solenostemon 'Molten Lava' (below)

Solenostemon 'Merlot'
Solenostemon 'Blackheart' (below)

Solenostemon 'Othello' (below)

S. 'Downers Ribbons' is a dark variety.

S. 'Ducksfoot Midnight' is low-growing with small, finely cut dark purple leaves and stems. Leaves are speckled light green.

S. 'Ella Cinders' has dark olive designs which are never repeating on dusky purple foliage. The colour changes in different light.

S. 'Gretchen' is black-purple.

S. 'Inky Fingers' is a striking, low growing form with wide leaf fingers, dark purple-black with a bright avocado edge. Great for trailing from baskets or tubs.

S. 'Juliet Quartermain' is a good maroon, fading in heat.

S. 'Jupiter' is a compact 'Molten Fire' with tiny furled finger leaves of deep blackish mahogany-purple edged avocado.

S. 'Kiwi Fern' is an old favourite with narrow, well-scalloped leaves, burgundy red with a golden rim.

S. 'Lord Voldemort' (Frieling) is vigorous with strong, erect stems having spruce green leaves and a burgundy stain sinking into veins.

S. 'Merlot' bears superb dark leaves, thriving in heat and sun, developing a contrasting slight green picotee as they age.

Solenostemon 'Palisandra'

S. 'Midnight' bears large, dark plum-purple to black leaves with lime green margins. 50cm (20").

S. 'Molten Lava' is an incredible combination of red-hot lava centre surrounded by black edges. Foliage appears as if blistered by the heat. Stunning from seed.

S. 'Mount Etna' is a dark leaved variety.

S. 'New Orleans' is very similar to 'Black Magic' with a burgundy centre and light green edge.

S. 'Night Skies' (Starry Night) features dark purple leaves strewn with lemon gold starry dots to give the impression of the sky at night. Makes a neat, low mound and is perfect for small containers.

S. 'Odalisque' bears deep maroon-black foliage with a golden green edge. With age, the centre darkens dramatically whilst the edge becomes lighter.

S. 'Othello' bears deep purple-black leaves which are richly fluted. This will keep going well after the first year. Smaller and darker than 'Jupiter'.

S. 'Palisandra' ('Black Giant') is a

Solenostemon 'Inky Fingers'

definite contender for the darkest seed type. Self-colour which is almost black with a slight purple hint to it, lush, velvety rich broad leaves. 45cm (18").

S. 'Plum Frost' is Downer's sport of S. 'Purple Emperor' with a crested black leaf and a rich green centre. Fades to purple olive in heat.

S. 'Purple Duckfoot' is very low and compact, small webfoot leaves in medium to dark purple, almost black in sun. Forms a dense mat and makes good ground cover.

S. 'Purple Emperor' is a lovely, vigorous plant bearing large, velvety deep purple-black leaves with wavy, scalloped edges. Very seldom branches. 45cm (18").

S. 'Purple Oak' bears dark purple oak-shaped leaves.

S. 'Purple Pumpernickel' is dusky maroon with a dark green edge in full sun with almost round leaves, a very compact, self-branching type.

S. 'Religious Radish' has warm red leaves, flushed almost black in the centre.

S. 'Saturn' has a light yellow or pale green centre, surrounded by a ring of dark purple. Superb contrast.

Solenostemon 'Kiwi Fern'

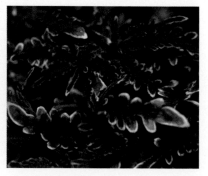

STREPTOCARPUS

The Cape primroses from wooded ravines in the Drakensburg mountains of South Africa were first introduced into England in 1826. Unbelievably velvet, dark flowers look so exotic and yet are so very easy to grow.

HOW TO GROW

Under glass, grow in loamless potting compost in bright filtered light. Shade from hot sun on an east or west facing windowsill. In growth, water freely, let compost dry out between waterings. Apply a high potash fertiliser every two weeks. Reduce watering in winter, keeping just moist and frost free. Repot each spring, and gradually commence watering and feeding. Keep slightly pot bound for the best flowers. Easy to flower from May to December. Remove faded flowers and stalks. Outdoors, grow in fertile, leafy, humus-rich soil, moist but well-drained in partial shade. Frost tender.

Surface sow seed in late winter or spring. Divide or take leaf cuttings in spring to early summer. Root stem-tip cuttings in spring.

Streptocarpus 'Kim'

S. 'Anne' introduced in 1993 has deep purple double flowers.

S. 'Black Ace' is admirably dark.

S. 'Black Beauty' (Ford 1999).

S. 'Black Gardenia' (Ford) has almost black-blue double flowers.

S. 'Black Magic' (Ford 1999) is a super black-plum. Fabulously dark.

S.' Black Panther' (Ford 1999) is a U.S. variety with deepest velvet purple flowers, with blackish hints. Two thin yellow bars emerge from the centre of the throat. Contrasts perfectly with the fresh green primrose-like foliage. The longest flowering for me, and a very big favourite. Supreme.

S. 'Bristol's Blackbird' (Robinson) has large, velvety very dark purple, almost black flowers.

S. 'Bristol's Ink Blot' is a velvety near-black with a tiny yellow eye.

S. 'Bristol's Nightfall' (Robinson) has very dark black-blue flowers with black veining into the bright yellow throat. A mature plant can produce up to sixty flowers. Stunning.

S. 'Bristol's Rare Stone' bears deep purple black velvety deepest

Streptocarpus 'Black Panther'

darkest burgundy flowers.

S. 'Bristol's Tricky Treater' is a heavy bloomer with myriads of very dark burgundy-black blooms. Easy growing and compact.

S. 'Elsi' is a spectacular colour with large flowers of the deepest purple with two small yellow flashes at the centre.

S. 'Kim' (Dibley 1991) is a very compact plant and an early bloomer with multi-flowered stems of smallish flowers of deep inky purple-blue.

S. 'Lord Fauntleroy' bears dark purple flowers, 5cm (2") wide, with a velvet appearance. 10-15cm (4-6").

S. 'Michael' is a very dark purple with a lighter yellow-splashed throat and heavy black-maroon striping.

S. 'Midnight Magic' (Ford) is a double-flowered form with deep blue-black flowers, with lighter shading on the petal backs giving a magical shadow effect.

S. 'Midnight Satin' (Sorano) bears velvety deep purple to near black flowers gently marked with white on the upper throat and yellow dots at the base of the lobes.

S. 'Olwen' bred by Lynne Dibley is a deep inky veined purple with a rich velvet sheen with slightly serrated edges. Medium sized flowers on a compact plant.

S. 'Ravens Wing' (Sorano) has deepest, darkest purple flowers with lighter shading on the upper lobes. This is compact but still a heavy bloomer.

S. 'Ulysses' is almost black-purple.

STROBILANTHES

Not many members of this interesting genus are in cultivation at present.

S. anisophyllus bears narrow leaves with a deep purple sheen in heat, losing its colouring in cooler temperatures. A shrubby perennial with glossy foliage for warm, humid areas. Grown in a well-drained soil enriched with organic material, this will reward you with pinkish mauve flowers in spring. Slim, gracious leaves.

S. dyerianus (Persian Shield) maintains its superb pink-purple foliage heavily lined in black even in heat. 8-10cm (up to 4"). Z. 9-11. 45-90cm (18-36").

S. lactatus bears shimmering purple-green leaves and zones of silver-white. An easy, reliable houseplant and makes good ground cover in a conservatory.

Strobilanthes dyerianus

SYMPLOCARPUS

Native American skunk cabbages are dark shade lovers.

HOW TO GROW

Grow in rich, moist, very retentive or wet soil in sun or light dappled shade. Fully hardy.

S. foetidus is normally grown from seed, obtain fresh seed if possible, the tubers are difficult to divide.

S. foetidus produces purple-brown flowers before the leaves appear which exude a strong, unpleasant smell when bruised. The flowers are not too pleasant smelling either, being pollinated by ground beetles.

S. nipponicus is a dwarf Japanese skunk cabbage which is very rare in cultivation. A miniature version of the above species, it grows to about a quarter of the size. Nearly black flowers are produced in spring.

TACCA

Bizarre is perhaps the word most often chosen to describe this genus, but the flowers have a beauty all of their own.

HOW TO GROW

Under glass, grow in equal parts of leaf mould and coarse bark with added slow-release fertiliser in bright filtered light. Water freely and mist in summer, reducing in winter. Apply a half strength foliar feed monthly. Pot on every 2 to 3 years and remove old, decaying rhizomes. Outdoors, grow in fertile, moist but well-drained, leafy, acid soil in partial shade. 13°C (55°F).

Surface sow seed in spring. Requires a high temperature and can be erratic and slow. Takes two to three years to flower from seed. Divide in spring.

T. chantrieri (bat plant, cat's whiskers or devil flower) is a curiously beautiful flower. An erect, rhizomatous perennial with oblong or lance-shaped green leaves. In summer, it bears five-petalled flowers of black, brown and green each with two pairs of black, brown or green floral bracts and black or maroon thread-like whiskers to 25cm (10") long. 1m (3ft).

T. integrifolia is similar bearing purple-red or brown flowers, with four deep purple or green floral bracts. Thread-like whiskers are suffused violet. 1.2m (4ft).

TELLIMA

Herbaceous perennials from western North America, providing purple or bronze leaves, suitable for ground cover in shady shrub gardens or woodland.

HOW TO GROW
Moist, humus-rich soil in partial shade, will tolerate dry soil and full-sun. Self-seeds freely. Hardy.
Sow seed in a cold frame when fresh or in spring. Divide in spring.

T. grandiflora Rubra Group ('Purpurea') bears evergreen leaves, boldly veined purple on the underside, green on the surface, turning reddish-purple to bronze in autumn and winter. In early summer, pink-fringed, green bells are borne on long spikes. 50cm (20"). Z6.
T. grandiflora 'Purpurteppich' is an improvement on the above with tougher leaves colouring maroon purple earlier in the year and holding their colour well. Pink stained rims to green bell flowers on dark stems in spring. 50cm (20"). Z6.

Tiarella 'Black Snowflake'

TIARELLA

Attractive, woodland herbaceous perennials offering some beatifully marked foliage. Versatile groundcover in shade or woodland gardens.

HOW TO GROW
Tolerate a wide range of conditions, but prefer cool, moist, humus-rich soil in deep or partial shade. Dislike excessive winter wet. Hardy. Z 4-11.
Divide in spring.
T. 'Black Snowflake' bears well marked, divided leaves with white flowers.
T. 'Black Velvet' (TN) has a black central mark on well-cut leaves with white flowers tinged pink in April to June. 45cm (18").
T. 'Braveheart' has a central maroon blotch.
T. 'Cygnet' has very narrow, dark marked leaves with scented beige flowers in April to June. 30cm (12").
T. 'Dark Eyes' bears glossy, maple-shaped leaves with a dark central blotch with bronze tones in winter and spikes of beige flowers from

Tiarella 'Iron Butterfly'

April to June. 30cm (12").
T. 'Dark Star' bears star shaped leaves with dark markings and beige flowers.
T. 'Elizabeth Oliver' has deeply lobed leaves and heavy maroon markings with light pink flowers.
T. 'Inkblot' has large dark markings which develop on mature leaves. Spikes of pinkish flowers from April to June or later. Suitable even in dry shade. 30cm (12").
T. 'Iron Butterfly' has deeply divided foliage, with central black markings on each leaflet, making an exceptional base 25cm (10") across for the fragrant, white flower spikes. 40cm (16").
T. 'Mint Chocolate' has maple-shaped leaves with a brown central blotch and pinkish flowers. Makes excellent ground cover. 30cm (12").
T. 'Ninja' makes good ground cover even in dry shade. Bears maple shaped leaves with a brown overlay turning blackish-purple, especially in winter and coral-beige flowers in spring. 30cm (12").
T. 'Tiger Stripe' makes neat clumps of green, crimped leaves each with a maroon-brown centre veining outwards. Pink spires of flowers on slender stems from May to August. Semi to full shade. 20cm (8").
T. wherryi 'Bronze Beauty' is a compact perennial, slowly making a clump of dark red-bronze foliage and light pinkish white flowers from March to December. An older, much admired variety. 20cm (8").

TRADESCANTIA

Fleshy purple-flushed leaves coupled with attractive flowers make *Tradescantia* worth growing. Ideal for hanging baskets.

HOW TO GROW
Under glass, grow in loam-based or loamless potting compost in bright filtered light. Water moderately in active growth, applying a balanced liquid feed every month. Reduce watering in winter. Pinch out to encourage bushy plants. Pot on each spring. Outdoors, grow in moist, fertile soil in full sun or partial shade. Fully hardy to frost tender. Tender species need a minimum temperature of 10-16°C (50-61°F).
Take stem tip cuttings of tender *Tradescantia* at any time, root in cuttings compost or water. Divide hardy species and cultivars in autumn or spring.

T. pallida 'Purpurea' ('Purple Heart') is a tender, trailing perennial. Stems are purple and the pointed fleshy leaves are a rich violet-purple. In summer, contrasting pink flowers are borne.

Tradescantia pallida 'Purpurea'

Leaves produce their best colour in bright sunlight, with the root zone slightly dry and cramped. Almost glow in the dark purple foliage. 40cm (16"). 0°C (32°F) Z 10-11.

The leaves of **T. spathacea** are green above and purple on the underside. White flowers are surrounded by prominent, long-lasting purple bracts throughout the year. Boat-shaped, purple bracts partly enclose tiny white flowers. Tender, semi-erect perennial. 30cm (12"). 5°C.

T. zebrina 'Purpusii' is a tender, trailing perennial bearing rich bronze-purple leaves and pink flowers. Leaf colour is usually better on the underside. 15cm (6").

TRIFOLIUM

Ornamental clovers have interestingly dark foliage.

HOW TO GROW
Grow in moist, but well-drained neutral soil in full sun. Ideal in containers. Makes quick ground cover. Hardy.
Sow seed in a cold frame in spring. Divide or detach and replant rooted stems in spring.

T. repens 'Purple Velvet' (pratense 'Chocolate') is purple-brown.
T. repens 'Purpurascens' is a chocolate brown clover with small white flowers. 10cm (4").
T. repens 'Purpurascens Quadrifolium' (Dark Dancer) bears lucky four-leaves. Easy and attractive maroon-black leaves with a green edging. White flowerheads.
T. repens 'Wheatfen' is a deep red clover with white flowers.

Trifolium 'Dark Dancer'

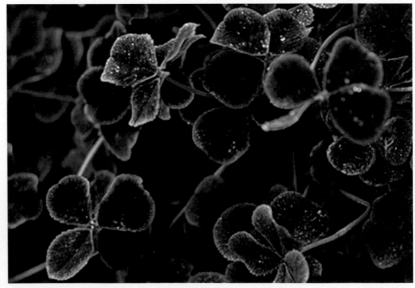

TRILLIUM

Ideal for the shady border or woodland garden, *Trillium* will not fail to please with their attractive, often mottled foliage and dark flowers.

HOW TO GROW

Grow in deep humus-rich, moist but well-drained preferably acid to neutral soil. Deep or partial shade is most suitable. Mulch annually with leaf mould in autumn. Most are hardy.

Sow fresh seed in a shaded cold frame. Leaves normally appear in the second spring and plants take 5-7 years to reach flowering size. Divide rhizomes after flowering, ensuring each section has at least one growing point, may be slow to re-establish.

T. angustipetalum bears dark plum-purple petals, longer than wide which roll as they age. Massive, purple-speckled leaves. Endemic to California and not often seen in cultivation. Paul Christian says it is a distinctive species, confused with *T. kurabayashii* in the Jepson manual and often with *T. chloropetalum*.

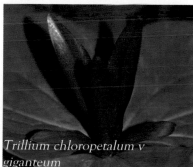

Trillium chloropetalum v giganteum

T. apetalon is a superb dark flower over plain green leaves.

T. chloropetalum is admirable, in both dark flowers and fabulous foliage. Z6.

T. chloropetalum v chloropetalum is a lovely, very upright, dark flower over darkish, silver mottled leaves.

T. chloropetalum v giganteum although the flower is not as dark as the species, this makes up for it in size. It is known as stinking Benjamin, I could not detect any malodour on the plants I photographed. It appreciates shelter from strong winds which should not be too much of a problem in a woodland setting. Good under deciduous trees. -12°C (10°F). Z 6.

T. cuneatum is often confused in horticulture, it bears long leaves and although silver marbled, it does not usually have maroon markings. The musk-scented, dark-maroon flowers have olive sepals and are stemless. Seedlings are variable. 45cm (18"). Z6.

T. decumbens is a fine, American wildflower, with mottled grey leaves usually without maroon markings that lie flat on the ground. Bears showy, upright dark

Trillium sessile

maroon-purple flowers. An easy species in shade.

T. erectum bears deep red-purple flowers with a black nose above plain leaves and is very dependable and easy. In the wild a green flower is more often encountered on this species. 50cm (20"). Z4.

T. foetidissimum bears small upright dark flowers over very attractive foliage.

T. kurabayashii is more or less confined to California. It is a handsome and robust species with broad-petalled upright, deep purple flowers, the largest flowers of all the sessile types. Slightly mottled leaves. Grows well throughout the U.K.

T. ovatum f maculosum bears white flowers, with dark purple-green blotches on the foliage which is unique among the pedicillate trilliums, however the markings are not consistent, yet it is possible to find wholly purple leaves in some forms. Z5.

T. petiolatum is found on the east side of the Cascades in the U.S. where it thrives in hot summers and cold winters in an arid terrain. It bears purple flowers near to ground level and tall, round leaves.

T. recurvatum has mottled green leaves with upright, elongated deep maroon flowers, with strongly recurving green sepals. 40cm (16").

T. reliquum has very upright, very dark flowers over attractive foliage.

T. rugelii x vaseyi bears pendent flowers with broad deep pink-purple petals, purple ovaries and a light fragrance.

T. sessile bears attractive marbled deep green leaves, the marbling often including bronze-maroon. Upright, red-maroon flowers are borne above the leaves on 15cm (6") stems from April to early June. An American native rarely seen in cultivation, *T. cuneatum* has been widely sold under this name. Easy. 30cm (12"). Z4.

T. smallii bears plain green leaves with tiny purple flowers. Z 4-8.

T. stamineum bears distinctive twisted deep maroon-purple flowers (not always that colour) with an unpleasant smell at very close quarters. Large, prominent stamens. Readily grown in neutral to slightly limey soil in leafy shade.

T. sulcatum has maroon, velvet-textured, very broad petals, like a superior *T. erectum* which name it is sometimes sold under, but it is taller. Petals have a turned back tip. Plain green leaves. Fungal odour.

T. underwoodii bears leaves mottled dark purple and grey with red-purple flowers. 25cm (10").

T. vaseyi bears nodding flowers of deep maroon-red (also green and white forms). Plain green leaves. This is the largest species for the garden similar to *T. sulcatum*. Sweetly scented or a pungent odour. Z. 6.

Most of the above can be variable producing other coloured flowers too and are best seen in bloom before you buy. Look out for **T. decipiens** and **T. gracile** which can produce dark flowers.

Tulipa 'Queen of Night'
(far right)

TULIPA

The most elegant addition to the dark garden. Cup-shaped flowers are a perfect combinaton with white or pastels. The symbol of love in Persia.

HOW TO GROW

Grow in fertile, well-drained soil in full sun, sheltered from strong winds. Dislike exessive wet and generally peat-based compost. Plant at a depth of 10-15cm (4-6"). Bulbs are best planted in November. Hardy. Z3-9.
Separate offsets after lifting in summer.

T. 'Arabian Mystery' is a fairly dark purple with a narrow feathered white margin. 50cm (20").

T. 'Black Hero' has double layers of exquisite deepest darkest maroon-black petals. Superbly ruffled peony type. Excellent cut flower. Forces well. 60cm (24"). Z3.

T. 'Black Horse' new from Holland, I am planting this up this year. Reputedly darker than *T.* 'Queen of Night'.

T. 'Black Parrot' is dark chocolate, maroon-purple and frilled at the margins of the petals. Excellent with *T.* 'White Parrot'. 55cm (22").

T. 'Greuze' is dark but not as good as *T.* 'Queen of Night'.

T. 'Havran' is maroon-black and can bear 2-3 flowers per stem. 45cm (18").

T. 'La Tulipe Noire' (Darwin) was raised by E.H. Krelage & Son in 1891, marginally lighter than *T.* 'Queen of Night'.

T. 'Negrita' is a very dark purple.

T. 'Queen of Night' produces distinctive single, velvety dark maroon flowers in late spring. Beautiful, stunning and still the darkest and best to my eye. Appear purple with the light behind them, otherwise very near black. The petals have a silky sheen. Elegant with *T.* 'Purissima', superb with *T.* 'Angelique' and quite sensational with *Allium* 'Purple Sensation'. Look out for a double form **T. 'Uncle Tom'**.

T. humilis 'Odalisque' is a deepish purple worth considering. 10cm (4").

T. humilis v pulchella Violacea Group black base bears deepish violet flowers each with a black base to the petals. 10cm.

T. humilis v pulchella Albocaerulea Group is a beautiful plant which should be grown more. Pure white petals are banded with a thin black line and a blue basal blotch. Early flowering, easy and fragrant.

T. 'Red Riding Hood' is useful for its maroon striped green leaves, bearing red-orange flowers.

TYPHONIUM

Incredible rare members of the aroid family, excellent in a woodland setting.

Cultivation as for *Arum*.

T. blumei bears a superb, dark purple almost flat spathe, with a darker spadix and fantastic leaves.

T. divaricatum bears limpish purple-black spathes, and large glossy green leaves.

T. giganteum (giraldii) is a rare Chinese aroid with extra large leaves to over 30cm (1ft) long. The 25cm (10") tall flower spike emerges purple with a sumptuous velvety black lining and a black spadix. Very handsome. Sun to light shade. Z 7-10.

T. hirsutum has a purple inner spathe and spadix.

T. pedunculatum bears a reflexed purple, near black large, silky spathe with a thin, near black spadix. Excellent.

T. roxburghii is an attractive species with deep purple, reflexed spathes which narrow to the tip, and a thin black spadix. Superb.

T. trilobatum has a purplish spathe and reddish spadix.

T. varians bears purple spathes with a greenish tip and an erect spadix near ground level. Leaves are well-veined.

T. venosum is really *Sauromatum venosum*, one aroid I am not fond of, I find little to recommend it. The spathe is floppy, an ugly spotted thing. It does not smell pleasant and is quite tender.

UNCINIA

Tufted reddish-bronze sedges, preferring damp or moist soil. Need replacing on a regular basis as they grow untidy quite quickly.

HOW TO GROW

Moderately fertile, humus-rich, moist soil in full sun or light dappled shade. In frost prone areas, grow in a sheltered site and mulch in winter. Frost hardy, tolerate temperatures to about -10°C (14°F) for short periods. I have grown U. rubra and U. egmontiana for several years in my Sheffield garden and never lost them. Temperatures drop to -7°C (just below freezing point in Fahrenheit) here for up to a week at a time.

Sow seed under glass in spring. Divide any time from late spring to midsummer. Can self seed mildly.

U. egmontiana is easy from seed and to my eye it has better form and colour than the other two.

U. rubra is an evergreen tufted perennial with short rhizomes. It bears abruptly pointed sharp leaves of a greenish red to brown and dark brown to black flowers. Divide frequently as they do get rather untidy looking quite quickly. 30cm (12"). Z8.

U. unciniata is smaller with reddish-brown leaves and brown flowers. 25cm (10").

VERATRUM

Almost black flowers on an imposing plant, a tower of dark stars above attractive foliage.

HOW TO GROW

Grow in deep, fertile, moist but well-drained soil with added, well-rotted organic matter. Choose a site in partial shade or in full sun where the soil is still retentive and will not dry out. Provide shelter from cold winds. Hardy to -35°C (-30°F) Z 4-10.

Sow fresh seed in containers in a cold frame. *Veratrum* seedlings develop very slowly and take many years to flower. Divide in autumn or early spring. Plants are usually very reasonably priced.

CAUTION: Contact with foliage may irritate skin. Please note all parts are highly toxic if ingested.

V. nigrum is an imposing rhizomatous perennial with pleated, deeply veined long basal leaves and few stem leaves. Leaves are hairless on the surface, but hairy-veined on the underside. In mid to late summer unpleasantly scented, star-shaped flowers are borne in terminal panicles of up to 45cm (18") long of a reddish-brown to nearly black colour with green striped backs. 120cm (2-4ft).

VIOLA

Surely the cheekiest plants and black suits them immensely. Violas and pansies are some of the prettiest little plants for the garden, much used in bedding schemes, containers or as fillers and ideal for black and white contrast.

HOW TO GROW

Grow in fertile, humus-rich, moist but well-drained soil in full sun or partial shade. Can seed themselves to death, so dead-head regularly. Cut *V. cornuta* back after flowering. Fully to half hardy.

Violas are easy from seed sown fresh or in spring in a cold frame. *V. x wittrochiana* (Pansies) can be sown in late winter for early spring and summer flowering, or in summer for winter flowering. Many Violas are short-lived so propagate regularly.

V. 'Black Ace' is an outstanding deep purple with an orange eye on smallish flowers.

Viola 'Bowles' Black'

V. 'Black from Black' has flowers with thick, rounded intense black petals from March to July and later. A strong grower with a good fruity scent. 15cm. (6").

V. 'Black Magic' from the U.S. is a superb *Viola* in containers, midnight black with a yellow eye. 20-25cm (8-10cm) which trails beautifully. Easy, free-flowering and useful as groundcover.

V. 'Blackjack' is small-flowered, velvety with a yellow eye.

V. 'Bowles' Black' (V.nigra) is actually a *tricolor* type with an orange eye, a touch of purple and near black flowers. Easy from seed and a favourite with me for its cheeky face and long-flowering from July to September, seeding itself gently.

V. cornuta 'Painted Black' from seed bears near-black flowers.

V. 'Mars' bears foliage with a brown-red centre and cream flowers in March-April.

V. 'Midnight Turk' bears delicate, wing-like purple-black flowers from May to October, mildly spreading.

V. 'Molly Sanderson' is a sexy, ravishingly black number with the

Viola 'Molly Sanderson'

darkest matt black petals with a yellow eye. Low habit and very compact but not very long lasting for me. Z4.

V. 'Raven' is a violetta with small deep purple flowers, easy to lose in the border and best in pots.

V. riviniana Purpurea Group (V. labradorica h) bears dark purplish green leaves and paler flowers. Can run and is more suitable for the wild or woodland garden in deep or partial shade. 10-20cm (4-8"). -23°C (10°F). Z 6-9.

V. 'Roscastle Black' holds near black and purple flowers well above the foliage from April to September. Almost like a larger flowered 'Bowles' Black', tending to legginess. 20cm (8").

V. 'Sawyers' Black' is similar to 'Bowles Black' bearing small, velvety purple-black flowers with a yellow eye. 15cm (6").

V. 'Sorbet Delight' is a 'Molly Sanderson' look-alike. An f1 hybrid if you feel you need one in the garden, good dark flowers.

V. x wittrochiana 'Black' bears black blooms with a yellow eye.

Viola 'Roscastle Black'

Viola f1 'Sorbet Delight'

V. 'Black Prince' and 'Black Devil' display large flowers, many of these look the same, **'Black Moon'**, **'Black Prince'**, **'Avalanche Black'**. A myriad of f1 strains circulate, choose from **'Black Beauty'**, **'Black Star'**, **'Zorro'**, **'Clear Crystals Black'**, **'Springtime Black'** or the f2 **'Black Princess'**. 20cm (8"). *Viola* make excellent fillers and are some of the blackest plants on offer.

V. x wittrochiana **Swiss Giants Group black** bears coal-black blooms. 20cm (8").

V. x wittrochiana **'Penny Black'** is short-lived.

Viola 'Avalanche Black' (left)
Viola 'Blackjack' (below)

VITIS

Oustanding dusky colour to clothe walls, screens and pergolas. This ornamental vine will wow all who are seeking a dark vertical accent.

HOW TO GROW
Best in sun in deep, moist, well-drained soil, preferably chalky.

The ornamental form **V. vinifera 'Purpurea'** bears attractive leaves, greyish at first, turning plum-purple then deep purple at maturity with a wonderful dusky bloom, maintaining good colour all summer. The fruits are unpalatable. A hardy, woody deciduous climber which can be used to good effect as a backdrop for paler colours in the garden. 10m (30ft). Hardy to -18°C (0°F). Z 7-10.

WEIGELA

Weigela are handsome deciduous shrubs with showy flowers. The most handsome of all, purple foliaged varieties have burst onto the scene.

W. 'Carnaval' (Courtador) bears good foliage, similar to 'Wine and Roses'

W. florida 'Foliis Pupureis' no longer really gets a look in, with its bronze tones.

W. 'Java Red' bears narrow rose-pink flowers with dark burgundy foliage.

W. 'Midnight Wine' is a superb dwarf forming a low mound of dark metallic burgundy-purple foliage. Use it at the front of the border or as groundcover.

W. 'Naomi Campbell' has stunning bronze foliage.

W. 'Wine and Roses' (Alexandria) is a lovely combination of excellent dark burgundy-purple foliage and rose-pink flowers. A much superior colour than *W.* 'Java Red'. Full sun will bring out the best colour.

Weigela 'Carnaval'

WISTERIA

Showy pendent racemes of fragrant pea-like flowers on these climbers which are so irresistible.

HOW TO GROW

Grow in fertile, moist but well-drained soil in full sun or partial shade. If grown into a tree, they will need no training, otherwise train against a wall, over an arch or pergola or as a free standing half-standard. Stems twine anti-clockwise. Hardy.

Species can be grown from seed but take many years to flower. Take basal cuttings from sideshoots in early to midsummer and root with bottom heat. Layer in autumn or graft in winter.

W. x formosa 'Yae-kokuryu' ('Black Dragon', often seen as 'Royal Purple' or 'Violacea Plena'). The real plant bears deep purple-violet flowers, hanging in racemes. Seek the double form, 'Kokuryu' double, with flowers of the same shade.

W. sinensis 'Blue Sapphire' has young bronze foliage and soft blue flowers. 10m (30ft).

Weigela 'Ruby Queen'

XANTHOSOMA

Blue taro has attractive arrow-shaped, pale purple leaves on deeper purple stems.

HOW TO GROW

Under glass, it needs a free root run. Best in loam-based compost with added leaf mould in moderate light. Water freely, applying a balanced feed every two weeks. Reduce watering in winter. Outdoors, grow in slightly acid, leafy soil which is humus-rich and fertile in partial shade. Frost tender.

Separate tubers at any time.

X. violaceum intermittently bears pale yellow flowers around spadices which are often violet. It is grown for the fabulous deep violet to purple stems and large leaves sometimes tinged purple. Edible tubers are pink inside. 2.5m.

Weigela 'Wine and Roses'

ZANTEDESCHIA

Another excellent choice for moist soil, both leaves and flowers are attractive and desirable.

HOW TO GROW

Under glass, grow in loam-based compost in full light. Water freely and apply a balanced liquid feed every two weeks until the flowers have faded. Keep just moist in winter. Outdoors, grow in humus-rich, moist soil in full sun. In frost prone areas, set deep in mud and protect *Z. aethiopica* with a deep winter mulch or grow as a marginal aquatic in water no deeper than 30cm (1ft). *Z. elliotiana* hybrids Z9. Sow seed under glass when ripe. Divide in spring.

These plants are known as arum lilies in England, but go under the name of calla lilies in the U.S.

Z. 'Black-Eyed Beauty' is an *elliottiana* hybrid with green leaves, heavily white-spotted. In summer it produces cream spathes each with a black central mark in the throat. A ready-made option for the black and white garden. 30-40cm (12-16").

Z. 'Black Magic' is another *elliottiana* hybrid with heavily white mottled green leaves, bearing yellow spathes, with black throats in summer. 75cm (30").

Z. 'Schwarzvalder' (Black Forest) (Keukenhof Gardens) takes pride of place. It is a deep claret-red *Arum* lily, definitely shaded black with a black inner throat almost forming a stripe to the tip of the flower. Use it as a container plant or cut flower. This requires a little less water than Z. aethiopica 'Crowborough' but is a wonderful companion for it. Stunning and a superb introduction which quickly went into my top ten of black plants for its exquisite dark flowers and spotted, elegant leaves.

ZINGIBER

Members of the ginger family, loving warmth and humidity.

Z. 'Midnight' incredible brownish black foliage, glossy and very desirable on arched stems. Flowers open creamy yellow changing to peachy apricot.

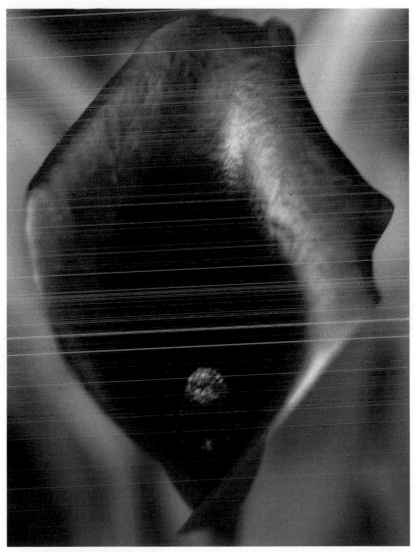

Zantedeschia 'Schwarzwalder'

179

POTAGER

A favourite gardening style is to mix fruit, vegetables and flowers in the potager. Dark leaves and fruits are not confined to flowers and you will encounter no problems finding edible plants to mix in the border. Vegetables offer their fair share of dark beauties and, of course, they are fit to eat.

For cut flowers in the potager, choose the dark *Lathyrus odoratus* varieties (sweet peas) on pea sticks, *Rudbeckia* 'Green Wizard' and darkest *Lilium*.

For arches which flank paths, choose *Vitis*, *Akebia*. or *Lathyrus* , along with *Rhodochiton atrosanguineus*, *Tropaeolum* (nasturtiums) with the darkest leaves or climbing beans with purple pods. A small specimen tree or fruit tree will provide a focal point and purple hedging can be used along with dark ivies to climb and clothe walls.

AUBERGINE

Known as eggplant in the U.S., these shiny dark beauties need high temperatures to form good fruits and are usually grown in a glasshouse. 'Mini Bambino' is excellent for the small garden, bearing dwarf 2.5cm (1") fruits which can be eaten whole. 'Black Beauty' was introduced in 1910 and its purple-black fruits are still popular today. 'Black Enorma' is very dark, early and prolific . 'Long Purple' is an unusual shape.

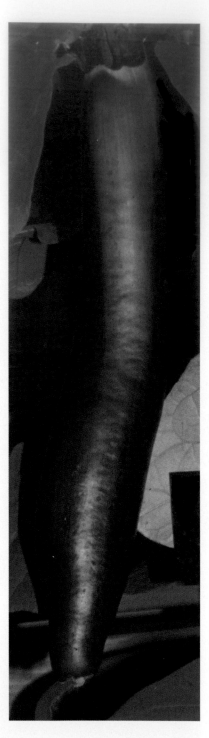

Aubergine 'Long Purple'

BEANS

'Purple Teepee' is a French bean which bears stringless pods which turn green on cooking. 'Royalty Purple Podded' is similar.

BEET

Purple-leaved beets enhance any planting. Beta 'Bull's Blood' has dark red foliage and 'McGregor's Favourite' offers brilliant narrow, recurved foliage of a deep blackish-purple, whilst 'Vulcan' has brilliant red foliage, all can be picked and eaten when young.

BROCOLLI

One of the earliest varieties is 'Rudolph' which produces tasty large spears from January onwards, from mid-February in colder climates.

CABBAGE

'Red Jewel' has large, tightly packed hearts with crisp, ruby-red leaves. Excellent standing quality and good storing ability. Delicious as a pickle or lightly cooked vegetable.

CAPSICUM

C. annuum 'Black Prince' is a perfect example of a dark ornamental pepper, with dark stems, small purple flowers and dark purple fruit. These fast growing annuals do best in warm, sunny positions. Sow seed under glass in spring.

Kale 'Redbor'

Lettuce 'Bakito'

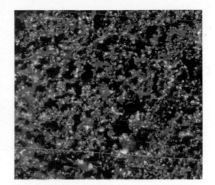

Lettuce 'Revolution'

CAULIFLOWER

Purple heads nestle amongst mid-green leaves on 'Violet Queen' up to 15cm (6") diameter. Turns green when cooked.

KALE

'Red Bor' with its crinkly purple leaves is highly decorative. It has excellent cold tolerance and crops during autumn to winter. 'Toscana di Negro' is absolutely fabulously dark and makes a very useful dark mound in the border. Once seen, never forgotten.

LABLAB

L. purpureus (Dolichos lablab) is a strong, tropical climber, useful in the ornamental garden for its purple-red pods.

LETTUCE

Lettuce come in shades from red to purple as well as the usual green. 'Lollo Rosso' is widely available, with frilled reddish brown leaves

but rather bitter I find. 'New Red Fire' is a dark red leaved variety with good flavour. 'Revolution' is a good bronze-black and the darkest I have seen yet is 'Bakito'.

ORIENTAL GREENS

Hon tsai tai is a flowering purple Pak Choi, both decorative and edible. Mustard Giant Red is also worthy of inclusion.

PEPPER

Such a wealth of peppers (capsicum) to choose from even in chocolate to black colours.
'Sweet Chocolate' has to be a favourite. An early fruiting, cold-tolerant sweet bell pepper which is the colour of plain chocolate. 'Chocolate Beauty' may well be the same thing. Looking for purple? Try 'Purple Beauty'.
In hot peppers you may come across 'Pretty in Purple', 'Chocolate', 'Black Dallas', 'Black Cluster' or 'Royal Black'.

CORN

'Red Strawberry' bears strawberry-shaped deep red cobs which can be popped or used decoratively.

RADICCHIO

Red Chicory has quite a bitter taste, but is good to mix with sweeter leaves. Colouring is good and the red leaves usually have white midribs.

TOMATO

Most of the following heirlooms have plum-purple skins. 'Black Crimea', 'Black Krim', 'Black Russian', 'Black Sea Man', the delicious, voted by many as the best tasting 'Black Brandywine'. You could also try 'Calabash Purple' or 'Prudens Purple'.

WHEAT GRAINS

Try Sorghum (broomcorn) or Triticum (wheat) for their dark ornamental value.

181

HERBS

Dark herbs such as Basil, come in lovely deep purples. Angelica, Orach (Atriplex) and Sage are included in the main section. Grow on their own in a herb garden or mix in the borders. Use in hanging baskets or window boxes. For picking, grow near the kitchen. Purple herbs are effective with silver or golden foliage.

BASIL (Ocimum basilicum)

'African Blue' is an unusual hybrid between 'Dark Opal' and the camphor basils, it retains the camphor odour which may be offputting, but is attractive for its purplish-blue cast. The variety 'Ararat' has striking foliage infused with purple markings.

'Dark Opal' has red-purple leaves and stems. Try it in basil vinegar. When launched it was extremely dark, but is now producing some green. Holy basil (*O.tenuiflorum* syn *O.sanctum*) is also available in a purple strain, 'Osmin' is perhaps the darkest. 50cm (20"). Purple basil, *O.basilicum v purpurascens* is an annual with strongly scented purple leaves. 'Purple Delight' upright strong growth, and colouring like the old 'Dark Opal'

Basil 'Red Rubin'

before it became greenish. 'Purple Ruffles' is an annual grown for its attractive ruffled leaves in deep purple. It is not the easiest to grow, damping off easily. Again, it is a strain which is showing some deterioration since it achieved award-winning status. Can be placed outdoors in a sunny position in pots. 'Mini Purpurascens Wellsweep' with its delightful pointed leaves edged in gold-green is wonderful.

FOENICULUM

Bronze Fennel (*F. vulgare* 'Purpureum' often sold as Bronze') is highly decorative with bronze-red lacy foliage. An excellent contrast to solid leaves.

GRAIN AMARANTH

Amaranthus hypochondriacus included in the main section can be cooked as a hot cereal or popped like popcorn. It can also be milled into flour. Edible landscaping with vibrant burgundy colour.

Foeniculum vulgare 'Purpureum'

JAPANESE PARSLEY

Cryptotaenia japonica f atropurpurea makes a handsome foliage plant with its trifoliate purple leaves with pointed leaflets, up to 7.5cm (3"). This strong, erect plant makes a mound on dark stems. Tip sprays of insignificant flowers can be removed. Also useful as a bog plant. 46cm (18").

MENTHA

M. spicata 'Nigra' bears dark purple to deep green colouring.

OREGANO

'Hopley's Purple' bears dark purple green foliage and has a compact growth habit.

RUMEX

Sorrel is another edible landscaping herb, the glossy red leaves of *Rumex acetosella ssp vinealis* are particularly good in winter and spring.

The Seed Search lists over 40 thousand varieties of seed and where to buy them all around the world, from over 500 seed spplier around the world. Includes over 33 thousand flowering plants from seed and over 9,500 vegetables. Order your copy now from the address at the front of the book.

ANNUALS

Perfect for filling gaps in borders and keeping the show going, annuals offer enormous potential adding quick colour, texture and fragrance to the garden. They can extend the garden season easily into autumn, filling unsightly gaps left by early flowering plants. Make use of them in new borders and new gardens, giving time for perennials and shrubs to establish. Tender perennials such as *Solenostemon*, *Pelargonium*, *Impatiens*, *Ricinus* and *Canna* are often used as annuals. *Impatiens* New Guinea types add dark foliage and hot coloured flowers to pots and containers. Tuberous *Dahlia* are best lifted and treated as an annual in colder areas. Keep pots of these to fill in any gaps which appear in borders.

Celosia cristata 'Amigo Mahogany Red' is a superb new plant available in the U.S. with rich dark purple foliage and amazingly dark maroon heads.

Centaurea cyanus 'Black Boy' has recently been re-introduced, offering some of the darkest flowers on an annual. Together with *Scabiosa*, *Nemophila*, *Papaver* and *Viola*, these are excellent fillers in borders and pots adding welcome dark accents to plantings. Add a little height with *Helianthus annuus*, sunflowers are now far from just yellow. A new breeding programme has been in existence in Russia for some time and darker sunflowers are on the horizon, although many of the flowers are on the brownish side. *H. debilis ssp cucumerifolius* 'Italian White' has creamy white petals around a black central disc.

Hibiscus trionum is a favourite with captivating, cream trumpet flowers and a near black centre. Adds a touch of mystery.

Allow dark-leaved *Tropaeolum majus* (Nasturtium) 'Chocolate' to weave around on poor soil. Useful for the base of pergolas and in containers too.

Celosia 'Amigo Mahogany Red'

BIENNIALS

Alcea (Hollyhock) is best grown as a biennial and not as a perennial. Some of the darkest flowers are found on *A. rosea* 'Nigra'. *Dianthus barbatus* (Sweet William) offers the unusual combination of dark flower and foliage.

PERENNIALS

Wonderful plants that please time and time again. Herbaceous perennials disappear underground to reappear afresh in spring, others are evergreen, some hardy, some tender. I grow all kinds, they all contribute to the garden. Long, rectangular herbaceous borders are wonderful if you have the space, but I admire just as much a mixed herbaceous border which is more suited to most smaller town gardens, particularly in the U.K. Glorious perennials are so versatile, use them in informal plantings mixed with other plants, bulbs, annuals, shrubs; as hedging, groundcover and specimen plants. Equally at home in the mixed border, an isolated border surrounded by grass, a meadow garden, rock garden, or planted into cracks in walls and paving.

There are numerous perennials from which to choose for their different attributes. Divide regularly to maintain vigour.

Graceful *Dierama*, bold *Eupatorium*, stately *Canna*, delicate perennial grasses all add a different quality to the garden.

Early flowering *Helleborus* are worthy of a place in the garden, the black ones are irresistible and they often also break dormancy with dark bronzed foliage.

Late-flowering perennials are valuable to extend the season and for the contrast of their flower colour. Try bronze-leaved *Kniphofia* and *Crocosmia* for their vivid flowers. *Eupatorium* combine well with silver grasses, *Stipa barbata* and *Miscanthus sinensis* 'Silberfeder'.

Dark-foliaged creeping perennials such as *Ajuga, Leptinella* or *Hemigraphis* in warmer climes make excellent ground cover. *H. alternata* (*H. colorata*) is known as red ivy owing to the undersides of its attractive leaves, and because it roots at the nodes. *H.* 'Exotica' goes by the name of purple waffle plant. Purplish-green leaves are puckered between the veins with a purple sheen, the underside is deep red. *H. repanda* has slender maroon-red stems which root down freely. Narrow leaves are red-flushed greyish-green, shading to purple above, and dark purple beneath. As an added bonus all

Hemigraphis alternata

three bear white flowers from spring to summer. Use in a tropical bedding scheme, contrasted with *Senecio cineraria, Solenostemon* (*Coleus*), *Colocasia* and *Canna*.

Easy, dark perennials include *Polemonium*. Unfussy plants, easy to grow virtually anywhere, three with dark foliage have sprung up in the last few years.

If a challenge is needed, try *Paeonia*, expensive plants if they do sulk and fail, but their fleeting beauty makes us want to succeed with them. Or why not try *Primula auricula*, given a good gritty soil, not overwatered or heated, their beauty is unsurpassable.

Unusual perennials include the incredibly handsome, dark-leaved *Eranthemum nigrum* with white flowers. *Phyteuma nigrum*, a class act from a bunch of difficult to grow, often weedy, usually rock-garden grown genus. It bears deep burgundy-black swirls of flowers. The exotic looking *Kohleria* 'Dark Velvet' is an admirable gesneriad grown for its dark leaves which are the most velvet-like of any leaf I have touched with bright flowers.

Nautilocalyx pemphidius is an evergreen gesneriad from tropical America, and suitable for the warm glasshouse. Its puckered chocolate brown leaves form a low rosette, its small white flowers are appealing. *N. bullatus* and *N. lynchii* have a purple or bronze sheen on the upper surface of their leaves and better, deeper colouring on the undersides.

SHRUBS

Choose well, these will become the main background of your garden whether grown in a shrub border or mixed border. Shrubs are also useful as hedges and smaller shrubs such as *Hebe* can be used as ground cover. *Acer* make superb specimens in pots or as a specimen in a lawn. There is an enormous range of purple to dark black-red foliage from which to choose, but shrubs which offer attractive flowers, autumn colour or berries offer that little bit extra, a plus feature. Most purple shrubs benefit greatly from full sun where the colours will sparkle.

One of the most used dark shrubs has to be *Berberis*, there are ones to suit different needs. Often used as a hedge, its prickly thorns are a deterrent to all things that want to climb into your garden; but equally useful as mounds, spires or standards. The best autumn colour is achieved when grown in full sun, where they fruit better too.

The spreading shrub, *Brachyglottis repanda* 'Purpurea' which grows into a magnificent 6m (20') tree in its native New Zealand, is better cut back each year when it rewards the grower with larger leaves. Employ it as an effective hedge or windbreak in coastal areas in well-drained soil in full sun. The frothy panicles of small flowers are produced in late winter to spring. Dark shrubs such as *Calycanthus* are captivating. The dusky, unusual flowers of *C. floridus* are similar to

Magnolia stellata with strap-like petals in dark red, brownish at the tips. *C. floridus* v *glaucus* 'Purpureus' has the addition of purple foliage on the underside as well as retaining the purple coloration on the surface of the shiny leaves into late autumn. *C. occidentalis* has larger foliage and flowers.

No purple garden should be without *Cotinus* for the fabulous foliage and plumes of 'smoke'. Often used as shrubs, they hover between the two categories of shrub and tree. They are the most used purple-leaved backdrop for contrasting plants.

More unusual dark foliaged shrubs include bronze *Coprosma* with their dark glossy leaves. Deep purple *Dodonaea viscosa* 'Purpurea' is not a shrub you see everywhere, but it is very dark and worthy. *Itea virginica* 'Henry's Garnet' is an interesting deciduous shrub with good purple summer colour in sun, staying the course in autumn. Also valued for its tassels of creamy flowers. The slightly tender *Leptospermum* and *Loropetalum* chinense cultivars offer foliage in good tones of purple.

Pittosporum is welcome for its dark, glossy leaves as well as the honey-scented brownish flowers. Available from small to large, these tender shrubs are very welcome in the garden. *Rhododendron* lovers can be placated with one or two dark flowers and bronzed leaves, but not so dark to get that excited

about. Dark red flowers are found in *R.* 'Black Hawk' (Azalea), *R.* 'Black Magic' and *R.* 'Black Knight', *R.* 'Queen of Hearts' and *R.* 'Ebony Pearl'. Other *Rhododendron* bear bronzed leaves, one good example is *R. vireya* 'Orange Queen' which is grown for its foliage alone, it is a non-flowering cultivar. These need to be kept under cover but are well worth any effort to grow. Once referred to as Malesian *Rhododendron*, these evergreen shrubs from tropical areas of S.E. Asia are frost tender. Containers can restrict the size of plants when grown in a cool conservatory.

Weigela are handsome deciduous shrubs with showy flowers and much improved purple foliaged varieties are readily available.

Weigela 'Midnight'

TREES

The mainstay of the garden, dark trees provide a backdrop. Their structure is so welcome, either in the border or as specimen plants. Some small trees are also suitable in large pots. Fastigiate forms are used to great advantage in small spaces where a tree with a spreading crown cannot be used. Positioning is important, catch the sun behind to shine through the leaves, the play of colour is one of the most entrancing aspects of the garden. Dark trees are valued for the intensity of their leaves, they stand centre stage in the garden. Many make excellent specimen plants and there are dark trees to suit most types of garden and soil. Extend the season by choosing early spring or late autumn colour. *Acer* are admired for their wonderful leaves, colouring well in autumn and many being interestingly pinnate or dissected. Autumn colour is better when plants are grown in neutral to acid soil. A specimen tree makes an arresting sight. They also fit well into the border and combine well with other plants and many of the smaller *A. palmatum* types are excellent container plants.

Agonis flexuosa 'After Dark' is a weeping tree with a graceful habit and an excellent specimen in frost free areas. This West Australian willow myrtle grows to 6m (20') and bears burgundy to purple foliage all year round. The tiny white flowers which appear in spring are silhouetted against the dark background. *Agonis* prefers good drainage.

The most well-known purple foliage tree, and sometimes the most hated, has to be *Fagus sylvatica Atropurpurea* Group. Fantastic when you can obtain a good coloured form. Used in landscaping it is a very visible exclamation mark and a superb specimen tree. From a very early age this became my favourite tree and still is, my passion for dark plants goes back a long way. I would make a point of looking for all the purple beeches when travelling by bus or car. I always got a buzz of excitement when I spotted one. I still feel a buzz when I see one now, especially with the sun coming through the foliage and positioning in full sun is essential for the best colour which is exquisite. The darkest is *F. sylvatica* 'Riversii', an old cultivar dating from the 1870's.

Gleditsia triacanthos 'Rubylace' is a wonderful purple-foliaged tree with the added fascination of sickle-shaped seedpods in autumn. This spiny, deciduous tree will appreciate fertile soil and a position where it will glow in late afternoon light to show the colour of its dark bronze, red-purple foliage to advantage. By midsummer, the leaves turn bronze-green.

Some of the most astonishingly beautiful flowers in the plant kingdom are to be found on *Magnolia* species. The darkest *Magnolia* available widely is still *M. liliiflora* 'Nigra' which bears dark red-purple flowers in a wonderful goblet shape, most elegantly in flower in early summer and intermittently thereafter. There are currently darker *Magnolia* about to be released from New Zealand. White flowered *Magnolia* with dark purple stamens or blotches can also enhance the garden, *M. x soulangeana* 'Amabilis' and *M. x soulangeana* 'Brozzonii' are admirable in this capacity.

Another excellent choice of tree for the dark garden is *Sambucus nigra* 'Black Beauty', now considered to be the darkest cultivar available. The dark, almost black foliage is combined with lemon-scented pink flowers in June, followed by autumn berries. In eight years you can have an excellent free-standing specimen tree of 3m (10ft) if the plant is left unpruned. Laciniate foliage is usually attractive, adding interest to the garden and a good contrast to solid leaves. Try *Sambucus nigra* 'Black Lace' teamed with pink flowers.

Sambucus nigra 'Black Lace'

BULBOUS PLANTS

Spring bulbs with dark colours are not numerous but well worth using to extend the season of dark planting. Try *Crocus* 'Negro Boy', the tender *Muscari latifolium* or *Hyacinthus* 'Menelik'. *Tulipa* 'Queen of Night' is the most planted dark bulb, but *T.* 'Greuze' is also popular in the U.S and *T.* 'Havran' in the U.K., though neither rival the 'Queen'. Watch for new ones from exciting breeding programmes in Holland. *Crinum purpureum* is one of the best deep purple leaved plants I have ever come across, still not in general cultivation and not to be confused with the red-leaved types or purple-flushed flowered types. A superb plant for which to yearn.

Fritillaria, superbly dark plants with dusky bells to entice and entrance. The dark petals add a touch of mystery and will have you hooked. Some are easy-going others quite a challenge. A favourite with me is the rather difficult to grow, but fabulous in flower, *F. persica*. *Hermodactylus tuberosus* is enchanting when given the right conditions to flower, rather demanding and needing a lot of heat and a long summer to enable a good flowering performance. It is a fabulous plant, worthy of every effort to satisfy its whims. Tubers need to be baked in a long hot summer, so give it your very hottest spot, at the base of a sunny, south-facing wall and pray daily. It is fully hardy and best planted at a depth of 10cm (4") in sharply drained soil in autumn. It can even be naturalised in grass in warmer areas, although I have never seen this, how I would like to, surely a sight to savour. The bluish green, linear leaves are handsome, as are the flowers of a most unusual colouring. They are a combination of greenish-yellow and a velvety blackish-brown. Their early flowers exude a sweet perfume in spring, prone to late frosts, so if in doubt, grow under cover.

Iris are stately and elegant and the perfect choice for a sunny spot in the garden where they can bake and bask in long, hot summers. In very hot sites, they appreciate a thin covering of soil. *Iris* dislike being in the shadow of other plants and also dislike nitrogen. Bearded *Iris* appreciate a slightly acid to alkaline soil. The worst thing about these wonderful plants is that they are a nesting box for weeds, those little dandelion parachutes just love to sneak in amongst the rhizomes and are almost impossible to dig out. Schreiner's *I.* 'Dusky Challenger' has topped the popularty polls for three years in the U.S., charming gardeners with the silky quality of its dark blooms which are hard to resist. The large flower is beautifully ruffled on a branched stem with four flowers often open all at once. The rhizomatous beardless *I. chrysographes* and its cultivars are some of the darkest flowers you will see, even though briefly with a short flowering time, these are still real wow plants.

Oxalis triangularis grow from tiny rhizomes with some garden worthy plants. The deep purple leaves of *O. triangularis* 'Cupido' or *O. triangularis ssp papilionacea* 'Atropurpurea' confused in horticulture offer foliage for which they are well worth growing, the latter has an attractive lighter purple splash. Foliage is truly magnificent all summer, but most welcome in late summer and early autumn when everything else is flagging. With the onset of frosts, I pop my pot in the cold frame, keeping on the dry side and growth begins again in late spring. The tubers can easily be split up at this time, and the plants will fill the pot by late summer. This was the second dark plant I came across after *Ohiopogon* and the two of them started me off on my never-ending quest for black plants. I have grown both plants ever since, and would not want to be without them. Although I find this *Oxalis* difficult to keep in open ground I have seen good use of this at flower shows, used at the edge of a border, in a formal bedding scheme and in a mixed border with other darks.

Oxalis

BLACK ORCHIDS

Black orchids are truly irresistible. *Coelogyne pandurata* is an impressive species with pseudobulbs on a creeping rhizome. Two long, dark green leaves are produced. The arching flower stems appear in spring with up to 12 flowers to 10cm (4") in diameter. Sepals and petals are a clear bright green. The lip is long and narrow, the crest is warted and black-veined, giving the plant its common name of black orchid. Hailing from Borneo and Malaysia, this species does best in the hot house in slatted baskets. The hybrid *C.* 'Green Dragon' also has a near black lip.

Columnara Wildcat v Bobcat is a mouthwateringly dark orchid in the plummy brown colour range. Delicate and delightful.

Cymbidium Pontac 'Mont Millais' is a good dark red, a little white for contrast, and darker purplish red on the edge of the lip. A very attractive plant, not least for the fact that *Cymbidium* are some of the easiest orchids to keep.

Dendrobium atroviolaceum bears upright spikes of up to 10 large, pendent flowers. The sepals and petals are creamy white and more often than not, heavily spotted with blackish purple. The flowers are exceptionally long lasting and need to be grown in a hot house.

Lemboglossum often produce brownish flowers, contrasting with lower pink petals. However, *Lemboglossum bictoniense* x Oda.

'Brocade' is a satisfying deep velvet red with black shading.

x Aliceara is fabulous, like a chocolate brown and cream dessert. *Miltonia* too produce spotted petals and sepals which are often brown. *Miltoniopsis* Charlesworthii x Seine delights with its pure white petals enticingly blotched black-red in the centre. *M.* Mem Ida Siegal has an incredible splotch of deepest burgundy in its centre appearing as if paint has been splattered onto the white petals edged pink, upper petals are mainly pink. On the brown side too are *x Wilsonara* Hamburen Stern 'Cheam' and the delightful, dark *Zygopetalum*, one of my favourites is *Z.* 'Adelade Meadows'. *Z.* (Yolanda x Blackii) x Skippy Ku is also superb. *Z.* 'Advance Australia 'Cute' x Helen-Ku 'Black as Black' should be black with a purple lip.

x Odontocidium 'Black Magic' is a plant to make your mouth water. These evergreen orchids are derived from hybrid crosses between the two species, *Odontoglossom* and *Oncidium*. Flowers are usually predominantly yellow or russet brown, so this is an unusual colouring for the hybrids. They are frost tender, needing a minumum temperature of 10°C (50°F) and only need to be divided when they are potbound. The flowers of this sumptuous orchid are fairly small, fuchsia pink with upper petals in near black-maroon. *Odontoglossum* 'Isler's Abendglut' has similar colouring, slightly lighter on a bigger flower. This is incredibly beautiful.

Paphiopedilum, the slipper orchids, are where one normally finds the darkest orchids. These orchids are the most resistant to red spider mite. They feature distinctive pouches and often look as if they are sporting a moustache. Grow in pots which constrict the roots and take great care not to overwater. *P.* Maudiae Prieta is the darkest I have seen with its deepest, darkest wine, near black flowers on a plant that blooms well. *P.* 'Black Maud' is a good example with its near black lip and purple colouring. *P.* 'Joanne's Wine' is a terrestrial orchid with greyish-green leaves with dark mottling to offset the dark flowers which are wine purple and green. *P.* 'Larry

Odontocidium 'Black Magic'

Paphiopedilum 'Black Maud'

Bird' has superb colouring with its almost black lip and very deep purple colouring with a hint of white around the edge. *P.* Maudiae 'Coloratum' which has dark wine flowers striped darker on the upper sepals. *P.* 'Red Glory' x 'Pacific Magic' is very dark. It is not too difficult to find *Paphiopedilum* with pouches that are near black. *P.* Croyland x Bright Alary is purple with a darker pouch, whilst *P.* 'Midnight Magic' can vary from dark purple to reddish, *P.* rothschildianum x mackayanum is a terrific dark cross. *P. delenattii* has delightfully mottled foliage, green marked with purplish brown spots, as is often the case.

Phalaenopsis 'Black Butterfly' is ravenously dark, slightly pinkish tips to petals, so too 'Black Ruby' with a paler throat. *P.* 'Ever Spring Prince' is equally desirable. *Pterostylis* 'Dusky Duke' bears almost black-red flowers with extended horn-like vertical petals. A naturally occurring hybrid (*curta x pedunculata*) blending the best of its parents, producing large flowers and deep colouration. Easy to grow in the U.K. and well worth trying outdoors.

Ludisia discolor, the Jewel Orchid, is a terrestrial with 7cm (3") elliptic maroon-green leaves with metallic red to gold veins. Small white flowers complete the charming picture. Requiring high humidity and warmth, they are easy in a terrarium. *Ludisia* 'Black Velvet' has deep green almost black leaves. *Dracula* orchids are fabulous too.

CLIMBERS

It is not difficult to find climbers in dark shades to run up bamboo poles, twiggy supports, cover fences and clothe arches, obelisks and pergolas, adding wonderful dark tones in spires. Some are very vigorous, such as *Aristolochia*, others are more gentle in their growth and easy to accommodate in the small garden. Apart from covering bare walls, climbers have an important role in the garden, invaluable as a vertical statement to lead the eye up. Choose different supports in varied materials to compliment the climber and the garden.

Akebia, all too infrequently mentioned in horticultural circles are a perfect dark climber for the dark garden. These twining shrubby climbers with their elegant foliage are hardy although their purple fruits are often not produced in the U.K. They need a rich, loamy soil to perform their best and they are worth pleasing, producing as they do, good dark flowers. *A. quinata* is a semi-evergreen climber with brownish purple flowers which emit a spicy scent. *A. trifoliata* is a deciduous climber with purple flowers in spring. Z 5-9.

Hedera, the classic climber, where the much overused and overrated *H.* 'Goldheart' still reigns supreme. Let me endarken you. The dark ivies create a superb backdrop. They are more stylish than some of the gaudy, vulgar variegated variations. *H. helix* 'Atropurpurea' ('Purpurea'), has large, 5-lobed blackish green leaves which gradually turn deep purple in cold weather. The attractive foliage is strongly veined green. This is an excellent climber for walls, reaching 25m (8'). *H. helix* 'Glymii' is less robust and is suitable for a chimney pot or small wall. Its medium-sized, entire or 3-lobed glossy, dark green leaves turn red-purple in cold weather. Each leaf is interestingly curled or twisted, a feature which increases as the weather turns progressively colder. A suitable dark ivy for a pot is readily found in *H. helix* 'Donerailensis' whose small leaves turn brownish-purple in winter. It retains its character best in a pot with restricted roots.

Hoya are such fascinating plants, rather fussy in their requirements, but extremely intriguing. Frost tender *Hoya* require an open, free-draining medium of compost to which has been added equal parts of leaf mould, sharp sand, pulverised bark and charcoal in which to really flourish. Indirect or bright, filtered light and high humidity are further necessities. They need a minimum temperature of 7°C (45°F). Still want to grow one? They are worth it, their waxy flowers are exquisite. *H. macgillivrayi* is a strong growing climber whose thick stems are twining. The rigid, thick, fleshy leaves are a lustrous green, often tinged red-purple when young. Cup-shaped, smallish flowers are borne 4-8cm (up to 3") across in spring to summer, the colouring of which is variable; anything from red, red-purple, purple or brownish-red to dark-maroon, even near black. Coronas can also be dark red or occasionally white. *H. purpureofusca* bears umbels of scented, deep maroon flowers.

Kennedia nigricans is a woody-stemmed climber from warmer climes in the southern hemisphere, bearing distinctive blackish flowers. Appreciates added sharp sand to a loam-based compost and a position in bright filtered light. Known as the black coral pea, this robust climber produces racemes of velvety darkest purple-black or dark chocolate flowers with the standard petals reflexed and boldly splashed with a yellow blotch. Thrives in poor sandy soils and is a good coastal plant, needing a frost-free environment and a temperature of 5-7°C (41-45°F).

Some *Nepenthes* species are climbing perennials. Plants I would describe as odd, not because they are dark, but for their curious pitchers and their most unusual habit of being carnivorous plants. What do you want for lunch today plants? Fly soup. I have always thought it quite an odd thing to have one's own personal fly catcher hanging in the greenhouse. Plants which stop people in their tracks and although never black, many have purplish-red pitchers. Pitchers can differ in colour on one plant. A lid protects against too much

rain entering the pitcher. Some species grow quite large. In cultivation cut back growth in spring to encourage larger pitchers and fresh foliage. Grown well they are a breathtaking sight, but heaven alone knows what one might find lurking in the depths of those receptacles. The curious pitcher plants secrete nectar from the thickened rim of the pitcher, to attract insects and small mammals which become trapped once tempted inside. All species need a warm greenhouse if temperatures normally fall below 10°C (50°F) at night, where they are best grown in baskets. *N. rafflesiana* and other lowland species need a much higher temperature, not falling below 15°C (59°F). These carnivorous plants hail from acidic open grassland or forest in Asia and are often epiphytes growing on

trees. *N. x ventrata* is a fascinating sight with many hanging, quite large, purplish pitchers and fabulously shiny green leaves. Pitchers come in a variety of shapes and sizes. *N. x mixta* shows wonderful coloration. Fresh seed of *Nepenthes* species can be sown on the surface of moist coir and placed in a tray of water in a shaded propagator at a constant temperature of 27°C (81°F). Cuttings with three to four leaves can be inserted into coir compost at a similar temperature. Air layer in spring or summer.

Nepenthes x ventrata

Nepenthes x mixta

SUCCULENTS

There are some fabulously dark succulents very worthy of growing in tufa containers, large or small. However, succulents seem to fall into two categories, there are those which I would suggest that everyone grows, and others which are for collectors.

The best dark succulent is *Aeonium* 'Zwartkop' for its fantastic, dark black leaves in full sun. A plant for every black enthusiast. The paler *A. arboreum* 'Atropurpureum' is a good companion. *Echeveria* 'Black Knight' is enjoyable for its green leaves are tipped in pale black. *Sedum* are so worthy of growing, both the small leaved ones, *Sedum spathulifolium* varieties which work so well underplanting *Ophiopogon* and the taller, larger leaved succulents, mostly from *S. telephium* such as *S.* 'Vera Jameson' or *S.* 'Betram Anderson', is its laxness a desirable quality or a nuisance? *Sedum* are becoming ever darker. There are also a large number of *Sempervivum,* favourites for pots. Growing well even in poor soil, in fact they are best in moderately fertile soil with added grit for drainage and appreciate full sun. Offsets need to be rooted in spring or summer as rosettes die after flowering. Fascinating succulents with very unusual flowers, but more difficult to grow and often with an off-putting aroma and there are few of us who want plants that smell anything but sweet, even if they are dark and attractive-looking. The scent attracts the pollinators and is not intended to offend the human nose. The unusual *Edithcolea grandis* is a perennial succulent with very dark flowers, which the uninitiated, who think dark plants are sombre, would perhaps call ugly. It reminds me of owls. *Huernia* are curious frost-tender succulents from hilly, semi-desert areas with a faintly unpleasant scent yet the flowers are interesting and quite beautiful. *Orbea* is sometimes placed under *Stapelia* to which it is closely related and bears the same unpleasant odour but extraordinary flowers of a unique beauty in summer and as a bonus, stems are often purplish. The star shaped flowers of *Orbeopsis albocastanea*, often found under *Caralluma* are dark and very distinct.

Catalpa erubescens 'Purpurea'

Leea coccinea

*Cercidiphyllum japonicum
'Rotfuchs'*

Prunus 'Royal Burgundy'

Diospyros eburneum

Mahonia gracilipes

*Hedera berries
Rheum palmatum
'Atrosanguineum'*

*Primula 'Garnet'
Rodgersia pinnata 'Superba'*

ALSO DARK

Consider the following flowers or foliage for inclusion in the dark garden. All make a valuable contribution to the dark theme.

Acanthus spinosus forms dark, architectural spires.

Achillea 'McVities' is an addition to the chocolate lovers garden.

Agapanthus 'Kingston Blue' bears royal blue flowers. *A.* 'Purple Cloud' is also dark. *A.inapertus* 'Graskop' has blue-black flowers.

Aloe petrophylla and *Aloe deltoideaulonta v contigna* are dark contenders.

Amorpha canescens (Lead plant) is an herbaceous perennial prairie plant with pubescent grey foliage and spike-like racemes of dark purple, near black flowers.

Apios americana bears clusters of scented chocolate-maroon pea-like blooms.

Artocarpus heterophyllus 'Black Gold' is a variety of jackfruit bearing large edible fruits with leaves so dark as to appear black.

Armeria maritima 'Rubrifolia' is a purple leaved thrift with dark burgundy foliage in full sun and deep pink flowers. A scree plant.

Asclepias cordifolia bears dark red-purple flowers, of interest are other Asclepiads such as *Caralluma* and the dark-spotted *Pachycarpus grandiflorus*.

Astrantia 'Hadspen Blood' is the darkest on offer.

Bartsia alpina is a distinctive and sought after rarity. The flowers, calyx and some of the upper leaves are suffused with a rich dark but somewhat subdued purple.

Billbergia amoena has varying shades of purple or red flushing. Cactus often have black spines.

Calceolaria arachnoidea bears rosettes of lance-shaped white, hairy leaves from which arise slender stems of deep purple flowers from summer to autumn. Best in an alpine house.

Cerinthe major 'Purpurascens' is borderline dark, but extremely beautiful so perhaps permissible in the dark garden. The darkest bracts are found wild in southern Spain. Bears navy blue flowers with hints of purple and grey.

Cirsium rivulare 'Atropurpureum' bears burgundy flowers.

Chamaesphacos illicifolius is like a purple-leaved dead nettle (Lamium). Can be seen at Wisley.

Chondropetalum, I only found one reference to this South African grass, resembling Carex and bearing tiny flowers in chaffy brown bracts.

Chrysanthemum 'Black Magic' is an early flowering outdoor reflexed type with dark velvety blooms, not as black as its name suggests.

Other dark *Clematis* hybrids, include 'Etoile Violette' or 'Niobe'.

Columnea 'Midnight Lantern' bears very dark leaves.

Crocus biflorus ssp alexandri, native to Skopje, Macedonia is a striking combination of deep purple and white.

Excellent container plants viewed close-up are found in *Cuphea* *ignea* 'Black Ash' and *C. silenoides*. Easy in good, rich, moist soil. 80cm (32").

Delphinium Black Knight Group bears very dark purple flowers with a black eye. *D. brunonianum* is an upright perennial with hairy stems and deeply lobed leaves. Short-spurred deep blue to purple flowers are borne with black-purple eyes, black spurs and heavy veining. Good for a rock garden. *D. speciosum* bears loose spikes of violet-black flowers above hairy leaves. 50cm (20").

Dierama 'Blackbird' has deep wine flowers from black buds. Many plants in cultivation obtained from seed, are not the real thing.

Diervilla x splendens has bronze-red tinged foliage all summer.

Dorstenia turnerifolia bears shiny green leaves and curious, very unusual fleshy purple flowers. Needs low light and high humidity.

Dracaena fragrans 'Compacta Purpurea' bears glossy leaves flushed purple.

Echium russicum for its dark rust-red spikes.

Epipactis gigantea 'Serpentine Night' bears purple tinted foliage.

Erica cinerea 'Velvet Night' bears blackish-purple flowers.

Erigeron 'Schwarzes Meer' you may find is darker than 'Dunkelste Aller'. *E.* 'Quakeress' has grey flowers, the foliage is grey-green.

Erythronium produce purple mottled leaves, try *E. americanum*, *E. helenae* or *E. dens-canis*.

Ferraria crispa bears few malodorous brown flowers.

Fumaria occidentalis is a rare British native found only in parts of Cornwall and the Isles of Scilly. White flowers age to red or pink with blackish-red wings of the upper petals, bordered with white edging.

Try dark *Gossypium* for their deep purple foliage with pink to cream flowers.

Graptophyllum pictum 'Chocolate' has dark sienna and creamy white variegation. *G. pictum* 'Black Beauty' bears darkest, glossy leaves.

Known as the purple velvet plant, *Gynura* 'Purple Passion' adds a little passion to your garden.

The deep reddy browns of *Helenium* are suitable candidates.

Helianthus 'Taiyo' is brownish red with a hint of yellow, flowers are small. *H.* 'Chianti' is reddish. *H.* 'Prado Red' is a multi-flowered type with up to 20 sunflowers on short stems. *H.* 'Velvet Queen' is brownish red.

Heliconia indica 'Spectabile' is coppery-brown.

Juncus ensifolius bears blackish flowerheads.

Kaempferia sp. mottled leaf bears large, deep green leaves heavily leopard spotted in near black.

One of my favourite brown-leaved plants is *Kalanchoe beharensis*.

Lagenophora pinnatifida produces mats of bronze-green foliage.

Leucadendron 'Safari Sunset' has stems and bracts of deep wine red in winter.

Leycesteria formosa has dark purple bracts surrounding white flowers.

Ligularia 'Britt Marie Crawford' claims to be the darkest in this genera. Mine was immediately eaten by snails, a gourmet delight.

Medicago sativa ssp falcata is sometimes black but can be variable producing flowers of other colours. They occur when sickle medic is crossed with lucerne. *Medicago lupulina* is known as black medic.

Melianthus major is a tender shrub which produces fabulous spike-like racemes of chocolate maroon to deep red flowers, but more often grown for its foliage alone.

Mucuna pruriens can have blackish flowers.

Nematanthus 'Black Magic' bears near black glossy leaves when young and wonderfully contrasting orange flowers. Very attractive. *N.* 'Black Gold' is similar.

Omphalogramma brachysiphon has black-purple bells whilst *O. farreri* bears deep purple flowers.

Orostachys furusei (Sedum) bears fleshy grey-brown rosettes.

Oryza sativa 'Nigrescens' is an ornamental rice bearing dark brown purple leaves.

Paris luquanensis bears blackish-green superb foliage with hidden deep purple stems.

Persicaria virginiana 'Filiformis' has red flushed foliage. *P. virginiana* 'Painter's Palette' for its dark chevron.

Petasites japonicus v giganteus f purpureus has large rounded leaves which emerge purple-black, maturing to purple-green.

Phlox paniculata cultivars with dark foliage include 'Le Mahdi', 'Starfire' and 'Windsor' or try *P. x arendsii* 'Anja'.

Plectranths ciliatus bears dark green foliage flushed black with purple undersides.

Potentilla atrosanguinea is a lovely dark red, *P.* 'Etna' even darker.

Protea longifolia is superb with its woolly black centre.

The dark red form of *Pulsatilla vulgaris*, suitable perhaps if you cannot get hold of the rare *P. pratensis ssp nigricans*.

If you find dark purples acceptable in flowers, you have a much wider choice including *Roscoea*, *Verbena bonariensis* or *Salvia verticillata* 'Purple Rain'.

Most Rudbeckias have black central cones to their daisy flowers, *R. occidentalis* 'Green Wizard' is a little more unusual. *R.* 'Black Beauty' is a clone.

Rubus parvus has dark or bronze-green leaves, paler beneath.

Scutellaria scordiifolia 'Seoul Sapphire' has deep black-purple flushed leaves and indigo flowers.

Synandrospadix vermitoxicus with a purple inner and green outer spathe and purple spadix.

Syngonium podophyllum 'Infra-Red' has purple-tinted bronze arrowhead leaves.

Torenia fournieri has deep-purple flowers in the seed mixture known as the Clown Series.

Xanthorhiza simplissima bears bronze leaves at first then turning red-purple in autumn.

THE SEASONS

Spring

In spring the renewal of the earth, only dreamt about huddled by the fires of winter, is so satisfying to watch. From the depths of the deep, dark earth buds emerge reassuringly, bulbs push through the cold earth to face the sun, herbaceous perennials begin to break through the soil and much is ready to come alive and blossom once more. The miracle of spring, the never ending cycle of nature.

In the dark garden, spring emerges with dark *Crocus* 'Negro Boy' raised in 1910 with its blackish blue petals, gold throat and silver edging and *C.* 'Purpureus Grandiflorus' an old deepest dark purple variety. In late spring the show stealer with regard to bulbs has to be *Tulipa* 'Queen of Night' known as the black tulip, superb planted with a white or pink contrasting tulip and blue Myosotis, (forget-me-nots) against a background of *Euphorbia,* the red-leaved *E. amygdaloides* 'Purpurea'. *Ophiopogon,* ever black through winter, is ready to send up new growth. *Primula* please us with their dark flowers or foliage, try *Primula* 'Garnet' next to the *Ophiopogon,* it does a capital job with its deep jewel red flowers combined with the feathery foliage of *Anthriscus sylvestris* 'Ravenswing' and *Ranunculus* 'Brazen Hussy', all looking at their best in spring. Woodland plants are coming into flower and there is so much to see and do. One of the wonders of gardening is that the eye always sees it afresh, it is always seen anew this rebirth of the garden. *Acacia, Akebia, Allium, Berberis, Bergenia, Euphorbia, Malus, Prunus* and *Ranunculus* are just some of the dark spring plants to enjoy. *Primula auricula* abound in dark forms, many of which are show auriculas and are best kept under glass although they do not appreciate heat in any form. Try the deeply cut leaves of *Geranium* 'Purple Heron' with *Ajuga reptans* 'Atropurpurea' and *Lamium maculatum* 'Silver Beacon'.

Spring brings a new joy to the dark garden which will diminish as the season progresses, the unfurling of some leaves are purple, good strong new tones are in evidence before leaves fade to green. Some leaves hold their colour much better than others. The following is a list of plants whose leaves emerge bronze or purple or are tinted so when young, thereby adding interest and a greater choice for the dark garden. It is of great benefit to incorporate some of these emerging dark leaves into the garden.

EMERGING DARK LEAVES

Abelia 'Edward Groucher' has glossy, bronze young foliage.

Acer offers good spring foliage.

Adonis amurensis 'Fukujukai' has emerging bronze buds opening to feathery-bronze leaves, later turning green.

Aesculus pavia 'Spring Purple' is a new introduction bearing new purple spring foliage.

The following *Astilbe x arendsii* cultivars all bear bronzed foliage in spring, 'Cattleya' has rose-pink flowers, 'Ellie van Veen' has white flowers, 'Obergartner Jurgens' is a new variety with remarkably dark foliage which contrasts well with the red flowers. 60cm (2ft). *A. simplicifolia* 'Bronce Elegans' is a beautiful dwarf form with green foliage darkened with bronze shadows which makes a good base for the arching sprays of tiny flowers in cream and salmon pink in July and August. 30cm (1ft). 'Dunkellachs' is a good hybrid, 'William Buchanan' bears pinkish-white flowers *A. glaberrima* also has bronzed leaves, but *A. glaberrima v saxatilis* is more widely grown with deep green leaves, red-tinted on the undersides. Spikes of white-tipped mauve flowers are borne in summer. Thrives in moist soil. 8cm (3"). *A. x crispa* 'Perkeo' has dark green mature leaves, bronze-tinted when young, on bronze stems with rose-pink flowers. 20cm (8").

The dark green leaves of *Buxus sinica v insularis* are often bronze-tinted.

Catalpa x erubescens 'J.C.Teas' has leaves which unfold purple, those of *C. x erubescens* 'Purpurea' are dark blackish-purple when young, gradually maturing green, flowers freely in the Midlands of England. *Corylopsis sinensis v sinensis* 'Spring Purple' and *C. sinensis v calvescens f veitchiana* 'Purple

Selection' have purple young growth.

Chelone glabra 'Black Ace' is a new introduction, a selection of the native U.S. white turtlehead by Craig Morck. Emerges with dark foliage with a black cast. In areas with hot summers, foliage will turn green by the time the white, snapdragon-like flowers appear.

Cotoneaster hummelii bears bronze young foliage whilst *C. insignis* bears branches which are reddish-purple when young and also bears blackish-purple fruits.

Daphne x houtteana bears purple foliage some of which retains its colour when the flowers appear in spring. Z 6-10.

The young leaves of *Diphylleia cymosa* are stained red.

Drimys lanceolata bears copper-tinted young growths, with purplish red shoots, a good addition to the woodland garden.

Dryopteris erythrosora has bronze, copper red foliage when young turning almost glossy green, so very useful in a moist site.

The shoots and leaf stalks of the deciduous tree, *Emmenopterys henryi* are bronze-purple when young, fully hardy when mature.

Epimedium x versicolor has copper-red and bronze leaves when young as do many other *Epimedium*, valuable additions for their handsome flowers and foliage in the shady or woodland garden.

The succulent spurge, *Euphorbia trigona* 'Purpurea' offers young tinted foliage.

The deciduous tree, *Euptelea pleiosperma* is grown for its attractive foliage, bearing young growths which are copper tinted. Young foliage needs protection from frost.

Garrya x issaquahensis 'Pat Ballard' is a male form with purple-tinged young foliage maturing to green tinged red, with the additional features of bearing reddish purple shoots and catkins. The young leaves of *Hamamelis vernalis* 'Sandra' are suffused plum-purple, becoming green but still retaining a purple flush on the underside.

Hypericum offer bronze leaves on *H. choisyanum* and *H. x dummeri* 'Peter Dummer', the latter also having a second flush in winter.

The attractive, heart-shaped leaves of *Idesia polycarpa* are purple-tinged when young. This hardy tree is deciduous, a good woodland candidate preferring moist soil in shade.

Ilex x altaclerensis cultivars can offer young reddish purple foliage such as 'Camelliifolia' and 'Moorei'. *I. aquifolium* 'Donningtonensis' has dark, blackish purple stems and purple-flushed leaves. *I. pedunculosa* bears bronze-tinted leaves when young and *I. vomitaria* is often purple-tinged.

Juglans regia, the common walnut tree, is bronze-purple when young.

Leea coccinea 'Burgundy' is a Burmese shrub producing deep red leaves, the species produces bronzed leaves when young. Leaves are highly glossy. The tender West Indian Holly makes an elegant houseplant.

Leucothoe fontanesiana 'Scarletta' has dark red-purple young foliage, turning dark green, with bronze flushing in autumn.

Lonicera nigra has deep purplish shoots, and the added attraction of green berries which turn purplish black.

Lophomyrtus offers good spring foliage, bronze or red tinged in *L. bullata* with the addition of deep black-red berries. *L. bullata* 'Matai Bay' differs from the species in that the new shoots are bright red, marturing to mahogany brown, and the *L. x ralphii* cultivars are a good choice here too, try 'Indian Chief', 'Kathryn' whose leaves are flushed a good deep purple, 'Purpurea', 'Red Dragon' which appears to be the darkest cultivar with brilliant reddish pink new shoots maturing to an outstanding blackish red and retaining its colour well, 'Wild Cherry' with foliage intensifying in winter or the dwarf forms, 'Lilliput' and 'Pixie' which are reddish.

Maddenia hypoleuca is an unusual rare shrub or small tree with cherry-like leaves which are bronze-tinged when young and bear small black fruits.

Mahonia aquifolium 'Moseri' has attractive bronze-red new growth. *M. gracilipes* has fine colouring in its attractive leathery leaves.

Some *Malus* species have bronzed or bronze-red foliage when young such as *M.* 'Aldenhamensis'.

Nyssa sinensis, a lovely deciduous

tree, bears bronze young leaves and reddish autumn colour.

Dark blackish purple new growth is a feature of the frost-hardy, evergreen shrub, the holly-leaved *Osmanthus heterophyllus* 'Purpureus'. *O. heterophyllus* 'Purple Shaft' also has young purple foliage.

Osmunda regalis has coppery-brown leaves as they unfurl in spring. *O. r.* 'Purpurascens' retains the colouring much better throughout the summer.

Parahebe catarractae has leaves tinged purple when young. This evergreen subshrub has attractive saucer-shaped flowers.

Parthenocissus thomsonii (Cayratia) has foliage which is reddish purple when young, turning purple-green in summer and finally bright red in autumn. On the reddish side, but what a way to cover a wall!

Another species to offer superbly coloured young growth is *Photinia x fraseri* with bronze to bright red foliage in the cultivar 'Robusta'. The cultivar 'Birmingham' offers bright purple-red foliage and that of 'Red Robin' is bright red. *P.* 'Redstart' is also bronze-red when young and the species *P. villosa* makes another good choice for young bronze leaves. Good in limy soils. Hardy to -18°C (0°F).

The young growths of many *Pieris*, such as *P. japonica* Taiwanensis Group and *P. japonica* 'Scarlett O' Hara' are bronze. They require an acid soil.

Polygonatum 'Betberg' has emerging leaves and stems stained purple.

Populus nigra has dark bark and bronze foliage when young, colours yellow in autumn. *P. x canadensis* 'Robusta' has bronze-red young leaves in mid-spring.

Many *Prunus* species and cultivars have bronze leaves when young, such as *P.* 'Kursar' and *P.* 'Pandora'.

Quercus glauca and *Q. laurifolia* bear bronze young leaves. The young foliage of *Q. robur* 'Atropurpurea' is red-purple, maturing to grey-purple, a wonderful smoky colouring, thriving in most reasonable soils, but preferring a rich, deep loam. *Q. petraea* 'Purpurea' has purple leaves and prefers a damp position. The architectural leaves of *Rheum palmatum* 'Atrosanguineum' emerge vivid red, the colour being retained better on the underside. *R. palmatum* 'Tanguticum' retains its purplish tints even better. These enjoy a rich, moist soil and are ideal close to water. Offer a rich diet of manure each year to see them reach their potential. Hardy to -23°C (-10°F). Z 6-9.

Some *Rhododendron* have bronze foliage when young. *R.* 'Bow Bells', *R.* 'Cowslip', *R.* 'Winsome' and the species *R. williansianum* and the new growth of *R.* 'Elizabeth Lockhart' is dark chocolate brown. The *Azalea* 'Berryrose' has coppery new foliage. These all make excellent woodland plants.

Rodgersia pinnata 'Superba' has mahogany-bronze burnished pinnate leaves when young.

The young foliage of *Rosa filipes* 'Kiftsgate' is richly copper-tinted, *R. longicuspis* has dark reddish-brown shoots and copper-tinted young foliage, its white flowers are banana scented. *R. x odorata* 'Mutabilis' has deep purplish young shoots and coppery young foliage.

Sarcococca 'Purple Stem', a valuable addition to the late winter, early spring garden for its scent, has young stems and leaf stalks of a purplish hue.

Staphylea holocarpa v rosea has bronze leaves when young, a deciduous shrub or small tree which is a good addition to the woodland garden. Bears whitish flowers and curious, bladder-like fruits. Appreciates moist soil which is well-drained.

The unfolding leaves of *Syringa oblata* are bronze-tinted but watch late frosts. Some lilacs such as *S. vulgaris* 'Charless Joly' bear dark purple flowers.

Veronica peduncularis 'Georgia Blue' (Oxford Blue) bears bronze-purple leaves when young.

Viburnum x bodnantense bears bronzed young foliage and *V. carlesii* 'Diana' has a distinct purple tinge. *V. farreri* has bronze young foliage becoming dark green and finally turning to red-purple in autumn. *V. tinus* 'Purpureum' has leaves tinged purple when young. *Viburnum* are excellent shrubs for woodland gardens.

Summer

The easiest time to achieve a garden full of interest, when there is lots in bloom and much to enjoy. The delights of the dark garden are abundantly evident in a balance of flower and foliage. Plants with early strong colour only, have, by this time, lost most of their purple tones and are looking green. Plants which retain strong colour throughout the summer include *Acer palmatum* 'Bloodgood', *Fagus sylvatica* Purpurea Group, *Phormium, Cordyline, Cotinus, Berberis, Begonia sempervirens* bronze and other rhizomatous and species *Begonia* and the year round black plants *Aeonium* and *Ophiopogon*. Deep purple-black foliage tones are enhanced in sun, but can be lost or intensified in heat. The spectacular bearded *Iris* are a favourite in flower in summer, the airy foliage of *Artemisia* combines well with dark flowered *Iris* hybrids, *Stachys byzantina*, dark *Tulipa*, and black *Papaver* are other good companions. Black *Viola* will flower all summer long in a damp site with a little shade. Dark roses reign supreme.

Tender plants and annuals come out in force to join the summer parade. Have plants ready in pots to fill gaps in the border, ensuring the continuance of the colourful carpet. A wealth of dark tender plants or annuals are useful as fillers or as bedding plants such as *Alternanthera, Canna, Centaurea, Nemophila, Lathyrus odoratus.*

Autumn

If summer is a blaze of colour, autumn is fiery in its intense foliage tones and a time not just for later autumn foliage tints and flowers but also of wonderful seedheads, chiefly amongst the ornamental grasses. Deciduous trees and shrubs still provide the dark background. The dark-leaved *Sedum* come into their own at this time of year. Dark *Helianthus* (sunflowers) tower over smaller plants. Tender plants such as *Solenostemon* (Coleus), *Salvia discolor* and *S. guaranitica* 'Black and Blue' and *Salpiglossis* are still going strong to the first frosts. So too the tropical foliage of *Canna, Ricinus* and *Musa* or *Ensete*, combined with the bright tones of *Dahlia* and *Crocosmia* flowers with dark foliage the show continues. Harmonious reds, bronzes, golden foliage turning to rust and bronze, the dark garden reflects a deeper harmony in shades ranging from bronze to copper through to dark purple. The low autumn sun shines through the leaves reflecting tones of violet, plum and deepest purple-black. Just as there are many plants whose leaves emerge with the desired darker tones, so the year draws near its end in a blaze of foliage which turns darker as the weather becomes colder.

SPECTACULAR COLOUR

Abeliophyllum distichum is a beautiful deciduous shrub related to *Forsythia* which sometimes turns purple in autumn, and is well worth growing with or without this change in colour.

Acer offer spectacular autumn tints.

Bergenia colour well in autumn and winter with the onset of cold weather. *B. purpurascens* 'Oeschberg' is one of the best. -23°C (-10°F) Z 6-9.

The perennial grass, *Bothriochloa ischaemum* has slender bluish leaves tinged purple in autumn.

Cercidiphyllum japonicum 'Rotfuchs' has excellent colouring in autumn. This beautiful, deciduous tree is superb on the edge of a woodland setting.

Clematis cirrhosa has leaves which are slightly bronze beneath and *C. cirrhosa v balearica* bears foliage which is bronze-tinged in winter. A wonderful addition to some of the loveliest of *Clematis* species. The flowers are usually well-speckled and highly desirable.

Cornus species offer rich purple-red foliage in autumn, choose from *C. controversa* which also bears small black fruits or *C. kousa* 'Satomi', or *C. mas.*

Corokia 'Frosted Chocolate' bears distinct chocolate coloured foliage in winter.

Cotoneaster can also offer purplish foliage in autumn, amongst the species are *C. sherriffii, C. tomentellus* and *C. villosulus* which also offers blackish purple fruits. *C.* 'Valkenburg' also becomes purplish in autumn.

Cryptomeria japonica 'Bandai-sugi' and *C. japonica* 'Elegans

Compacta' both have dense foliage which turns bronze in winter. The Japanese cedars are evergreen, coniferous trees.

If standing in water in full sun, *Darmera peltata* has superb large leaves which colour well in autumn.

Deschampsia cespitosa 'Bronzeschleier' has silvery flower plumes, ageing to bronze on this very handsome ornamental grass.

Some *Erica* are bronzed in autumn such as *E. carnea* 'Heathwood', *E.* 'Ruby Glow' and *E.* 'Corfe Castle'. Most prefer acid soil in full sun, but these winter flowering species will normally tolerate slightly alkaline soil.

Euonymus fortunei 'Coloratus' bears leaves which are purple throughout winter, particularly when the roots are starved or controlled. *E. fortunei* 'Dart's Blanket' turns bronze-red in autumn. *E. hamiltonianus* 'Fiesta' bears leaves blotched with creamy-yellow and pink, turning purple in autumn. It is shy-fruiting. *E. oxyphyllus* bears leaves turning purple-red in autumn with dark red fruits.

Forsythia x intermedia 'Spectabilis Variegated' bears cream variegated leaves turning deep maroon and pink in late summer and autumn.

Fraxinus americana 'Autumn Purple' turns reddish purple in autumn, at other times the leaves are dark green. *F. americana* 'Rosehill' turns bronze-red, *F. angustifolia* 'Raywood' can turn plum-purple although this

sometimes drops its leaves beforehand, and *F. chinensis* sometimes gives wine-purple autumn colour. *F. nigra* merely offers dark brown winter buds.

The glistening green leaves of *Galax urceolata* become bronze in winter. This evergreen perennial from woodland in southeastern U.S. needs lime-free soil and provides good ground cover in a shady site. White spike-like flowers are attractive, when persuaded to make an appearance.

Hakonechloa macra 'Aureola', a marvellous bright yellowish green grass has purple stems and the leaves age to a wonderful reddish brown. Best leaf colour is found when growing in partial shade.

Hamamelis japonica v flavopurpurascens has petals suffused dull red and the calyx is dark purple on the inside.

Hebe 'Blue Clouds' has dark glossy green foliage, purplish in winter.

Leiophyllum buxifolium, an evergreen shrub from acidic woodland in the U.S. is tinted bronze in winter. Suckers spread quite widely.

The leaves of *Leptospermum rupestre* turn purple-bronze in very cold weather, its stems are reddish.

Leucothoe fontanesiana bears leaves which turn a rich beetroot-red or bronze-purple especially in exposed positions. The bronze-yellow leaves of *L. grayana* are tinged purple in autumn. Needs acid soil.

Some leaves of variants of *Libertia ixioides* turn orange-brown in

winter. A plant I much admire, worth protecting from frost, but borderline hardy.

The dark green leaves of *Ligustrum obtusifolium*, a type of privet, are often purplish in autumn, and those of *L.* 'Vicaryi' are bronze-purple in winter.

Another species which offers wonderful autumn colour, though rather reddish on the whole, is *Liquidambar*. The cultivar offering the darkest foliage colour is *L. styraciflua* 'Lane Roberts' which has reliable dark blackish crimson foliage over a long period in autumn, or *L. styraciflua* 'Burgundy' being dark purple or perhaps *L. styraciflua* 'Worplesdon' but this does not retain the good purple colour for very long before becoming orange-yellow, *L. styraciflua* 'Golden Treasure' turns reddish purple edged with yellow, and *L. styraciflua* 'Moonbeam' has pale creamy yellow leaves, turning green and becoming red, yellow and purple in autumn. The leaves of the dense, shrubby *L. styraciflua* 'Gumball' turn orange-red and purple in winter. The species *L. formosana* also has purple tints in autumn amongst red and orange.

Some *Malus* cultivars are bronzed in autumn.

Nandina domestica 'Harbour Dwarf' turns dark red in autumn.

Parrotia persica turns yellow, orange and red-purple in autumn. There is also a weeping form.

Parthenocissus species offer excellent colour in autumn plus the bonus of blue or black berries, which can cause mild stomach upsets if ingested. Try *P. tricuspidata* 'Veitchii' for its dark-red purple foliage or *P. tricuspidata* 'Beverley Brook' tinged purple in summer, but red in autumn, or *P. tricuspidata* 'Lowii' which is bronze-red with purplish hints. *P. himalayana v rubrifolia* offers attractive, rich purple young foliage on a vigorous climber.

Persicaria affinis 'Superba' bears rich brown foliage in autumn.

Prunus besseyi has rusty purple leaves in autumn, those of *P. spinosa* 'Purpurea' become deep reddish purple.

Pyrus ussuriensis bears foliage which turns bronze-crimson in autumn.

The deeply cut leaves of *Quercus ellipsoidalis* are quite beautiful in form and turn red-purple in autumn. The foliage of *Q. velutina,* the black oak, turns red-brown in autumn, the bark is dark brown, almost black hence the common name. *Q. coccinea* is fabulous in autumn, but probably too red for the purposes of the dark garden.

Rhamnus imeretina bears leaves which are usually bronze-purple in autumn.

The leaves of *Rhododendron davuricum* 'Hiltingbury' are bronze in cold weather and the pubescent leaves of *R. tosaense* turn crimson-purple in autumn.

Rhus trichocarpa offers red-purple foliage in autumn, and *R. typhina* offers purple tints whilst *R.*

aromatica turns orange to red-purple.

Rosa elegantula bears purple and crimson autumn foliage, as does *R. nitida* and the small, suckering shrub, *R. virginiana* bears glossy green leaves which turn purple, then orange-red and finally crimson and yellow in autumn. *Shortia* have foliage often suffused red in autumn. These evergreen perennials from woodland in East Asia and one U.S. species are grown for their attractive leaves and flowers. Shade lovers perform best in areas with cool summers.

Sorbus reducta and *S. scalaris* offer red and purple foliage.

Suaeda vera, a small, native, maritime sub-shrub can turn totally bronze-purple in autumn.

Taxodium, handsome evergreen coniferous trees, suited to swamp forest by riverbanks, turn rust brown in autumn, offering a superb display.

Vaccinium arctostaphylos offers red-brown foliage when young turning to red-purple in autumn with the addition of blue-black berries.

Viburnum x burkwoodii 'Chenaultii' is a compact shrub which turns bronze in autumn.

The foliage of *Zelkova serrata* is bronze or red in autumn.

Winter

Dark berries will play a part in the winter garden. Stems too, such as those of *Cornus* add interest at this all too often bare and bleak time in so many gardens. The copper foliage of *Leucothoe, Photinia* and if you are in frost free areas, *Phormium, Cordyline* and *Pittosporum* will keep the interest going through the winter. *Bergenia* colours well at this time of year, and before Christmas, *Helleborus orientalis* black will be sporting its wonderfully seductive black flowers. *Ophiopogon* exhibits its black berries and its foliage looks fine all the way through winter. It is an admirable sight to see those black spidery legs peeping through the white snow. A time to plan ahead, to reflect, whilst much is dormant, on how you want the garden to look the following year, a time to look forward to the re-awakening of spring.

PODS, FRUIT AND BERRIES

These are evident in all seasons and again can be used to enhance the dark plantings. The following, varying from clusters of tiny black berries, to large purple cones are interesting for their fruit and berries of purple to black hue.

Conifers, such as *Abies* species make an addition to the dark garden with violet-blue cones.

The seed pods of some *Acacia* species are tinged red or purple.

Acmena smithii can bear edible red-purple berries, but they can also be white or pink. *Acoelorraphe wrightii*, the saw palm, bears black fruit.

The berries of *Actaea* are highly toxic if ingested, *A. erythrocarpa* bears maroon berries and *A. spicata* (nigra) bears black berries.

Ailanthus altissima bears red-brown fruit.

Amelanchier species bear spherical or pear-shaped purple to maroon fruits, in addition to their colourful autumn foliage.

Ampelopsis megalophylla, a vigorous woody climber, bears bunches of black fruit.

Aralia species, suitable for a shady border, bear spherical fruits which are usually black as in the case of *A. elata* and *A. spinosa*, but dark purple on the species *A. racemosa*.

Arctostaphylos alpina bears purple-black fruit and *A. patula* has dark brown to black fruit.

Arenga pinnata, the sugar palm, often dies after fruiting, its fruits are black.

The autumn fruits of the evergreen, tender shrub, *Aristotelia chilensis* are purple ripening to black.

Aronia melanocarpa, the black chokeberry bears black berries and those of *A. x prunifolia* are purple-black. These hardy shrubs are suitable for a border or as specimen plants.

Baptisia pendula has large blackened drooping seedpods.

Many *Berberis* species offer dark fruit, the colour varying from purple, blue-black to black.

The long, red fruits of *Berchemia*

racemosa, a deciduous, twining, woody climber ripen to black, and those of *B. scandens*, a vigorous climber are blue-black.

The fruits of *Billardiera longiflora* are unusual in their shade of deep purple-blue.

Callitris oblonga, the frost-tender Tasmanian cypress pine bears shiny black female cones.

The fruits of *Carissa*, evergreen shrubs and small trees from woodland in tropical and subtropical Africa and Asia, can vary from red to purple-black.

The edible sweet fruits of *Celtis* species ripen to varying shades of purple and black. *C. sinensis*, bears dark orange fruits which ripen to red-brown.

Cestrum species such as *C. elegans, C. fasciculatum, C. parqui* and *C. psittacinum* all bear dark berries.

Chamaecyparis thyoides has angular female cones which are purple-black to red-brown.

The small fruits of some *Chamaedorea* species are black.

Chionanthus retusus, Chinese fringe tree, bears blue-purple or blue-black fruits.

Cinnamomum camphora bears black berries.

The dry, unpalatable berries of climbers, *Cissus antartica* are black, those of *C. striata* are glossy black and those of *C. hypoglauca* and *C. rhombifolia* are blue-black.

The red fruit of the bushy, evergreen shrub, *Cleyera japonica* ripens to black.

Clintonia uniflora, a spreading

perennial from woodland in western N. America bears blue-black berries.

Coriaria terminalis, a deciduous subshrub has fleshy, dark blackish-red fruit to 1cm across.

Cornus alternifolia, C. controversa and *C. macrophylla* all bear blue-black fruit and that of *C. sanguinea* is dull blue-black.

Corokia buddlejoides bears bright red-black fruit.

Cotoneaster affinis bears dark purple-black fruits.

Daphne bholua bears fleshy, spherical blackish-purple fruit. *D. caucasica* mainly bears black fruit although the colour can vary and *D. laureola* and *D. pontica* both bear black fruit.

Decaisnea fargesii bears unusual and highly decorative pendent, dull blue fruit to 10cm (4") long in autumn.

Dictyosperma album, the Princess palm, bears purplish black fruit.

Disporum cantoniense and *D. flavens* bear dark black or blackish berries.

The midribs of the leaves of *Dryopteris wallichiana* are covered with dark brown or black scales.

Eleutherococcus species, mostly thriving in full sun, bear black or purple-black fruits.

Empetrum nigrum has black berries, *E. purpureum* reddish purple.

Eurya emarginata and *E. japonica* bear purple-black and black berries respectively. These are tender subjects with inconspicuous flowers for the shrub border.

Fatsia japonica bears spherical black fruit.

Forestiera neomexicana, the desert olive, bears black egg-shaped fruits.

Fraxinus excelsior bears conspicuous black buds in winter.

Fuchsia usually bear edible, purple fruits, unpleasant to my palate.

Gaultheria forrestii, *G. myrsinoides*, *G. nummularoides* and *G. pyroloides* all bear dark blackish fruits.

Gaylussacia baccata, the black huckleberry bears edible glossy black fruit.

Hakea from the *Protea* family bear warty dark brown seed pods.

Mature *Hedera*, ivy, can bear black fruit.

Holboellia bear sausage-shaped purple fruits.

Hovenia dulcis, a deciduous tree bears spherical black fruit.

Ilex have male and female flowers borne on separate plants, both are needed to produce berries. *I. crenata* cultivars such as 'Convexa', 'Golden Gem' and Mariesii' and the form *f. latifolia* often bear black berries.

Juniperus species bear bluish black fruits.

Lardizabala bear edible sausage-shaped purple berries 5-8cm (2-3") long.

The female cones of *Larix*, larch, are usually purple.

Leycesteria formosa, an attractive shrub, bears red-purple berries.

Ligustrum species, privet, can bear blue-black to black fruits.

Some *Livistona* species, fan palms, bear brownish red to black fruit.

Lonicera giraldii, *L. henryi*, *L. involucrata*, *L. japonica*, *L. ledebourii*, and *L. nitida* all bear blue-black, purple-black or black berries, those of *L. pileata* are violet-purple.

Lophomyrtus bullata and *L. x ralphii* bear deep black-red berries.

Luma apiculata bears purple berries, *L. chequen* black berries.

Mahonia species bear mostly purple to black berries.

Manglietia insignis sometimes bear purple fruit.

Melicytus bear decorative purple berries.

Meliosma have dark fruits of varying hues from red through violet to black.

Menispermum, moonseed, bear grape-like glossy black fruit on female plants.

Morus nigra, the black mulberry, bears edible red fruits turning dark purple in late summer.

Some *Myoporum spp*, evergreen shrubs and trees from dry areas, bear purple berries.

Myrtus communis bears purple-black berries.

Interesting black pods are to be found on *Nicandra physalodes*.

Ochna species, shrubs and trees from tropical woodland, can bear lustrous purplish to black fruits contrasting with the thickened and enlarged calyces and receptacles.

The immature green fruits of *Olea*, the olive, ripen to black.

Ophiopogon species bear blue-black berries, which persist well into winter.

Many *Osmanthus* species bear blue-black or dark purple fruit.

Osteomeles species are shrubs or small trees which bear red-brown, blue-black to black fruits.

Paris quadrifolia bears blue-black, spherical berry-like capsules.

Parthenocissus species may produce dark blue or black berries.

Pavetta capensis bears glossy black fruits.

Peltophorum pterocarpum is a frost tender, evergreen tree, related to *Caesalpinia*, bearing winged purple-brown seed pods.

Phillyrea species are evergreen woodland shrubs with glossy green foliage which bear blue-black fruits.

Some *Phoenix* species bear edible brown or black fruits, including the date palm.

Some female cones of *Phyllocladus*, the celery pine, can be black. Purple male cones are catkin-like.

Phytolacca species, pokeweed, bear dark red to purple-black fruits. Often highly toxic as in *P. americana*.

Polygonatum species often bear black fruits.

Polyscias, evergreen shrubs and small trees from tropical areas, usually bear small purple to black berries.

Prunus species such as *P. x cistena* bear dark purple fruits, whilst *P. serotina*, the black cherry, bears edible red fruit ripening to black.

Pseudopanax species, evergreen trees and shrubs from forest and scrub in the southern hemisphere bear purple-black to black fruits.

Rhamnus species, usually thorny

shrubs and trees, bear berries which ripen to black.

Rhodotypos scandens, a hardy deciduous shrub of the rose family, bears black fruits.

Rhoicissus capensis bear tiny flowers followed by red to purple berries.

Some *Ribes* species bear black fruits or red berries which ripen to black.

Robinia, unless sterile, usually bear dark brown seed pods.

The hips of *Rosa pimpinellifolia* are purplish-black.

Rubus species often bear black fruits including the edible blackberries and the unpalatable berries of *R.cockburniana*.

Rumex species, dock, bear brown to red-brown fruit.

Salix gracilistyla 'Melanostachys' is distinguished by its beautiful black catkins with red anthers that turn bright yellow. Well worth growing.

Sambucus nigra bears glossy red fruit whilst *S. canadensis* bears spherical purple-black fruit.

Sarcococca species bear dark berries from blue-black or purple to black.

Schefflera species often bear spherical black or blue-black fruits.

Sinofranchetia chinensis, a hardy, twining, woody climber from woodland in China, bears grape-like purple berries.

Solanum jasminoides bears ovoid black fruit. Aubergine (eggplant) and peppers also belong to this genus, providing dark edible fruits. If pollinated, *Stauntonia* bears edible purple fruit to 5cm (2").

Symphoricarpos orbiculatus bears dark purple-red fruit which can cause a mild stomach upset if ingested and contact may irritate the skin.

Syzigium aromaticum (Eugenia), the clove, bears ellipsoid purple fruit.

Tetrapanax papyrifer, the rice-paper plant, bears clusters of black fruit.

Tetrastigma voinierianum, a tender, attractive, very dark green leaved climber found in tropical woodland, bears small, acidic, grape-like, black berries.

The seed pods of the very attractive *Thevetia peruviana* are black, each contains one or two highly toxic nut-like seeds. Glossy green leaves and delightful flowers are the reasons to grow this shrub from tropical America.

The male cones of slow-growing, evergreen conifer, *Thujopsis dolobrata* are dark violet.

The spherical or kidney-shaped fruits borne on female plants of *Trachycarpus* are blue-black.

Trapa nutans, the water chestnut bears spiny, hard black fruits.

Vaccinium includes the blueberries and bilberries which are grown primarily for their fruits and are interesting additions to the potager or fruit garden.

Many *Viburnum* bear blue-purple-black fruit. Others produce red fruits which ripen to black.

Vitis amurensis bears unpalatable or edible blue-black grapes.

Some ornamental species of *Zea mays*, maize, produce black cobs.

BARK

Snake-bark maples offer interesting striped or flaky bark. One example is *Acer davidii* 'Serpentine' which has strongly contrasting stripes on a deep purplish brown bark, but unfortunately not purple leaves. Autumn foliage is yellow, orange and dull scarlet. *A. triflorum* bears greyish-black bark.

Betula nigra has reddish bark which, when young, peels like wallpaper when steamed. Mature trees have darker, fissured bark which is blackish or grey-white.

The trunks or stems of tree ferns are often blackish, such as the slimline *Cyathea medullaris* or the chunkier *Dicksonia squarrosa*.

Dacrydium cupressinum has dark brown bark which flakes.

Diospyros ebenum has incredibly black bark, for which it is known as the highly prized, ebony.

Fraxinus nigra has dark bark, so too the black walnut, *Juglans nigra*, whilst *Quercus nigra* has smooth brown, then dark grey bark. If anything the bark of *Quercus velutina* is even darker being almost black.

Xanthorrhoea australis known as Blackboy, has gorgeous deep black trunks contrasting with the falling green of the grass 'hair'.

STEMS AND SHOOTS

Acer negundo v violaceum bears purple maroon young shoots.

Adiantum pedatum bear wiry, brown or black stems.

Some *Astilbe* such as *A. x crispa* 'Perkeo' have bronze stems.

Baptisia australis bears black swollen seedpods on dark, upright stems.

Bamboos such as *Gigantochloa atroviolacea*, Bambus lako (G. 'Timor Black') and *Phyllostachys nigra* have beautiful black canes.

Colchicum speciosum 'Atrorubens' has purple stained stems.

Cornus alba 'Kesselringii' provides colour in winter with its brownish black stems, and the added bonus of plum-purple leaves in autumn too, whilst the stems of *C. stolonifera* 'Kelsey's Dwarf' are purplish red.

Daphne longilobata bears purplish stems.

Drimys lanceolata has purplish red shoots.

Eriogonum crocatum has almost black stems.

Hebe decumbens has purplish black shoots, whilst *H. ochracea* and *H.* 'Carl Teschner' have blackish main stems, and those on *H.* 'Mrs Winder' are red- brown.

Heliconia bihai 'Purple Throat' has maroon stems.

Helionopsis orientalis bears dark red stems.

The fronds of *Hemionitis* are borne on shining black stalks.

Hydrangea nigra has striking black stems.

Ilex x altaclerensis 'Hodginsii' is a male form with dark purple stems.

Kniphofia 'Dorset Sentry' and *K.* 'Mount Etna' both have brownish stems.

Lachenalia species sometimes have mottled stems, marked with purple or brown.

Ligularia 'The Rocket' and *L. przewalskii* have almost black stems.

Lychnis x arkwrightii 'Vesuvius' has dark stems.

The stems and leaf veins of *Pachyphragma macrophyllum* are purple tinted in winter.

The stems of *Penstemon digitalis* 'Husker Red' are beetroot red.

Some *Philadelphus*.

Phlomis tuberosa 'Amazone' bears dark purple branching stems.

Pilosella aurantiaca has black hairy stems.

Some *Salix* species bear dark or even purple stems as in the case of *S. hastata* 'Wehrhahnii', those of *S. acutifolia* 'Blue Streak' are blackish-purple, covered with a vivid, blue-white bloom. *S. daphnoides* has white-bloomed, purple-violet shoots.

Schefflera elegantissima has dark blackish stems.

Stachyurus species bear red-brown shoots.

Tamarix tetandra has purple-brown shoots.

Tetrastigma voinierianum has red-brown stems.

Trapa nutans, the water chestnut produces red stalks.

Veltheimia bracteata has yellow-spotted purple stems.

DARK ON THE UNDERSIDE

Often leaves have green upper surfaces but are dark, usually purple-red on the underside. A perfect contrast to the surface colour of the leaves and are still visible, particularly when the leaves are unfolding, or when the plant is suitable for a hanging basket.

Admirable *Acer pseudoplatanus* 'Atropurpureum' offers dark-red purple on the underside of its leaves with red leaf stalks.

Aeschynanthus 'Black Pagoda' is a sumptuous gesneriad with green leaves, purple beneath having green and orange flowers.

Alpinia luteocarpa bears red-maroon undersides.

Calathea are attractively patterned on the surfaces and usually red or purple beneath.

Ctenanthe are frost tender plants which can be grown in a shady border in the tropics, but here in the U.K. are best as houseplants. Related to *Maranta*, they have attractively marked leaves on the surface. *C. burle-marxii* has deep purple leaves on the underside, those of *C. oppenheimiana* are wine-red and *C.* 'Greystar' is spectacularly purple beneath.

Dioscorea discolor is purple underneath.

Hebe 'Ettrick Shepherd' and *H.* 'Midsummer Beauty' are purple on the underside.

Hedychium greenei has maroon on the reverse of its leaves and stems too.

Hoheria populnea 'Foliis

Purpureis' bears leaves of plum-purple on the undersides whilst *H.* 'Purpurea' is coppery and *H.* 'Osbornei' purplish.

Kohleria 'Dark Velvet' has dark leaves, purple on the underside with slightly pouched tubular flowers of bright orange. *K. warscewiezii* has dark velvet leaves, larger than the above.

Silvery leaves of *Ledebouria socialis* have purple undersides.

Pseudowintera colorata bears pale yellow-green leaves above, flushed pink underneath, edged and blotched with dark crimson-purple. The dark red to black fruits are rarely produced in the U.K.

The large leaves of *Rheum palmatum* 'Atrosangulneum' are reddish on the underside.

The leaves of *Rhododendron forrestii* and those of *R. tephropeplum* are purple beneath. The leaves of *Rosa longicuspis v sinowilsonii*, a climber with reddish-brown stems are purple-flushed on the undersides.

Ruellia devosiana has spreading purplish branches and leaves are purple on the underside only.

Streptocarpus wendlandii is a curious, unusual species bearing one solitary, enormous leaf which is dark purple-green on the surface and red-purple below.

Stromanthe 'Stripestar' is dark purple on the underside, very prominent as the leaves unfurl.

Tradescantia spathacea has fleshy leaves deep purple underneath.

Viola walteri has purple leaves on the underside.

DARK-CENTRED FLOWERS

Dark centres, eyes and blotches in shades of purple, black and reddish maroon.

Allium nigrum bears large heads of white flowers with black centres. Dark-centred *Anemone* include *A. x fulgens* and *A. pavonina*.

Arctotis 'Zulu Prince' has creamy flowerheads with a dark disc.

Calochortus luteus has maroonish markings at the base of the petals.

Catananche caerulea 'Bicolor' has white flowers with purple centres.

Some *Cistus* are marked with crimson such as *C. x cyprius*.

Clematis florida 'Sieboldii' bears single white flowers and large bosses of purple stamens.

Clianthus formosus has black blotches on a scarlet flower.

Codonanthe gracilis has maroon spotted white flowers.

Codonopsis lanceolata bears pendent, mauve-flushed, greenish-white flowers veined with violet.

Delphinium 'Sandpiper' bears white flowers with brown eyes.

Dianthus 'Alice' bears ivory white flowers with a crimson eye, *D.* 'Forest Treasure' has double white flowers flecked red-purple.

Dietes bicolor bears small brown marks on the yellowish petals.

Dimorphotheca pluvialis 'Tetra Pole Star' has pure white flowers with a black disc.

Geranium ocelatum and *G. psilostemon* have magenta flowers with a black eye.

x Halimocistus wintonensis 'Merrist Wood Cream' bears creamy yellow, dark-banded flowers with a yellow centre.

Halimium 'Susan' has yellow flowers with red-purple centres.

Helianthus 'Italian White' bears primrose petals with a dark disc.

Hemerocallis 'Pandora's Box' bears pale cream flowers with a purple base and a green throat.

Hibiscus calyphyllus is yellow with an astonishing purple-brown eye. *H. trionum* bears creamy yellow flowers with a brown centre.

Ixia 'Hubert' bears brownish red flowers and black centres.

Leptospermum lanigerum bears white flowers with brown calyces.

Lilium duchartrei bears white flowers deeply spotted purple.

Magnolia x weisneri and *M. wilsonii* are white flowered with purple stamens.

Ornithogalum saundersiae bears creamy-white flowers with prominent black ovaries.

Osteospermum 'Whirlygig' for its unusual twisting petals.

Paeonia suffruticosa ssp rockii has white petals with maroon bases.

Ranunculus asiaticus is a pure beauty, usually white with a purple-black centre. Tender.

Romulea sabulosa bears scarlet and black flowers.

Sanvitalia procumbens and *Thunbergia alata* bear orange and black flowers.

Spiloxene capensis (Hypoxis) often has deep purple centres. A small, perennial corm preferring sandy soil, water in winter, dry in summer. 0°C.

Tolpis barbata is yellow with dark maroon.

INDEX

The main alphabetical sections are not included below.

ACKNOWLEDGEMENTS

I would like to express my grateful thanks to all those who had a part in this book, however small.

To the team at Proven Winners, especially Josh, for their support and their faith in the 'Black Magic' range of plants.

To my son for his technical help, technical, without him this book would not be the same. To my mother and my friend Karen.

To Thompson & Morgan, Ipswich for their support of the International Black Plant Society.

Thanks to Secret Seeds for giving the black seed line an airing.

My thanks to the following for loan of photographs in the book. Key: b bottom, t top, m middle, r right l left.

Proven Winners P3,8,12,19,32r,45, 48,55tl,55br,77,87,91,116,118,167tr,1 70,172.

J. Schneider for Dracunculus P96

Dan Heims,TerraNova Nurseries P32l,115 ml,br,149,167br.

J. Amand Arisaema griffithii p63.

T.Wood, Spring Meadow, P82,160 bl,178 br, 185,186, Prunus 192.

Karchesky Canna P83

OHGB P.84.

Thompson & Morgan P131bl,151br, 181tr.

Lynne Brennan P.111 topl, 3rd l, bl.

Cyberlily Gardens P. 2nd l, br. P112l.

Pat Stamile, H. 'Dakar' P111.

JohnPeat P. 113

Ted Petit P.112 m

Schreiner's, Oregon for all Iris except the one in bud on P.18.

Shuo Wang for Paeonia bl and br P.138.

Howard Wills, Fernwood Nursery top 3 r and br P164.

Wayside Gardens P183.

SUPPLIERS

The following supply dark plants.

U.K.
SEEDS
Secret Seeds
Turnpike Cottage
Salcombe Regis
Sidmouth
Devon. EX10 0PB
www.secretseeds.com
See the range of **Karen Platt 'Black Magic and Purple Passion'** seeds.

PLANTS
Gardener's Catalogue
Thompson & Morgan
Poplar Lane
Ipswich
Suffolk. IP3 3BU
T&M are supporting the IBPS.

Avon Bulbs
Burnt House Farm
Mid-Lambrook
South Petherton
Somerset. TA13 5HE.
www.avonbulbs.co.uk

Beeches Nursery
Village Centre
Ashdown
Saffron Walden
Essex CB10 2HB
www.beechesnursery.co.uk
Excellent range

Edrom Nurseries
Coldingham
Eyemouth
Berwickshire
Scotland TD14 5TZ
www.edromnurseries.co.uk
Excellent range, a favourite nursery

Dibley's.
Llanelidan.
Ruthin.
Denbighshire.
Wales. LL15 2LG.
www.dibleys.com
Streptocarpus

Europa Nursery.
PO Box 17589.
London.
E1 4YN
www.europa-nursery.co.uk
Epimedium, Asarum

Fernwood Nursery
Fernwood
Peters Marland
Torrington
Devon. EX38 8QG.
www.fernwood-nursery.co.uk
Sempervivum, Jovibarba

Great Dixter Nurseries
Northiam
Rye
E.Sussex. TN31 6PH.
www.greatdixter.co.uk

Jacques Amand
The Nurseries
145 Clamp Hill
Stanmore
Middlesex. HA7 3JS.
bulbs@jacquesamand.co.uk

Oakland Nurseries
147 Melton Rd
Burton-on-the-Wolds
Loughborough. LE12 5TQ.
www.oaklandnurseries.co.uk

Shirley's Plants
6 Sandheys Drive
Church Town
Southport. PR9 9PQ.
www.stbegonias.com

Slade Park Plants
Old Slade Lane
Iver
Bucks. SL0 9DX.
dayvidslilies@aol.com

Winchester Growers Ltd
Varfell Farm
Long Rock
Penzance
Cornwall. TR20 8AQ.
www.wgltd.co.uk
Dahlia

Viv Marsh Postal Plants
Walford Heath
Shrewsbury
Shropshire. SY4 2HT.
www.PostalPlants.co.uk
Zantedeschia, Arisaema, Phormium

U.S.
PLANTS

Proven Winners distribute the **Karen Platt range of 'Black Magic and Purple Passion'** plants available throughout the U.S. Ask at your nearest garden center for details or visit
www.provenwinners.com

www.asiatica.com (Aroids)
www.centrecommons.com
www.crownsvillenursery.com (Solenostemon)
www.dansdahlias.com
www.dutchgardens.com(Bulbs)
www.glasshosueworks.com (Exotics)
www.heronswood.com
www.mtmaples.com (Acer)
www.oldhousegadens.com (Bulbs)
www.plantdelights.com (Unusual)
www.robsviolets.com
Begonia, Streptocarpus, Episcia
www.schreiners.com (Iris)
www.springmeadow.com (Shrubs)
www.terranova.com (Heuchera)
www.waysidegardens.com

CHINA
PLANTS
Shuo Wang
Hexe Prefecture Imp & Exp Corp.
17 Xing Cai Rd. Hexe City.
Shandong Provincer.
P.R.China PC 27 4012. (Paeonia).

For further information join
The International Black Plant Society or contact the author

k@seedsearch.demon.co.uk
www.seedsearch.demon.co.uk